Truman
Defeats
Dewey

Truman
Defeats
Dewey

GARY A. DONALDSON

THE UNIVERSITY PRESS OF KENTUCKY

Publication of this volume was made possible in part by a grant
from the National Endowment for the Humanities.

Editorial and Sales Offices: The University Press of Kentucky
663 South Limestone Street, Lexington, Kentucky 40508-4008

03 02 01 00 99   5 4 3 2 1

Library of Congress Cataloging-in-Publication Data
Donaldson, Gary.
    Truman defeats Dewey / Gary A. Donaldson.
        p.   cm.
    Includes bibliographical references and index.
    ISBN 0-8131-2075-6 (alk. paper)
    1. Presidents—United States—Election—1948. 2. Truman, Harry
S., 1884-1972. 3. Dewey, Thomas E. (Thomas Edmund), 1902-1971.
I. Title.
E815.D66   1998
324.973'0918—dc21   98-24424

This book is printed on acid-free recycled paper meeting
the requirements of the American National Standard
for Permanence of Paper for Printed Library Materials.

Manufactured in the United States of America

FOR JENEE

Last but not least

Contents

Acknowledgments

I wish to acknowledge people who assisted in the completion of this book. I received several small travel grants from the Bush-Hewlett Foundation, and without them this work could never have been completed. The grants were awarded through Xavier University, and I am indebted to those at Xavier who saw promise in my scholarship. I am particularly indebted to the members of the History Department at Xavier for their encouragement. I also wish to thank the archivists at several libraries, including those at the Truman Library, the libraries at the University of Iowa, the University of Rochester, the University of Wisconsin, and Clemson University. Without their kind assistance, the research for this work would have been impossible. Last, I thank my family for undying support and assistance. Thank you for being quiet.

Introduction

Every four years at election time the image of Harry Truman is trotted out by the popular press, and comparisons are made between today's candidates and the no-nonsense president from Independence, the man who pulled off the greatest of election upsets against all the odds and against the predictions of all the pundits and pollsters. The nation's interest in the election is understandable. The election of 1948 was a spectacular upset and a great victory for Truman and the Democrats. It was also, in many ways, the beginning of a new, modern political era in American history. By election day, November 2, Truman and his advisers and campaign strategists had put together a large, loose-fitting, temporary coalition that pushed the president over the top in the balloting. Everyone, it seems, except the president himself, was surprised by the outcome. Even Bess Truman doubted that her husband could win.

This 1948 Democratic coalition was made up of many of the main parts of the old New Deal coalition that had kept Roosevelt and the Democrats in power through the decade of the mid-1930s to the mid-1940s. But the coalition that formed around Truman in 1948 was also very different. The times had changed, new factors had been introduced into the American political scene, and, of course, many of the players were different. The war and then the Cold War changed America. The nation's confrontations with the Soviet Union altered the nature of politics and even the way Americans voted. On the left, for instance, several of the Democratic party's old coalition groups broke apart over the issue of communism; communism also changed voting patterns in such important groups as the progressives, the liberals, and labor.

The coalition was different after the war also because several of the groups that had supported Franklin D. Roosevelt were not nearly as important to Truman and his strategists, whereas groups that were of little significance to Roosevelt emerged after the war years as power brokers in the party. The South was the most obvious loser. A major player in the Roosevelt administration, the South had been a chief benefactor of New Deal programs, and every four years the region had returned the favor with reliable votes. But after the war the South's small electoral numbers foretold a future of weakening power within the party structure, particularly in close elections. Truman and his political strategists believed that the South was safely Democratic. It became clear immediately after the war that a black-urban-liberal coalition in the Northeast, Midwest, and California made for more lucrative political ground to plow than the Old Confederacy. These groups, particularly African Americans, whose changing voting patterns had placed them in a position to demand a hearing from the federal government and the Democratic party, gained new power. The changing political situation forced the Democrats, for the first time, to choose between the segregated South and the growing African-American voting strength in the northern cities.

The left was also out. Once a powerful wing in the Democratic party, the left had been the backbone of the New Deal. Henry Wallace, Harold Ickes, Henry Morgenthau Jr., and other New Dealers were the policymakers who kept the New Deal on line and running. Truman and the postwar Democratic party had no use for these men. Truman called them "crackpots." Wallace's lack of appeal in 1948 more than anything else made it clear that the Democratic party's left wing was gone and that the party was now controlled by those who leaned toward the center of American politics.

Organized labor also had been a strong and important part of the New Deal coalition, and Roosevelt had aided its cause to gain its support. The Wagner Act, which gave labor the right to organize, was the payoff it received for supporting the administration. In addition, as the New Deal sought to aid the lot of the common man, wage earners, along with farmers, benefited the most. Although labor remained inside Truman's coalition in the 1948 election, it had changed as well. Labor was divisive after the war, and it had begun to purge itself of its far left and move toward the center along with much of America.

Truman's problems with labor revolved mostly around the nature of the postwar economy, which differed greatly from the economy of the prewar years. Truman had to grapple with the problems of an economy of inflation. Roosevelt had fought an economic depression. The answers to America's economic problems were the direct opposite in each case. Truman could not maintain political support, as Roosevelt did, by bestowing economic programs to the advantage of specific groups. In fact, Truman was forced to restrain economic growth in various sectors of the postwar economy, particularly in labor and industry. Moreover, American workers had been deprived of economic prosperity during the Depression, and they had sacrificed further to win the war. After the war, most earnings for factory workers had fallen below prewar levels. When, in 1945 and 1946, Truman attempted to keep the economy in check by holding down wage increases along with other inflationary practices, he alienated labor.

So for the Truman administration, both the economic and political equations of the postwar period were vastly different than they had been in the 1930s. The groups may have had the same titles and names, but they often had a different makeup, a different power base, even different goals, demands, and tactics than they had as part of the prewar New Deal coalition. The progressives and the left were gone, and the South's power had diminished considerably. In addition, the nation's postwar economic structure had changed from one of depression to one of inflation, forcing the administration to hold a rigid economic line that was often politically unpopular. It is not enough to say that Truman simply put back together the old New Deal coalition and made it work in 1948. He did more than that.

The Republicans, in contrast, emerged from the war with many of the same old problems they had carried around for decades, in addition to several new ones. Out of power since 1933 (and in the minority in Congress since 1931), they were little more than an opposition party through the 1930s and 1940s. Life for Republicans had been difficult through the New Deal era.

The Republican party was fiercely divided. The liberals (still often described in the 1940s as progressives) had little in common with the party's Old Guard—the conservatives and isolationists. Roosevelt and the Democrats had made political hay through four national elections by blaming the Great Depression on the Republicans, and the Republican liberals had, in turn, maintained power in their party by laying blame for the party's woes on the conservatives. The result was liberal Republican candidates for president: Alf Landon in 1936, Wendell Willkie in 1940, and Thomas E. Dewey in 1944. To Old Guard conservatives like Robert A. Taft, this course was little more than "me-tooism," and it offered little chance for success against the Roosevelt juggernaut. As liberal Republicans continued to lose, the Old Guard argued for a new approach, and their power in the party grew.

Not only had the Democrats forced the Republicans to carry the political blame for the Great Depression, they had also successfully blamed the Republicans for a tremendous foreign policy mistake: isolationism. Several Republican isolationists, mostly from the Midwest, had opposed America's entrance into the war. But, when the war ended, it became clear that entering the war had been the right thing to do. The postwar foreign policy (as devised by FDR, carried on by Truman, and accepted by many Republican liberals) was known as "internationalism." It was a popular policy with the American people, who had come to see the United States as the leader of the postwar free world. The old prewar isolationists in the Republican party appeared to be from another era, and the image hurt the party at the polls.

For Republicans, however, there seemed to be some light at the end of the tunnel. The postwar economy grew rapidly, and New Deal measures appeared no longer necessary to maintain prosperity (and political power for the Democrats). Also, FDR's death in April 1945 brought in Harry Truman, who was clearly incapable of holding together the diverse Democratic coalition that had kept FDR in power for so long. By 1946 the Republicans seemed on the verge of regaining power; the nation appeared prepared, finally, for a turn to the right. But the party remained severely split. In 1946 Taft and the right gained control of Congress, but in 1948 it was the liberals who nominated the party's presidential candidate, and the two sides could not unite during the campaign to win an election that most said they could not lose.

The 1948 election was the first presidential election after the war and the first since Roosevelt's death. The nation had changed, voting patterns had changed, issues had changed. Powerful interest groups and political groups in both parties made bids for power. At times, it even appeared that the party system might be in for a realignment—either to the left or the right. Instead, the two-party system persevered and the political center held.

It is no wonder that the election of 1948 still holds the imagination of the nation. It was the election of the feisty Truman, of the whistle-stop tour, of the *Chicago Tribune*'s headline "Dewey Defeats Truman," and of "give 'em hell, Harry!" It was an upset, a victory by an underdog who everyone said had no chance to win. For Dewey and the Republicans it was the lost mandate and the election that slipped away at the last moment. It was also an election of complicated grand strategy, severe political infighting, special interests, and issues that ranged all the way from the communists in the nation's capital to the fish in Oregon's streams. By every possible definition, the election of 1948 is at the very foundation of America's postwar political heritage.

1

"Had Enough?"
The Elections of 1946

If there is anything akin to a natural phenomenon in American political history it is that the minority party generally gains congressional seats in an off-year election. Some call it merely a swing of the pendulum, a natural cycle of events, but clearly American voters are prepared to register their disenchantment with the administration they elected two years earlier and to voice their dissatisfaction with the progress of their politicians' programs and promises. It is always a strong signal to the embarrassed majority party: it must either alter course or expect more defeats in the general election, just two years away.

Consequently, as the 1946 congressional elections approached, the Republicans prepared for a significant gain in their congressional power. As early as June, the Democratic National Committee (DNC) was willing to admit privately that the Democrats might lose control of the House. For that to occur, they would have to lose twenty-six seats. To lose control of the Senate, the Democrats would have to give up nine of sixteen seats up for reelection.

Minority party victories in midterm elections may be common in American political history, but that pattern was regularly broken by the Democrats themselves between 1932 and 1946. In those fourteen years, the all-powerful FDR-built New Deal coalition remained strong, and the Democrats controlled both houses of Congress with large majorities. In fact, the Democrats had maintained a majority in Congress since 1930, when they took control of both houses in the midterm elections two years into Herbert Hoover's first and only administration. For the Republicans in 1930, the outcome of the midterm elections was a warning that a change would come if Hoover and the Republicans failed to solve the nation's growing economic problems. In November 1932 that threat was made good when FDR and the Democrats swept into office on a wave of anti-Republicanism. In 1946 President Truman and the Democrats faced much the same situation that the Republicans had faced in 1930. The problems of the volatile postwar economy were not being solved. American voters would send a message in 1946: alter course or face big losses in the general election in 1948.

The Democrats were burdened with a variety of problems in 1946, not the least of which was President Truman's crashing popularity ratings, which had dropped from 87 percent when he took office in April 1945 to 50 percent a year later. By November, as voters were casting their ballots, the numbers had plunged again to a pathetic 32 percent.[1] Much of this decline had to do with the perception that Truman lacked leadership ability. Of course, part of the problem was that he was constantly measured against his talented predecessor. FDR oozed leadership qualities and charisma, and he was a dynamic speaker who inspired the nation. When it became apparent that Truman lacked these qualities, America began to see him as little more than a caretaker president, filling out FDR's fourth term. Truman himself did little to dispel this image, and the passivity showed.

Truman also suffered from inexperience, a poor image, and bad advice. Between his first days in the White House and the 1946 elections he spent most of his time learning the ropes of the office and finding his way. His choices for cabinet officers and advisers were not always popular, and as the old New Dealers fell away, the White House took on a new appearance that was a far cry from the image of efficiency, urbanity, and intellectualism of the Roosevelt presidency. After twelve years with Roosevelt, many Americans disliked the contrast of Truman's homespun, ward-heeler style of leadership. Then as the nation's economic problems worsened, Truman's image became so tarnished that Democratic National Committee chairman Robert E. Hannegan decided that the party would best be served by keeping the president out of the public eye in the months before the elections. Consequently, Truman did not campaign for the party. In the last days before the balloting, Hannegan resorted to radio broadcasts of old FDR speeches, each a supposed response to how the great man would have dealt with the problems of the day.[2] *Newsweek* called the strategy "defeatism." Republican National chairman Brazilla Reece called it "one of the cheapest and most grisly stratagems in the history of American politics."[3] At a time when American voters believed they needed strength and leadership in Washington, their president was directed by his own advisers to sit out the election.

Truman's poor image also hurt his ability to hold the diverse Democratic party together, and that contributed significantly to the party splits that would plague the president and the Democrats until November 1948. FDR had built a coalition that only he could hold together. *U.S. News* wrote that "Mr. Roosevelt built the organization and it kept him in power as long as he lived. But he built it of such diverse and divergent fragments that no other hand could make it function. Perhaps even Mr. Roosevelt could not have won another election with it."[4] By the summer of 1946 it seemed to many in nearly every camp of the New Deal coalition that Truman was unable to hold the party together. Liberals, southerners, African Americans, organized labor, farmers, all had strong complaints, and Truman could do little to solve the problems and patch the differences.

When Truman took office, he told FDR's cabinet members and chief advisers that they could stay on indefinitely, that America was in a time of crisis and it was important not to make changes in the front line. But Truman had no use for Roosevelt's New Dealers, social reformers, and Ivy League–trained economic planners. Privately, he called them "crackpots" and "the lunatic fringe."[5] Consequently, through the rest of 1945 and into 1946, several old New Dealers became annoyed with the new way of doing things in the White House, and they slowly fell way. Within four months of FDR's death, Truman had accepted the resignations of all cabinet officers except Henry Wallace and Harold Ickes.[6] Certainly, Truman needed his own people at his side and not the advisers to another president, but to American liberals and old New Dealers who expected FDR's programs to move forward, the spirit of the New Deal seemed to be gone from Washington. To make matters worse, Truman then replaced the venerable New Dealers with Missouri cronies, old war buddies, and political lightweights such as Harry Vaughan, Ed McKim, Fred Vinson, Edwin Pauley, and Tom C. Clark. To the press they became the "Missouri Gang," supposedly reminiscent of Warren Harding's corrupt "Ohio Gang."[7]

Not only did the nation's liberals dislike Truman's attitude toward FDR's New Deal and the New Dealers, they also believed he was too tough on the Soviets, too tough on labor, and not moving fast enough to achieve civil rights for African Americans. Just as this disenchantment was setting in, Truman fired his secretary of commerce, Henry Wallace, the august leader of the American left, just six weeks before the 1946 elections. For liberal America it was the last straw. The scorn this action brought Truman and the Democrats could be measured in a lackluster turnout by liberals in November. Truman and his advisers would learn a lesson that would serve them well as the general election approached in 1948. The president would have to make amends with the liberals.

One important aspect of the 1946 election was that it was the origin of the Republican party's postwar anticommunist campaign against the Democrats. This campaign lured away many political conservatives who had spent the Depression and the war at FDR's side to vote Republican.[8] One month before the election, J. Edgar Hoover told an American Legion convention in San Francisco that there were as many as one hundred thousand communists running loose in America. He added that ten sympathizers stood behind every Red cardholder "ready to do the party's work. These include their satellites, their fellow travelers and their so-called progressive and liberal allies."[9] *U.S. News* characterized the Republican anticommunist campaign as "accusing the Democratic party of being one that preaches radical doctrines and engages in radical practices. The main tenor of the Republican campaign theme is that the Democratic Party is leading the country toward Communism." Two weeks later, the magazine added: "Republicans are still accusing the Administration of being pro-Russian in its policies and are accusing the Democrats of permitting men with communistic ideas to dictate the Administration policy. This is a clear note of the campaign."[10] Through the summer and fall of 1946, the Republicans accused the Democrats of being "red fascists" and of the "Three Cs": "Confusion, Corruption and Communism." After the campaign, Marquis Childs concluded that the anticommunism issue "was one of the most potent forces in the shift from the party in power to the opposition."[11] Clearly, Republicans campaigning on the issue of anticommunism struck a nerve in the American postwar electorate.

A major part of this Republican anticommunist attack on the Democrats was grounded in Cold War foreign policy, specifically in the events surrounding the Yalta Conference. It was at Yalta, the Republicans argued, that Roosevelt tried to appease Joseph Stalin by handing over Eastern Europe. There was no truth to the claim; by February 1945, when the Yalta Conference convened, Stalin was in firm control of Eastern Europe and refused to withdraw his troops. Roosevelt's only options were to accept the situation or remove the Soviets by force, which he was unwilling to do. But the Republicans saw it as a blatant act of appeasement and constantly accused the Democrats of being soft on communism for their willingness to negotiate with the Soviets. As the Cold War hardened through the late 1940s, the Republicans continually blamed the Democrats and their Yalta decisions for causing the world's problems.

The Republican frontal assault against communism in 1946 was directed most often at Henry Wallace, certainly the most liberal and supposedly even the procommunist figure inside the Truman administration. Even though Truman fired Wallace in September, the Democrats had to carry the considerable weight of his liberal leanings into the election just a few weeks later. Wallace spent the time between being fired and election day traveling about the country, speaking on behalf of liberal Democratic candidates. The left wing flocked to his side. As the election approached, however, most Democratic candidates generally shunned Wallace, and many even hoped that his ouster from the Truman administration would help them with conservative voters who saw Wallace as far too liberal. By November it was clear that Wallace had kept large numbers of both liberal and conservative Democrats from voting Democratic. The conservatives saw the party as too liberal because of the influence of Wallace and the far left, while the liberals saw Wallace's removal as a sign that the party was moving to the right. The liberals generally stayed away from the polls, while conservative Democrats voted Republican in overwhelming numbers. In 1948 Truman and his advisers would look back on 1946 and see the potential disaster that a loose cannon like Wallace could cause and keep him as far away from the campaign as possible.

Conservative Democrats in the South joined the other groups in the Democratic party with their own criticisms of the administration. Truman's 21-Point Plan, laid out before Congress in September 1945, was a liberal blueprint to extend the New Deal, but it quickly alienated southern conservatives. They feared the growth of organized labor, but they especially feared the power a growing northern liberal-labor coalition in the Democratic party that by 1946 had come to include an important contingent of African Americans.

During the war, southerners had vehemently opposed FDR's Fair Employment Practices Commission (FEPC) that was designed to end racial discrimination in the war industries. FDR, however, had recognized that African Americans (particularly those moving to northern cities) were quickly becoming an important factor in American politics. The result was concessions from the White House, including the establishment of a wartime FEPC, the naming of prominent African American William Hastie as assistant to Negro affairs in the War Department, and in the military the establishment of the Tuskegee Airmen and the commission of the first African-American general. Southerners complained, but FDR made certain that the South was appropriately appeased. The New Deal continued to pump aid into the South, and war industries and military bases helped the southern economy during the war. Although the president's wife made overtures to African Americans, Roosevelt continued to toe the line on most issues dear to the South. Then as the 1944 election approached, Roosevelt folded under pressure from powerful southern congressmen (in coalition with northeastern urban bosses) and abandoned Henry Wallace for Truman as his vice-presidential candidate. In effect, FDR worked to keep the South in line while successfully laying the groundwork for a political relationship with northern urban blacks.

When President Truman came to office, he wanted to continue FDR's success of winning African-American votes while maintaining control of the South. Truman was not unfamiliar with this strategy; as a Missouri politician he had received support from both black voters and the Ku Klux Klan in the 1920s, and when he ran for the Senate in 1934 he received as many as 130,000 black votes in a state that maintained strong southern values and prejudices. But despite his past successes at balancing these groups, President Truman, at least before 1946, showed that he either had not learned from FDR's wisdom or he lacked FDR's political savvy for maintaining such a delicate balance. In Truman's defense, however, that balance was much more difficult to sustain in the postwar years than before 1945. By the time Truman became president, African Americans were making greater demands, their leadership was stronger, and their position as a political force in the northern cities had increased considerably. In addition, conservative southern Democrats voting with the Republicans were capable of wielding a conservative majority in both houses of Congress, and that coalition was powerful enough to halt Truman's domestic programs. Truman was thus placed in another pincer as the 1946 elections approached.

The president's response to this political problem was to mollify the South at the expense of black voters, or more exactly, to pay lip service to the demands of African Americans while making sure that their demands were not met. The best example of this ill-conceived attempt at fence-riding was Truman's handling of the FEPC. It was scheduled to expire in June 1946. Several times Truman called for a permanent FEPC, but he never confronted the powerful congressional opponents of the bill for fear they would desert him on other issues. In December 1945 the president issued an executive order removing the FEPC's only effective enforcement weapon, its power of "cease and desist," thereby reducing the FEPC to an impotent fact-finding agency. Finally, in June the members of the FEPC resigned when funds were cut; thus the FEPC was sacrificed to the cause of political unity in the Democratic party.[12]

In November, the South remained solidly in the Democratic column. Democratic victories in the South were so secure in 1946 that several of Truman's advisers began to speculate that the region would surely hold in 1948 even if the president made major overtures to civil rights.

At the same time, Democratic congressional candidates lost in several northern urban districts at least in part because African Americans chose either to vote Republican or to stay at home on election day. Many were disenchanted by Truman's lack of enthusiasm for civil rights, while others were put off by Democrats running white racist campaigns in the South during the summer of 1946. Southern Democrats Governor Eugene

Talmadge of Georgia and Senator Theodore Bilbo and Representative John Rankin of Mississippi conducted overtly racist campaigns in 1946, and they were elected because of their views. *U.S. News* reported that the election of these southern Democrats had "sent many Negroes to wondering why they have been voting a ticket that embraces these men. So they are returning back to the Republicans."[13] In addition, Truman made it clear by his lack of support for such initiatives as antilynching and anti–poll tax legislation that southern white votes meant more to him than northern African-American votes. For large numbers of black Americans (even those in the North who had escaped the racism of the South) a Democratic party that harbored such a powerful racist wing and an obviously sympathetic president held little appeal—and in November 1946 many African Americans either voted along the old Reconstruction loyalty lines for the party of Lincoln or did not vote. The gains that the Democrats had made in the Roosevelt years in bringing African-American voters into the New Deal coalition all seemed lost in 1946. "With Mr. Roosevelt gone and Mrs. Roosevelt no longer in the White House to offset the outburst of rampant Southerners, the Negroes are shifting away from the Democratic Party in many areas," reported *U.S. News* just before the election.[14] All this, together with the GOP's active attempt to court black votes through the National Association for the Advancement of Colored People (NAACP) by promising postelection concessions and a "square deal" for African Americans, brought Republican victories in close races in New York, Philadelphia, Detroit, and Chicago. After the election, *Fortune* reported that 15 percent of African-American voters switched to the Republican party in 1946, and most of those were in the northeastern and midwestern urban areas.[15] Again, the lesson to Truman and the Democrats was clear. Significant voting strength in these cities could win for the Democrats in the 1948 election the large electoral votes of such states as New York, Pennsylvania, Michigan, and Illinois. The African-American vote was crucial for 1948. The South, it seemed clear, would hold.

The Republicans, however, missed a golden opportunity to wrap up the northern African-American vote in 1948; they let it slip away because of their own overconfidence as a result of the 1946 victory. After the 1946 elections, the new Republican Speaker of the House, Joseph Martin, told a group of African-American leaders what they could expect from the Republican party in the future: "I'll be frank with you. We are not going to pass an FEPC bill, but it has nothing to do with the Negro vote. We are supported by New England and Middle Western Industrialists who would stop their contributions if we passed a law that would compel them to stop religious as well as racial discrimination in employment. . . . We may as well be realistic."[16] African Americans learned their own important lesson from the election: the Republican party had nothing to offer them. Just as Truman had learned that he needed African-American votes to win in 1948, African Americans realized that they needed the Democratic party if they were to win any civil rights concessions in the future. Everyone learned.

The problems facing organized labor added to Truman's troubles. The labor situation in the immediate postwar era is an excellent example of the dramatic changes in the years after the war and how Truman, the first leader in this new age of American history, came face to face with entirely new situations. Truman's problems with labor also exhibited the new president's confrontational style, which was a hindrance in the first few months of his presidency but would become an asset after 1946 as he went head-on with the Republicans on almost every issue and almost always to his own political advantage. FDR had not succeeded by butting heads with the opposition, and to Americans who had lived since 1933 under the peaceful coexistence in American politics, Truman's confrontational posture was annoying, if not unacceptable. In no other situation was this more true than his handling of the nation's exasperating postwar labor troubles.

A clash was inevitable. Wartime price controls had kept prices low, and most unions had agreed to refrain from wage demands until the war ended. But when Japan surrendered in August 1945, strikes broke out in nearly every industry. By October, 275 strikes were under way, four hundred thousand workers were out, and the National Labor Relations Board had received notification of 416 additional strike votes. By January 1946, 4.6 million workers were out on strike. In the spring Truman seized several industries, including coal, oil, meatpacking, and the railroads. The war's end brought an almost immediate rise in the cost of living, while the president seemed determined to keep wages down to wartime levels. In May 1946 labor leaders felt Truman went too far when he demanded the power to draft strikers. In September he fired Henry Wallace, labor's self-appointed representative in the White House, and organized labor responded by staying away from the polls on election day, just a few weeks later. Others went farther. A.F. Whitney of the Trainmen vowed to raise millions of dollars to end Truman's political career, and the Congress of Industrial Organizations's Political Action Committee (CIO-PAC) began a campaign to brand Truman a "fascist" and a "labor-hater."[17] From all this Truman and his advisers had learned lessons taught over and over by the factionalism in the Democratic party: the coalition must be maintained at all costs, and disenchantment can keep voters at home on election day.

At the same time, the incessant strikes that had paralyzed the country between the summer of 1945 and early 1946 had angered voters, and Truman received most of the blame. The strikes had taken the nation to the verge of economic collapse, had caused power cuts and brownouts, and resulted in shortages of basic consumer goods. Annoyances seemed to reach a boiling point on the eve of the 1946 election, when a dockworkers' strike in New York caused a national shortage of sugar while sugar sat rotting in ships in New York Harbor. Then John L. Lewis called a strike of the United Mine Workers (UMW) just one week before the election. In a desperate effort to avoid the rancor that would accompany a UMW walkout, Truman gave in to Lewis's demands at the last minute and averted the strike.[18] Organized labor was satisfied, but to moderates in the party the president appeared weak and conciliatory while Lewis seemingly had wielded extreme power at the expense of the administration.

Organized labor had been an important link in the Democratic party coalition since the mid-1930s. Thus it should not be surprising that American voters blamed the Democrats for the nation's problems with labor, and in November they responded by turning the Democrats out in droves. Of the eight most liberal labor-supporting senators, only one survived the election. All five senators supported by the CIO-PAC were defeated. Of the sixty-nine most liberal representatives, thirty-seven were defeated.[19] As the general election approached two years later in 1948, Truman and his advisers would remember this lesson and push to win labor votes by opposing Republican antilabor legislation, but they would also work to keep labor in line by neutralizing such disruptive labor leaders as John L. Lewis.

Labor had learned a valuable lesson as well. By staying away from the polls (which then gave a Republican Congress the power to pass antilabor legislation) it became obvious to organized labor that a moderate Democrat like Truman was far better than trying to deal with the Republicans. As the 1948 election approached and labor had felt the sting of Republican antilabor legislation, organized labor was willing to accept Truman at nearly any cost.

Another factor in the 1946 loss was Truman's handling of reconversion, the process of converting the nation's economy from wartime back to peacetime production. And Truman and the Democrats learned from that lesson as well. During the war the federal government maintained an elaborate system of controls designed to focus the economy on the war effort. This system, managed by the Office of Price Administration (OPA), regulated wages and prices and also controlled wartime production. To most Americans the inconvenience of such a system was a necessary cost of winning the war. At the same time, the controls allowed the average American worker to build up considerable savings during the war years at least in part because there were few products on the market to buy. In addition, much of the savings that accumulated were invested in war bonds. By 1945, $48 billion in war bonds were in the hands of American consumers, and most of that was readily cashable. Spendable wealth was thus at an all- time high; Americans were chafing at the bit to spend the money they had been saving for four years. In addition, more Americans were working than ever before. But when the war ended (more abruptly than anyone expected), the war industries ground to a halt, laying off as many as eight million workers. Add to that figure twelve million soldiers who were demanding a discharge and a job, and it became clear to most observers that the United States was headed for a dual shot of high inflation and unemployment—at least until industry could begin meeting the growing consumer demands and hiring the workers. Several of Truman's advisers, particularly Chester Bowles of the OPA, believed that problem would not occur for at least two years. Bowles convinced Truman to hold the line, to maintain wage and price controls through 1946 until industry could retool, reconvert, rehire, and get back to the American way of meeting consumers' demands.

For the old New Dealers who had dug the country out of economic depression in the 1930s by inflating the currency and spending the money on liberal programs, the postwar economic situation was a perplexing turnabout. Reconversion replaced the New Deal as the management plan for the nation's economy, at least for the moment. And that meant keeping prices and wages artificially low, the very reverse of the New Deal strategy. In his State of the Union message in January 1946, Truman called for a balanced budget to deal with the country's economic problems. From FDR's wartime budget of over $67 billion, Truman proposed a budget of $35.9 billion and an ultimate end to the $4.3 billion deficit. Such a plan was no less Keynesian than the New Deal (economist John Maynard Keynes had called for balancing the budget in times of inflation), but for many liberals the turnaround brought fears that New Deal social programs might be sacked as the price of the new economic tack. Truman spent much of 1946 trying to belay such fears by cutting military spending rather than social programs.

On August 18, 1945, just three days after V-J Day, Truman called for Americans to "hold the line" against inflation; wage and price controls would continue. Consumers, however, had come to believe that when the war ended they would put all the economic hardships behind them. Now, their new president was telling them that the products they had been denied for so long would remain unobtainable for just a while longer. American consumers complained bitterly at first, but when the OPA lifted controls on a few products and prices immediately shot up, public opinion polls showed that consumers were generally willing to live with price controls for a while longer to keep inflation under control.

Much of Truman's problem with reconversion can be blamed on organized labor. After four years of agreeing to hold the line during the war, labor refused to do so when the war ended. As strikes erupted throughout the country and in nearly every corner of industry, wages and then prices rose. Steelworkers, for instance, received a 15 percent wage increase that translated into a $45 per ton increase in the cost of steel.[20] The price of automobiles immediately rose, followed by price increases in other industries using steel. Truman moved to curb such obvious snowball effects by trying to stop the strikes, but it badly damaged his relationship with labor.

One troubling result of reconversion was the growth of an active black market. This illegal activity subverted the intentions of the OPA, making it impossible to control prices in many sectors of the economy and in many areas of the country. For example, at least half the lumber sold in 1946 found its way to the black market, and nearly 80 percent of the butchers in New York City sold their meat illegally, above the price limits assigned by the OPA.[21] As consumers continued to buy more and more products on the black market, the OPA's authority dwindled and the entire program began to appear unenforceable. Black market activities also gave Republicans ammunition to blame the Democrats for the economic problems of the average American, while warning the voters that all the regulations and government intervention in the economy was just a few steps from the deprivations and shortages of communism.[22]

The image of Americans purchasing products on the black market, illegally, openly, and with an attitude of accomplishment in their ability to circumvent the controls, conjured up recollections of Prohibition, when the portrait of the American government became tarnished for its inability to enforce unpopular laws. *Fortune* said that such activity lowered the moral standards of the American people.[23] As the 1946 elections approached, the economic demands of the OPA became untenable, even ridiculous in some quarters, with strawberries rotting in the fields because the OPA refused to lift the controls on the production of wood cartons. Veterans were living in cars because of the scarcity of building products. Automobiles were being sold at the OPA price but with a spare tire thrown in at an additional $500. Store owners sold controlled products only if certain other products— not controlled and at highly inflated prices—were purchased as well. By November, Truman's reconversion was a popular joke.

Truman did not help. One of the OPA's biggest problems was controlling the price of meat. In the summer of 1946, Truman went along with farmers' demands to lift controls on meat prices. Overnight, the price of veal went from forty to ninety cents per pound and steak rose from fifty-five cents to a dollar per pound.[24] In late July, Truman tried to plug the break by reimposing price controls on meat and rolling prices back to wartime levels. By October (just one month before the election) a virtual farm strike broke out against Truman's policy. Livestock producers held their stock off the market with the result that beef and pork became an unattainable luxury outside the black market. The press reported experiments with horse meat and soy curd as substitutes. Finally, on October 14, with his back to the wall, Truman again lifted the controls on meat. By then, however, both farmers and consumers were mad and blaming the administration.[25] Three weeks before the 1946 election, the president once again appeared weak and in-decisive, even foolish.

In the days before the election, *U.S. News* reported that a majority of congressmen believed that the most important issue was price controls, followed by shortages and then foreign policy and the threat of domestic communism.[26] After the election, *Time* reported that America had spoken out against "price muddles, shortages, black markets, strikes, Government bungling and confusion, too much Government in too many things. The majority of the people were fed up with all that."[27] On November 9, four days after the election, by executive order, Truman removed all controls on wages and prices.[28] On the economy, the people had spoken. Truman would not move on toward the 1948 election with the millstone of wage and price controls around his neck. The OPA was dissolved in the first months of 1947.

In the weeks before the 1946 election, the smell of defeat for the Demo-crats was clearly in the wind. The only surprise was the severity of the loss. *Life* had predicted a Republican landslide, and a Gallup Poll had reported that 56 percent of the voting public was unhappy with the Democratic party's track record.[29] But when the smoke cleared, no one expected such a debacle. The Republicans won twelve seats in the Senate and fifty-five seats in the House. Only four of eleven Democratic incumbents in the Senate won outside the South. The Democratic party's three most renowned cham-pions of reform were cast out of the Senate: Joseph Guffey of Pennsylva-nia, James Mead of New York, and Orrice Abram Murdock of Utah. In the House, the Democrats lost over 40 percent of the contested seats outside the South. In addition, the Republicans won a majority of the nation's gov-ernorships, something that had not occurred since the 1920s.[30] Of the eight most liberal senators, only one survived; of the sixty-nine most liberal representatives, only thirty-two won. Of the seventy-seven congressmen who were rated at or above "80 percent liberal" by the *New Republic,* forty-one were sent home. And of one hundred candidates supported by the political capital of the administration, forty-seven were voted out of office.[31]

Organized labor was hurt worse than any interest group. Five of the top laborites in the House were defeated and another four in the Senate, while three states voted to bar the closed shop. Of the 78 candidates rated by the CIO-PAC at "100 percent" in support of labor, 42 were defeated, while 108 of the 132 the CIO-PAC stumped against were reelected. *Newsweek* reported that railway workers sat out the election because Truman broke their strike in the spring and that the CIO stayed away because Truman had fired Henry Wallace. *Time* suggested that large numbers of voters may have voted Republican because the Republicans had promised to weaken organized labor and stop inflation.[32] Simply, it was an astounding victory for the Republicans and a horrible defeat for the Democrats.

Truman even suffered a humiliating personal defeat in his home state. Congressman Roger Slaughter, a Missouri Democrat, managed to incur Truman's wrath by standing in the way of several of his domestic bills, including the bill to establish a permanent FEPC. Truman had supported Slaughter when he first ran for Congress in 1942 and then again in 1944, but in 1946 Truman pushed to have Slaughter defeated for the Democratic nomination. Truman's big mistake was asking the Pendergast machine in Kansas City to aid in Slaughter's defeat. Of course, it was Tom Pendergast and his unscrupulous Kansas City machine that had catapulted Truman to national prominence in the 1930s, and Truman had always had to face accusations that he was a dupe and a puppet of that organization. In the 1946 Democratic primary in Missouri, Truman's candidate, Enos Axtell, defeated Slaughter for the Democratic nomination, but the *Kansas City Star* uncovered election irregularities tied to the Pendergast machine, and Truman suffered the consequence in the press. After all the trouble and all the political chips spent by Truman on Slaughter's ouster, Axtell lost in November to a conservative Republican.[33]

Probably the most important aspect of the 1946 election was that the Republicans misread its results. They felt they had been handed a mandate for change, that the era of New Deal liberalism had ended, and that they could now dismantle the New Deal programs. *U.S. News* reported that a new cycle in American political history was beginning and that the Republicans could be expected to remain in office for up to sixteen years.[34] *Newsweek* speculated that the New Deal was at its end and announced, "An

Era Begins."[35] To Republican Senate leader Robert Taft, the Republican mandate was "to cast out a great many chapters of the New Deal, if not the whole book."[36]

The victory also gave the Republicans tremendous overconfidence. No party had ever won the midterm elections and then gone on to lose the White House two years later, and the Republicans began to plan for the probability of controlling both houses of Congress and the White House after 1948. Their attitude seemed to be that they could do as they pleased (at least on domestic issues) without worrying about suffering the repercussions in the presidential election. Thus the Republican-dominated Eightieth Congress had little concern for compromise or building coalitions outside its own conservative power base. Also, many Republicans were simply content to wait out the two years until one of their own would be elected president, to do nothing until they controlled both branches of government. By 1948, all this overconfidence would turn in Truman's favor.

The election of 1946 also had a major impact on the balance of power inside the White House. Truman had chosen a cabinet that was basically conservative, and that group had maintained considerable influence over the president in the first eighteen months of his presidency. Men such as Secretary of the Treasury John Snyder, Secretary of Agriculture Clinton Anderson, and Truman's chief assistant John Steelman pushed for a conservative response to most important issues such as labor relations, race issues, and general economic policies. After the election, however, liberals in the administration including Special Counsel Clark Clifford, Leon Keyserling of the President's Council of Economic Advisors, and several others at the assistant secretary level were able to persuade Truman that the election results had shown that a move away from the basic policies of the New Deal had confused the American voter, that a liberal swing—a reaffirmation of the New Deal—would, in fact, bring voters back to the party in 1948. Truman was reluctant, but the 1946 defeat forced him to listen to Clifford and his liberal advisers in his administration.

The campaigns in 1946 had little to do with foreign affairs. In a spirit of postwar cooperation, the two parties were supposedly working together to solve the monumental problems that plagued the world after 1945. Any show of divisiveness, it was thought, would send the wrong signal in this crisis time. But to Truman, the results of the election had shown that American voters wanted something done about communism, both in the United States and abroad. Clearly, voters had responded eagerly to Republican Red-baiting. Labor had taken big losses largely because of accusations by Republicans that the unions were lousy with communists. Henry Wallace's demands that the United States cooperate with the Soviets on several issues had obviously hurt liberal candidates, and Wallace himself was successfully labeled a communist by the Republicans and shunned by all but the most liberal Democratic candidates—and most of them lost. Although Truman said after the election that he did not see the results as a mandate to harden his policies against the Soviets, he must have believed that the voters had spoken against communism because he almost immediately began to take a tougher stance against Moscow.[37] This hard line developed into the foreign policy of containment and military and economic aid to Greece and Turkey; finally in March and June 1947 the administration institutionalized the containment policy in the Truman Doctrine and the Marshall Plan. One result of the 1946 election was a hardening of the Cold War.

One month before the election, Arthur Schlesinger Jr. pointed out in *Atlantic Monthly* the gravity of the situation. It was, he said, the first election since FDR's death, the first since the atomic bomb, the first since the end of the war, "the first since the dark growth of the sense of irrepressible conflict between East and West. The most grave and consequential issues are poised for judgement."[38] All of that was true, but the election also turned out to be a lesson to both parties that they needed to learn as the American political system moved into a new era in the years after the war. It was also Truman's nadir as president. His popularity in the polls was lower than for any president in the twentieth century. And to make matters worse, Democratic senator William Fulbright of Arkansas suggested immediately after the election that Truman name a Republican secretary of state (at that time next in line to succeed the president) and step down, like a British prime minister who had lost a vote of confidence in Parliament. The idea was taken so seriously in Washington that Truman felt compelled to respond, saying that he had no intention of relinquishing the presidency.[39]

The obvious deciding factor in the 1946 election was Truman himself. The Democratic party had been held together in one victory after another for sixteen years by the Roosevelt magic. Whatever charisma Roosevelt had, Truman lacked it, and the party factions responded by disintegrating. "The old groups that had been towers of strength for Franklin D. Roosevelt crumbled," reported *U.S. News.* "It will take long and arduous work for the Democrats to bring [the coalition] up to election-winning efficiency again."[40] All Truman could do was move on to 1948, with the lessons of 1946 as a guide for the future.

2

Clark Clifford and Democratic Party Campaign Strategy

The 1946 election hit the Democrats hard. The message from the voters seemed clear: postwar America was moving to the right, the era of the New Deal was over, and if Truman and his administration had any chance of staying in office after 1948, they also would have to take big steps to the right. How could political pundits, strategists, and theorists think otherwise? Americans had not only given the Republicans a congressional majority, they had elected a large number of congressmen who sympathized wholeheartedly with the Republican Old Guard, several prewar isolationists, and not a few rabid anticommunists from the outermost reaches of the far right. The voters, it appeared, had responded to the conservative philosophy, the Republican call. It seemed true enough, as *Newsweek* reported a week after the election, "An Era Begins."[1]

A few liberals in Truman's administration saw the lessons of 1946 differently. Some were advisers in the White House, a few were deputy cabinet officials. Most had some ties to the New Deal, and all can be described as liberals, at least in some fashion. They came to believe that the Democrats had lost in November because Truman had been pulled to the right by conservative forces in the administration, which had led to an abandonment of liberalism and the basic tenets of the New Deal that had kept the Democrats in power since 1933. Within weeks of the 1946 loss these men began meeting to discuss the nature and future of the Truman administration. Their political strategy sessions were held every Monday evening at the Wardman Park Hotel suite of Oscar Ewing. The purpose of the meetings, one of the members recalled, was "for achieving better results in the 1948 elections than the Democratic party had managed in 1946."[2] They also set out to redefine liberalism for postwar America.

Ewing was an official in the Democratic National Committee during the Roosevelt years. He was about to leave his job as special assistant to the attorney general to become director of the Federal Security Agency. It was

Ewing who chose the participants for these meetings, brought them together at his Wardman Park apartment, and even provided the steak dinners that preceded the sessions.

Among the most continuous members of Ewing's exclusive club were Leon Keyserling and C. Girard (Jebby) Davidson. Keyserling, a lawyer and economist and a former administrative assistant to Senator Robert Wagner, was by 1947 the most liberal member of the Truman administration's Council of Economic Advisors. Davidson, assistant secretary of the interior, had attained a reputation as a militant defender of civil liberties and an advocate of a government-managed economy. Other regulars included David Morse, assistant secretary of labor; Charles Murphy, a White House aide; and Clark Clifford, special counsel to the president. Others met with the group occasionally, most hoping to have their plan or opinion approved by the group and then presented to the president, but it was these six men who became the chief strategists for Truman's 1948 campaign.[3]

The members of the Wardman Park group met informally over dinner, apparently as equals with no chosen leader. Nearly all participants, however, accorded Clark Clifford a special status within the group.[4] A successful St. Louis lawyer and a naval officer, Clifford rocketed to the White House top levels as Truman's chief adviser by filling an important vacuum left by Samuel Rosenman, Roosevelt's special counsel, who left the Truman administration in the summer of 1946. After 1946 Clifford emerged within the administration as a liberal around whom other young liberals rallied against the powerful conservative coalition building inside Truman's cabinet. Clifford was pragmatic (even a bit cynical) about politics—an attitude that would greatly affect the Wardman Park group. As the president's special counsel, he had considerable influence with Truman, and that made him the key to the success of the group meeting at Wardman Park. They decided what opinions and ideas should be presented to the president, and Clifford approached Truman with the group's consensus arguments. "I was their link with the President," Clifford stated.[5]

These liberals came to believe that the 1946 defeat had shown the necessity for coordinating liberal thinking in the administration to offset the strong conservative influence on Truman. Jebby Davidson recalled these concerns: "We felt that our little group constituted the 'Liberal wing versus the old timers and the conservatives in the Cabinet.'" The group came together, he remembered, because Democratic National Committee chairman "Howard McGrath, [Oscar] Ewing, and others who were running the Committee, did not like the type of advice that the President was getting from some of his Cabinet officers to try and outdo [leading Republican presidential contender Thomas] Dewey in being conservative."[6] The result was that the Wardman Park group formulated liberal political strategy to counter the conservative voices in the administration.

This powerful conservative coalition of advisers and cabinet members included Presidential Assistant John Steelman, Secretary of Commerce Averell Harriman (and later Charles Sawyer), Secretary of the Treasury John Snyder, Secretary of the Navy James Forrestal, and Secretary of Agriculture Clinton Anderson. They were often joined by Secretary of State George Marshall and a few others. The conflict between this group and the liberals in the administration became acute after the 1946 debacle. Clifford later recalled: "There was a very real imbroglio within the administration, and it was generally known that there was a conservative-liberal struggle going on. . . . It was two forces fighting for the mind of the President."[7] This conflict, however, did not bypass Truman. In fact, he made use of it. Several advisers recalled that the president was well aware of the conflict and, in fact, considered it healthy even to the point of asking representatives from each side to engage in debates on various issues in his presence.[8]

Truman liberalism differed from Roosevelt liberalism. The postwar world was no longer focused on the problems of poverty and the burdens of inequality. Instead, a new liberalism emerged that was concentrated on the equitable distribution of the new abundance and the rise of a new and powerful middle class.[9] The members of the Wardman Park group understood this well. Clifford, in fact, saw the group as new thinkers, "a new generation of post-Roosevelt officials who felt that new circumstances required new solutions. They believed that the basic tenets of the New Deal should be adapted to the postwar environment, not abandoned."[10] The group, recalled Clifford, hoped "to make every effort it could to see that [the] prosperity was participated in by all and not just a favored few." The group was, he added, "opposed to what was known as the 'trickle down' theory."[11] Liberalism in this period was moving toward Truman, Clifford, and the members of the Wardman Park group and away from the style of liberalism of Roosevelt, Harry Hopkins, and Wallace—the representatives of the downtrodden and helpless. As the crises of the Depression and the war years gave way to the prosperity of the postwar era, liberalism naturally took on a new character away from the left.

After 1946 Clark Clifford was the primary representative of this new style of liberalism. Clifford was pragmatic in his outlook, and his pragmatism soon overtook the members of the Wardman Park group. He believed, as he later wrote, that the liberals like himself in the administration were "misunderstood by most of the old . . . ideological liberals." Therefore, he added, "we did not include in the group 'professional liberals,'" those men "whose ardor and search for ideological purity outweighed their discretion and their judgement." The Wardman Park group was, instead, made up of practical men who were looking for definable results of their work. "To me," Clifford wrote, "the question has always been, What is the most that can be achieved—in short, what is the best *possible* outcome?" The group, he added, followed his lead in wanting to "marshall the power and authority of the government for the benefit of all mankind."[12] The pragmatic liberal philosophy of the Wardman Park group had a tremendous impact on the direction taken by the Truman administration for the next three years.

They may have originally assembled to bring their style of liberalism to bear on the Truman administration, but the Wardman Park group quickly turned into a campaign strategy committee focused on electing the president in 1948. Clifford recalled this change of purpose. The group, he remembered, was organized after the 1946 election "to promote the interest of those in the administration who believed that the liberal principles should continue to guide the Truman administration." He added, however, that "within a period of a few months the political overtones of these decisions began to become apparent and we were clear beyond question . . . that through '47, as the record was being made, [the Wardman Park group] would either make a contribution to [the election of] '48 or be a burden to '48." As the election approached, Clifford noted, "Every decision [we] made . . . had some political connotation." Keyserling agreed: "The Ewing group branched into a wide range of other matters which really culminated . . . in the stance of the President in the campaign of 1948."[13]

The group advised the president, through Clifford, to rebuild a coalition that would include organized labor, moderate liberals, and northern urban African Americans. The president should move aggressively to satisfy each of these groups, the committee contended, through specific concessions that would win their votes in 1948. "It was my idea," Ewing recalled, "that we should try to develop a pattern of things for the President to do that would convince the various groups of voters that President Truman was pitching on their team. You've got to direct your efforts at these great large groups," he added. "We made a drive at labor. . . . We made a real drive for the Negro vote." By election time, Clifford recalled later, the president could show these groups that the administration was on their side.[14]

The group also originated the campaign strategy of attacking the Eightieth Congress, a strategy that would virtually dominate Truman's campaign and be a major factor in his victory. "I thought the 80th Congress was a good target," Davidson said, "and one that should be attacked. . . . This whole idea of giving the Congress hell, I think, really came from this little Monday night group." The group also advised the president to support national health insurance, fair employment legislation, unification of the armed forces, federal housing, an extension of Social Security benefits, and the establishment of a Jewish state in Palestine. The president followed the advice and pushed these issues.[15]

It has been suggested that Truman was not influenced by the Wardman Park group, that their opinions, philosophy, and strategy simply matched his.[16] Clifford himself stated, "It is everlastingly to the President's credit that his basic inclinations were along liberal lines, or I think the group never would have succeeded."[17] Truman may have had liberal inclinations, but the Wardman Park group seems to have influenced him on several important political issues, forcing him into a liberal posture while others in the cabinet were pulling him to the right in response to the Republican victories in 1946. "This group," said Keyserling, "was set up for the purpose of reexamining the position of the Democratic administration and its policies, and it was quite influential with the president." Davidson felt the Wardman Park group influenced the president as much as the cabinet did. And Clifford (although he was willing to give Truman a great deal of credit) said, "Out of the group . . . I think came the major impact of liberal thinking on the Truman administration in '47 and '48."[18]

While the Wardman Park group debated the various objectives of liberalism—and how Truman might win the 1948 election—a piece of campaign strategy emerged that would become the primary agenda for Truman's 1948 victory. The author of this strategy memorandum predicted coming political events with an almost eerie accuracy, and he gave advice to Truman and his advisers that would send them on a direct route to victory in November 1948. This now-famous memo was written by James Rowe, a political analyst in the Roosevelt administration, and placed in Truman's hands by Clifford, who again became the conduit for the political strategy that would elect Truman.

This memo has long been credited to Clifford, who received it from Rowe in September 1947 and gave it to Truman a month later. In fact, Clifford made almost no significant changes to Rowe's original memo before he delivered it to Truman. Clifford was certainly important here. Without his access to Truman, Rowe's memo would never have become the guiding light of the president's campaign strategy. But Clifford was not the author.[19]

Rowe had been an important political adviser in the Roosevelt White House. When FDR died, Rowe moved on to become a partner in a prestigious Washington law firm headed by onetime Roosevelt aide Thomas Corcoran, but he continued to maintain contacts with the Truman administration and the Democratic party through Truman's budget director, James Webb. In 1946, at Clifford's request, Rowe began writing political studies that Clifford used to formulate his own political advice to the president. One such study concerned the problems the president would face in dealing with the Republican Eightieth Congress and how that impending conflict could be used to the president's political advantage.[20] A second study, entitled "The Politics of 1948," was the memo that Clifford used to mold the strategy of Truman's 1948 campaign.

This memo had to go through Clifford because Truman disliked Rowe, or, more exactly, Truman disliked "Tommy the Cork" Corcoran. And when "Harry Truman dislikes someone," Clifford recalled, "he would often extend that hostility, in the spirit of old Missouri feuds, toward his enemy's associates—and that most definitely included Tommy the Cork's partner James Rowe." Consequently, when the memo first came to Truman (through Webb) and under Rowe's signature, Truman passed it on to Clifford without reading it. Clifford took it to the Wardman Park group. "The Monday-Night men were unanimous," Clifford recalled. "The Rowe draft was consistent with our views and contained the core of a very perceptive strategy for the 1948 election."[21] He made some changes, had it retyped, and sent it on to the president under his own signature.[22]

In a letter to Webb that accompanied the original memo, Rowe explained how he came to his ideas. He wrote that the research for the document was done through "a large number of conversations with labor leaders, professional politicians, newspapermen[,] etc." These conversations were carried on in an "idle fashion and were all in social settings, and 'accidebtally' [sic] pushed into political channels. No one knew that I was writing anything for anyone on politics."[23]

Rowe began his memo by making two important predictions: New York governor Thomas Dewey would win the Republican nomination in 1948, and Henry Wallace would run as a third-party candidate. He then went on to argue that the nation's political system had changed since the war and that the party's political machines could no longer be relied on to deliver votes. "They have been supplanted in large measure by the pressure groups—and," he added, "the support of these must be wooed since they really control the 1948 election." He identified these groups as farmers, organized labor, and progressives, and he added to the list "racial groups who have learned to use the vote as an economic weapon and who can no longer be satisfied with a Tammany turkey on Thanksgiving." The key to a Democratic victory in the 1948 election, Rowe argued, was to satisfy these various groups, to give them what they wanted, and to see that they voted Democratic.[24]

Of all these groups, it was labor, Rowe wrote, that was the most crucial to Truman's 1948 campaign: "President Truman and the Democratic Party cannot win without the *active* support of organized labor." If workers were not inspired and not politically satisfied, he added, they would do what they did in 1946: stay home. "Labor must be cajoled, flattered and educated. Above all its leaders must be taken into the Administration's councils and must be given a far larger voice than they now have on matters of policy."

Of those on the left in the party, Rowe distinguished between two groups: the liberals and the progressives. The liberals, represented in Rowe's analysis by the Americans for Democratic Action (ADA), included most of the old Roosevelt New Dealers. This group, Rowe pointed out, had broken with the group he called the progressives over foreign policy issues, with the liberals supporting an anti-Soviet stance while the progressives had wanted the United States to join the Soviet Union in a postwar alliance. Both the liberals and the progressives, Rowe added, were numerically small. "But, similar to manufacturers and financiers [in] the Republican Party, they are far more influential than mere numbers entitle them to be." These groups exerted unusual influence because they were articulate, Rowe wrote. "The 'right' may have the money, but the 'left' has always had the pen. If the 'intellectual' can be induced to back the President, he will do so in the press, on the radio, and in the movies."

Another group Rowe targeted was African Americans: "A theory of many professional politicians is that the northern Negro voter today holds the balance of power in Presidential elections for the simple arithmetical reason that the Negroes not only vote in a bloc but are geographically concentrated in the pivotal, large and closely contested electoral states such as New York, Illinois, Pennsylvania, Ohio and Michigan." But, he added, the African-American voter was disenchanted with the Democrats because of the influence of southern white racists in the party. African Americans must be reminded constantly during the campaign "that the really great improvement in the economic lot of the Negro of the North has come in the last sixteen years only because of the sympathy and policies of the Democratic Administration." But unless Truman made "real efforts (as distinguished from mere political gestures which are today thoroughly understood and strongly resented by sophisticated Negro leaders) the Negro bloc . . . will go Republican."

Any campaign strategy that played to liberals and African Americans threatened to alienate southern conservatives, a powerful wing of the Democratic party and a large and important bloc of voters. Rowe, however, advised that any strategy to elect Truman should not consider the South. "It is inconceivable," Rowe wrote, "that any policies initiated by the Truman Administration no matter how 'liberal' could so alienate the South in the next year that it would revolt. As always, the South can be considered safely Democratic. And in formulating national policy it can be safely ignored."

Rowe identified other groups and their political needs. The Jews, he wrote, were important only in New York and were concerned only with the administration's handling of Palestine. Catholics, he added, were fearful of communism and "actively distrustful and suspicious today of any group which gives even an appearance of neutrality towards foreign or domestic Communists." He then added observations about Italians and "The Alien Group," or first-generation immigrants.

Rowe continued his memo with another series of predictions and some advice. He warned the administration that the bipartisan foreign policy would become a casualty of the campaign, and he insisted that relations with the Soviets would intensify as the election got closer. "The worse matters get," he argued, "the more is there a sense of crisis. In times of crisis the American citizen tends to back up his President." That is, foreign policy crises could substantially aid the president's campaign.

Rowe also predicted that domestic issues in the campaign would focus on high prices and housing. He added that the administration's conflict with the Eightieth Congress would increase as the election approached. He added that the administration would fail to have its domestic agenda approved by Congress because the Republican-dominated Eightieth Congress would not allow any such victories in an election year. Therefore, Rowe argued, the president's domestic policy "must be tailored for the voter, not the Congressmen," and it must also "display a label which reads 'no compromise.'" Bills introduced by the administration and defeated by Republicans in Congress could be pointed to in the campaign as an attempt by Truman to aid a specific agenda, while suffering no adverse political consequences.

In the fall of 1947, Wallace was moving toward announcing his candidacy on a third-party ticket, and most political analysts considered him a real threat to Truman's coming campaign. Rowe advised that Wallace should be "insulated . . . put under attack whenever the moment is psychologically correct." These attacks, Rowe added, should come from loyal liberals in the party "*and no one else*. . . . They must point out that the core of the Wallace backing is made up of Communists and the fellow-travelers." But, Rowe continued, the simple strategy of labeling Wallace a communist sympathizer would not be enough to remove him from the campaign. Rowe added that Truman must make significant moves toward the political left, which would cut the ground from under Wallace and steal his support. Only that, said Rowe, would end the Wallace threat.

Rowe continued his memo with a long discourse on what he saw as a drastic need to improve Truman's image. Roosevelt, of course, had successfully maintained a spectacular image in the American mind, and as the first presidential election since Roosevelt's death began to unfold, image was now a problem for Truman and for the other candidates in the campaign as well. Rowe advised that the press be coddled, that Truman be seen with important Americans, and that he use his office as often as possible to make news.

Rowe's predictions, as it turned out, were exactly right. The memo so influenced Truman, Clifford, and the Wardman Park group that it became the backbone of the administration's campaign strategy. From another suggestion in the memo a campaign research staff was established in the Democratic National Committee to direct campaign strategy. The strategy devised was based on Rowe's memo, and it directed Truman through the campaign.

The memo is the key to understanding Truman's campaign and the key to his November victory. The strategy that was devised in the Wardman Park group and then among the campaign research staff was essentially the same: move to the left and focus on building a coalition of groups that centered on organized labor, liberals, and northern urban African Americans. It was a winning plan.

In his letter to Webb that accompanied his memo, Rowe wrote an obvious truth in late 1947: "I do not know whether Mr. Truman would be elected if everything in this memo were done to perfection. But I *do know* that if no attempt is made to do the major suggestions, us Democrats ain't got a chance in hell."[25]

3

The Eightieth Congress and the Question of Mandate

The love-hate relationship between President Truman and the Republican-led Eightieth Congress is legendary in America's twentieth-century political history. On domestic matters, it was a bare-fisted affair with the president vetoing seventy-five bills in the two sessions, five of which were overridden. The 1946 elections had strengthened the Republican–southern Democrat coalition of conservatives, and that coalition generally overran Truman's domestic initiatives. Consequently, very little was accomplished, giving the president an issue that set the tone of his 1948 campaign. On foreign affairs, however, the two parties generally worked together through much of both sessions establishing a bipartisan Cold War foreign policy (based on the containment of communism) that prevailed for another forty years and gave Truman the popular reputation as the president who took a strong stand against the spread of international communism. After Truman's victory in November 1948, Representative Charles Halleck, an Old Guard Republican from Indiana, seemed to see the decisive roll the Eightieth Congress played in Truman's election: "It . . . galls me to think that Harry Truman won in 1948 by attacking the Congress which gave him his place in history."[1]

In January 1947, as the members of the Eightieth Congress took their seats, the Republicans were badly divided. Out of power in Congress since 1930, they now clashed openly and loudly over how the country should be run under their leadership. On the left were the Republican liberals. They were still occasionally referred to as progressives, but that term had changed its meaning since the early years of the century. This group did not fear big government, and they often supported federally sponsored social programs as a means of maintaining economic prosperity. On foreign policy issues, these liberal Republicans were internationalists, in opposition to the old midwestern isolationists in the party, and generally in support of the Truman administration's foreign policy initiatives. Republican mayors, governors, and congressmen with large urban constituencies (particularly in the Northeast) usually fell into this group. Often referred to as "me-too" Republicans for their willingness to go along with the Democratic party's agenda, these liberals made up the smallest of the Republican factions and were the least represented in the Republican Eightieth Congress.

To their right, ideologically, sat the moderates. They wanted to stop government growth, although they were usually willing to accept some New Deal social programs, only with reduced funding. Generally, they considered the New Deal acceptable but inefficient, and given the opportunity they believed they could run the New Deal social programs better than the Democrats. They usually supported lower taxes, a balanced budget, and an internationalist foreign policy. The moderates were a large and important part of the Republican Eightieth Congress, and they often held the balance of power on major issues, both foreign and domestic.

On the right were the conservatives, better known as the Old Guard. Their forebears had been in power in the 1890s, then again in the 1920s, and now it seemed they were on the verge of another run of national power and prominence. In 1947 they controlled national Republican party machinery, and they were in firm control in Congress, particularly in the House. Their most popular refrain was to accuse the New Deal of being the pathway to communism, or communism itself, and they had already achieved considerable political success by accusing others of being communists or, often, "soft on communism." They also believed in limiting the growth of government and government spending. A balanced budget would result, and that would bring on increased business confidence and, ultimately, real prosperity, as opposed to the artificial prosperity being handed out by New Deal programs. On foreign policy they were often isolationists, believing that the nation's energies and money should stay at home and that the United States could only lose by becoming involved in the world's entangling alliances.

The split in the Republican party between the Old Guard on the right and the moderates and liberals had its origins deep in the Republican past, but it was during the New Deal era (and over the question of the New Deal itself) that the split widened considerably and then became a major problem for the party in the postwar years. In the 1920s, the last great period of Republican dominance, the Republican party maintained a powerful coalition of prosperous midwestern farmers, African Americans who maintained their loyalty to the party of Lincoln, urban workers, small businessmen, and powerful corporate moguls. But the Depression ate deeply into that coalition. Roosevelt and the Democrats in 1932 succeeded in convincing voters that Hoover and the Republicans were responsible for the nation's woes. Over and over again between 1932 and 1944 the Democrats laid that blame at the feet of their Republican opponents and won elections. While in office, Roosevelt was able to build a new Democratic coalition by dispensing the nation's wealth to a variety of identifiable groups through the New Deal programs. As an economic program, the New Deal may have achieved only nominal success, as historians of the period point out, but as a political program the success of the New Deal has been unmatched in the twentieth century. By 1945 the powerful Democratic coalition included African Americans, southerners, ethnic urban voters and urban political machines, organized labor, farmers, and urban intellectuals. Through the Roosevelt era, the Republican right tried to maintain its Old Guard conservatism and its new anti–New Dealism, but the moderates and the liberals in the party moved to the left in the face of successive defeats and began to argue that Roosevelt's New Deal programs were acceptable but inefficient and would be better managed in their hands. Consequently, the split between the two wings of the party widened over how the New Deal should be challenged.

In 1936 the liberal-moderate coalition in the Republican party nominated Alf Landon, who was promptly trounced by Roosevelt. Afterward, the Old Guard argued persuasively that "me-tooism" was not the answer to the party's troubles and that given a viable, conservative alternative to the New Deal the nation's voters would again come back to the Republican party. Consequently, Landon's defeat strengthened the Old Guard. Four years later, however, the liberal-moderate coalition again pulled the strings at the convention and nominated Wendell Willkie, a man whose political leanings need little more embellishment here than to note that he voted for FDR in 1932. Willkie improved on Landon's 1936 showing, but, as the Old Guard Republicans argued again, "me-tooism" was a loser. The Republicans, however, went through one more cycle of this defeatist plan in 1944 when they passed over Willkie and nominated Thomas E. Dewey, the well-known New York City gangbuster and popular New York state governor. Despite predictions of victory from the likes of Walter Lippmann and an endorsement from labor leader John L. Lewis, Dewey was defeated fairly handily (54 to 46 percent), although he had gotten closer to Roosevelt than either Landon or Willkie. The defeat again strengthened the Old Guard argument that the answer to the Republican party's losing streak must come from the right and not the left. The 1946 victories brought in large numbers of conservatives to both houses, and it appeared that 1948 would not only be a GOP year at the polls but a year for the Old Guard to control, possibly, both Capitol Hill and the White House.

Domestic policy had defined the Republicans through the Roosevelt decades of the 1930s and 1940s. Generally, they either opposed the New

Deal outright, or they opposed the way it was managed. Postwar foreign policy, however, presented ideological problems for many Republicans. The old prewar isolationism still held on for many in the party, particularly those from the Midwest, where isolationism had been the strongest before December 1941. However, to stop the spread of international communism, large amounts of U.S. aid would be required, money that many in the Republican party believed should be used instead to balance the budget and then returned to the public in tax cuts. Right-wing isolationists in Congress such as William Jenner of Indiana insisted that foreign aid doled out to every little country that believed it was being challenged by communism would ultimately bankrupt the United States and lead to what he called a "bloodless takeover" by the Soviet Union.[2] Republican isolationists, in the years after the war, fought U.S. aid to Great Britain, opposed the establishment of the International Monetary Fund, and many opposed the Marshall Plan.[3]

While Jenner and other isolationists on the far right continued to complain about costs and commitments, most of the old prewar isolationist Republicans had come to the conclusion that isolationism had failed in the prewar period and that the United States must continue its involvement in world affairs to avoid future wars. They wanted to maintain a strong stand against the spread of the Soviet Union's power, but they also believed that all foreign dealings must be done alone, without the commitments of entangling alliances, thus they became known as "unilateralists." They wanted a strong military, placing a great deal of emphasis on the superiority of U.S. airpower and the nation's nuclear monopoly as deterrents against war. They also advocated protective tariffs and opposed foreign aid.

The undisputed leader of the Republican Eightieth Congress was Robert A. Taft, the son of a president, a consummate politician, and the only member of his party who could command the sobriquet of "Mr. Republican." Taft came to the Senate from Ohio in 1938 pledging to end the excesses of the New Deal. We must, he said, "break with the corrupting idea that we can legislate prosperity, legislate equality, legislate opportunity." Prosperity, equality, and opportunity, he added, "came in the past from free Americans freely working out their destiny. . . . That is the only way they can continue to come in any genuine sense." By 1947, when the members of the Eightieth Congress took their seats, he was the leading anti–New Dealer in the Senate, and his sights were set on dismantling as many of Roosevelt's programs as possible.[4]

Taft may have seen it as his mission to destroy the New Deal, but he was no right-wing ideologue. He believed strongly in active government and its responsibility to help Americans who had fallen through the cracks of the free market system that he defended so strenuously. He spoke openly of the need to prevent hardship and poverty in America, and he often supported federal aid to education and public housing in situations where private enterprise had failed to do the job. In 1947, as the Republicans looked to the promises of victory in the 1948 presidential election, Robert Taft was the undisputed powerhouse in Congress, and at that moment he was also considered the party's leading contender for the 1948 presidential nomination. It was undoubtedly the crowning moment of Taft's political career.[5]

Taft was the undisputed party leader on domestic affairs. His counterpart on foreign affairs was the venerable Arthur Vandenberg, senator from Michigan and chairman of the Senate Foreign Relations Committee in the Eightieth Congress. Vandenberg had been a leader of the Midwest isolationists before the war, but after Pearl Harbor he began slowly moving toward the internationalism of the Roosevelt administration. In the postwar years, Republicans with internationalist leanings like Vandenberg came to support Truman's foreign policy, ostensibly to maintain a united front in the face of the growing Soviet threat but in fact because both the Republican internationalists and the Truman administration foreign policy experts had the same general philosophy toward foreign affairs. That philosophy was to present a hard line against international communism, while giving the United States a significant role in the world. As the Cold War grew colder, the relationship between the Republican internationalists and the Truman administration grew closer. It was no surprise that a hard-line anticommunist like Truman's secretary of state James F. Byrnes shared a foreign policy philosophy with Vandenberg and other Republican internationalists.[6] Consequently, the Truman administration regularly called for a bipartisan foreign policy, courted Vandenberg and kept him informed, and occasionally hailed the Michigan senator as a statesman for having the fortitude to keep politics from influencing his foreign policy stance.[7]

The Republican Eightieth Congress is often described as having been led by Taft on domestic policy and by Vandenberg on issues of foreign affairs. It is true that Vandenberg almost always deferred to Taft on domestic issues. But Taft, with traces of isolationism still flowing through his veins, was hardly willing to defer to Vandenberg on foreign policy concerns. Taft believed strongly that it was the job of the Republicans in Congress to form an opposition—on all fronts—to the Democrats, that it was necessary to present the American people with two distinct choices at election time. He believed, in fact, that the more clearly contrasted the two major parties were on the issues, the better choice voters would be able to make and the stronger the nation's political system would be as a result. For Taft, bipartisanship meant a weak political system. At the same time, he was not prepared to allow foreign affairs issues to split his party between the isolationists and the internationalists; harmony within the party was more important. Also, Taft needed conservative southern support to push through his domestic agenda, and southerners almost always fell in behind the administration's internationalist foreign policy. For these reasons, Taft remained mostly quiet on foreign affairs issues during the first session of the Eightieth Congress.[8] When the press found hints of a split between Taft and Vandenberg over foreign policy, Taft wrote an open letter to Vandenberg designed to end the speculation and maintain party harmony: "I suppose there may be some differences as there always are, but I approve without qualification your whole position as I know it."[9]

Despite the mask of harmony, the Republicans were deeply divided over foreign policy. The Old Guard, steeped in isolationism, opposed the bipartisan internationalists on a variety of issues, including the Marshall Plan. Also, the domestic leadership was Old Guard, while international affairs were generally under the leadership of moderates and liberals. The big question remained: How could America contain communism overseas without huge amounts of foreign aid, tax increases, and a large, expensive standing army—all anathema to the Republican philosophy? Foreign policy was a difficult problem for Republicans in the immediate postwar years.

When the Republicans came to Capitol Hill in January 1947, there was a great deal of speculation in the country. For the first time since 1930 they were in control of Congress. *US News* dubbed the event the beginning of "a new cycle in American political history." A month later, the magazine added that the Republicans were on their way to a victory in 1948.[10] Representative Joe Martin, the new Speaker of the House, felt, as the new Congress took its place, that it was "the revival of the Republican Party, the ultimate proof that the party had survived the ordeal of the Thirties."[11] For Republicans, redemption had finally come. It was a jubilant time.

But what was the mandate? Why had the nation sent a Republican-dominated Congress to Washington? The Republican campaign slogan had been "Had Enough?" And Republican candidates believed they were asking further "of the New Deal?" It seemed clear enough that voters had answered with a rousing affirmative. One congressman handed out brooms to all Republicans as they took their seats. Each broom carried a sign that said, "Here's yours. Let's do the job."[12] The job to be done, of course, was to clear out the New Deal. To Taft, the mandate was apparent: "The main issue in the election" of 1946, he told Congress, "was the restoration of freedom and the elimination or reduction of constantly increasing interference with family life and with business by autocratic government bureaus and autocratic labor leaders." And they intended to fulfill that mandate, to do the job they believed they had been elected to do, to cut taxes drastically, to deregulate business and industry, to crush the power of organized labor, and to balance the budget at all costs. We are here, Taft told Congress further, "to cast out a great many chapters of the New Deal, if not the whole book."[13]

It would soon become clear, however, that the Republican members of the Eightieth Congress had badly misinterpreted the mandate they received in the 1946 elections. The message sent by voters reflected more a disgust with the administration's policy of reconversion than a desire to see the New Deal torn down. It should be no real surprise, however, that the Republicans misinterpreted the election results. Conditions requiring the New Deal had ended. The economy was different in 1946 than it had been during the Depression. There was now high employment, inflation, and a rapidly expanding economy—the opposite of the problems facing Roosevelt in the 1930s. There was a growing middle class, relatively satisfied with their economic situation and for the most part with no great desire to come to the aid of others. So it appeared that Americans neither needed nor wanted the New Deal programs. Consequently, the Republicans saw the 1946 election results as a mandate to end the reforms of the New Deal, reforms that were designed to relieve economic problems that no longer existed.

The committee assignments in the Eightieth Congress revealed much about the divisions in the Republican party—and of what was to come. The position of Speaker of the House went to Joseph Martin from Massachusetts. Martin was elected in 1924 and had been his party's floor leader since 1932. He had supported Wendell Willkie in 1940, but he was very conservative and an avid anti–New Dealer with strong ties in the House to conservative southern Democrats. The job of majority leader in the House was contested between the two main wings of the Republican party. Indiana congressman Charles Halleck, who was being pushed by Republican presidential hopeful Thomas Dewey, was locked in a fight with Clarence Brown of Ohio, who was supported openly by Taft. It was eighteen months before the Republican convention would convene in Philadelphia, but this struggle signaled the opening shots between Taft and Dewey in the campaign for the party's 1948 nomination. Finally, Halleck, with Dewey behind him, won the caucus vote, scoring Taft's first defeat in the Eightieth Congress.[14]

The chairmanships in the House were filled mostly by Old Guard conservatives, rabid anti–New Dealers, and prewar isolationists.[15] During the tenure of the Eightieth Congress, the House would be considerably more conservative than the Senate, and the Senate often found itself in the position of moderating House bills. Conservative southern Democrats in the House (a group Speaker Martin called "stout allies") voted regularly with the Republicans on domestic issues, following an unspoken understanding that in exchange Republicans would support southern Democrats against the efforts of their liberal party members to change southern segregation laws. This agreement was forged on the philosophy of states' rights shared by both Republicans and conservative southern Democrats.

Leadership in the House was divided among several influential Republicans, but in the Senate Taft was the undisputed leader. His place in the party was secure enough for him to take the position of Senate floor leader, but he expected to be shackled with the burdens of running for president during the second session in 1948 so he allowed that time-consuming job to pass to mild-mannered Wallace White of Maine. Taft then simply controlled White, to the point that White openly deferred to Taft on all issues by looking back from his Senate seat twelve rows to Taft for signals that told White what to do. Taft instead chose to head the Senate Steering Committee, which allowed him to control all committee assignments and set the party's legislative agenda. It was from this position, his biographer William White has written, that Taft was able to run the Republican-dominated Senate "like the Commanding General at Supreme Headquarters."[16]

Taft, however, had a stiff personality. He was often described as pedantic, cold, and abrupt. He was fact-driven and generally considered boring.[17] Although well respected by members of both parties for his political skills, Taft was a long way from being liked by his colleagues. Over his years in office, he had made enough powerful enemies in his party to stand in the way of his nomination for president. These things together produced a Republican postulate that Taft could not be elected, that even if he won his party's nomination he might not be able to beat a Democratic candidate, even Truman, in 1948. This hypothesis had gained momentum over the years, and in 1940 and again in 1944 his party had pushed him aside in favor of a more moderate, less controversial figure. But Taft believed he could win his party's nomination and then the election in November 1948 on the record of the Eightieth Congress—a record he would create.

Taft also used his power to have himself named chairman of the Labor and Public Welfare Committee. Republicans in the Eightieth Congress expected to produce an important piece of labor legislation, and Taft, in taking the committee chairmanship, expected to be a major player in that final product. But the job was very controversial. It was not the place in 1947

Robert Taft expected to run for president in the 1948 election. From the collections of the Library of Congress.

for an aspiring presidential candidate to endear himself to voters. The power of organized labor was an emotional issue in 1947, and whatever stand Taft chose to defend would surely bring down upon him the wrath of either labor or management—and probably both. But Taft saw the work of the labor committee as important to the success of the Eightieth Congress, to the Republican party, and possibly to the future of the nation. "Since the success of the whole session depended on this job being done right," he told Alf Landon, "I thought I had to accept it."[18] Such was the character of Bob Taft. The resulting labor bill that carried his name, however, did little to enhance his electablility. The party leadership's concern that "Taft can't win" grew even stronger.

Taft carried the banner of the Old Guard, but he was hardly the anchor of his party's far right. Several senators were well to the right of Taft, and they saw his willingness to reach workable compromises with the Democrats as no less than cavorting with the enemy. Consequently, they did not trust him. The Senate majority whip, Kenneth Wherry of Nebraska, for example, said of Taft: "I like [Taft], goddamit, even if we have had a hell of a time to keep him from climbing up in [liberal Democrat] Claude Pepper's lap."[19] But ultimately it was the Taftites who controlled most of the major committees in the Senate. Styles Bridges of New Hampshire chaired Appropriations. Wayland Brooks of Illinois headed the Rules Committee. Chan Gurney of South Dakota chaired Military Affairs. Eugene Millikin of Colorado took over Finance.[20] Their appointments were all a testament to Taft's control. The success or failure of the Eightieth Congress would rest squarely on Taft's shoulders.

An important figure in the Republican Eightieth Congress was the newly elected senator John Bricker. Like Taft, Bricker was from Ohio, and also like Taft, Bricker had shown an interest since 1944 in running for his party's presidential nomination in 1948. Bricker had served as Ohio's governor for four consecutive two-year terms and had made a run for president in 1944, settling for the number two spot on the Republican ticket with Dewey. Bricker was no Taftite; he spoke his mind often, and he made it clear that he opposed Taft's stands on education and public housing. After 1946 it appeared that Taft and Bricker would be the leading Republican contenders for the 1948 nomination, but Bricker announced almost immediately that he would defer to Taft and not run.[21]

Other newcomers included John Sherman Cooper, the first Republican elected from Kentucky in twenty-two years; William Knowland, who defeated the popular Will Rogers Jr. in the California Senate race; and James P. Kem, who threw out the Missouri incumbent Democrat who had been appointed to fill Truman's Senate seat in 1945. Montana sent Zales Ecton to Washington, the state's first Republican senator in thirty-three years. These new faces, many of them important before they entered Congress, became an immediate problem for the Republican leadership in the Eightieth Congress. These freshmen considered themselves on the cusp of a new conservative revolution, with a mandate to change the course of the nation. Change was in the air, and they wanted to be a part of it. But the seniority system in Congress counted them out—or at least delegated them to the periphery of the major decisions. In addition, several new Republican members of Congress had come to Washington to make names for themselves. Joseph McCarthy, William Jenner, William Knowland, and Richard Nixon began looking for a vehicle to take them to the top of their party's structure. Taft, forever loyal to the seniority system that he now controlled, tried at first to quell their energy, then he tried to appease them with positions on the party's policy committee. But through the two sessions of the Eightieth Congress these men continued their revolt against the congressional seniority system in their attempt to make themselves heard.

If the Republicans misinterpreted the 1946 mandate, Truman did not, and in several ways he moved quickly to shore up those weak points in his administration that had given the Republicans the issues they needed to win the 1946 elections. The outcome of those elections had shown, if nothing else, that the nation's voters were fed up with the administration's attempts to control postwar inflation through price controls. Simply, reconversion had cost the Democrats control of Congress. On November 9, within a week of the election, Truman ended all wage and price controls except those on sugar, rice, and rents. On December 31 he proclaimed an end to wartime hostilities, which instantly ended eighteen additional emergency powers. Thirty-three other powers were scheduled to lapse in six months. Not only did the move deprive Republicans of an issue, it allowed the president to cut his losses and bring an end to reconversion before the new Republican Congress could grab the opportunity when it convened in January.

The Republicans had also made political hay out of the issue of communism, claiming that communists had infiltrated federal government agencies. Just three weeks after the election, in an attempt to beat the Republicans to the punch on that issue, Truman appointed the Temporary Commission on Employment Loyalty. The commission was to examine the government's procedures for investigating and removing employees deemed disloyal to the government of the United States. On March 21, 1947, after the commission filed its report, Truman set up the Loyalty Review Board, headed by conservative Republican Seth Richardson. The move deprived the Republicans of another issue.[22]

The president's loyalty program succeeded in heading off the Republican charge of being soft on communism that was quickly becoming a Republican campaign slogan directed at all Democrats and even some moderate Republicans. The program allowed Truman to continue to avoid that deadly issue clear through the 1948 campaign. The price paid for neutralizing the issue, however, was very high. Nearly three million federal workers were investigated at an exorbitant cost to American taxpayers of over $20 million. Civil liberties were ignored. Those investigated were presumed guilty, never charged, and never able to confront their accusers. Careers were destroyed. Two hundred twenty-one government employees ultimately lost their jobs as a result of Truman's loyalty program. None were ever convicted or even indicted. Truman was responsible for turning up the heat on the long-burning issue of communists in the government.

The president's State of the Union message, delivered just after the new year and before Congress convened in 1947, was moderate compared to his message of just a year earlier in which he laid down his 21-Point Plan, his ambitious attempt to carry the New Deal forward after Roosevelt's death. In 1947 he outlined a more modest program that included a call for a labor relations bill that would end jurisdictional strikes and secondary boycotts and expand the Department of Labor to aid in the settlement of disputes. He asked for a broadening of Social Security, bills to increase housing and health care, and an increase in the minimum wage. He called for antimonopoly legislation in addition to federal assistance to new industry and small businesses. He asked Congress to balance the budget and to formulate a long-range agricultural program. And Truman promised that civil rights would be dealt with soon. On foreign affairs he called for free trade and international control of atomic energy. It was a moderate program, possibly a sincere attempt to cooperate with the Republicans.[23]

A few days later, Truman sent an economic report to Congress that echoed much of what he had asked for in his State of the Union message. But he added a request that Congress not cut taxes, a proposal that did not sit well with members of the Republican right such as Congressmen John "Meat Axe" Tabor and Harold Knutson, both of whom had promised drastic tax cuts in the 1948 budget. Truman's budget proposal totaled $37.5 billion, and in his budget message he again asked that Congress not reduce taxes, arguing that all surpluses should be used to pay off the national debt, which exceeded $260 billion.[24]

The budget became a problem for the Republicans. For sixteen years they had criticized the Democrats for overspending. Now in power, they were obliged to make good on their promises and slash the budget. But immediately a power struggle erupted between the moderates and the Old Guard in the party over the extent of the cuts. The Joint Committee on the Economy, under right-wing leadership, wanted a $6 billion cut, but Taft won a hard-fought compromise in the Senate for $4.5 billion. The House, however, rejected the Senate compromise and adopted the Joint Committee's proposal of the original $6 billion. The House-Senate conference committee deadlocked, and the Eightieth Congress adjourned without a budget, forced to approve spending throughout the year on individual appropriations bills.[25] For Truman, it would be another issue in the coming campaign that would focus on an inept Congress. For the Republicans, it caused a further split between the Old Guard in power in Congress and the moderates. Out of power for so long, the Republicans seemed inexperienced, hobbled by their own differences and ambitions, powerless to move forward and accomplish much of anything.

There were few conflicts between Truman and the Eightieth Congress in the first few months of 1947, at least partly because the Republicans were divided and unprepared to take on the president. Truman, at the same time, was willing to hand over domestic policy initiatives to Congress while he made decisive and far-reaching moves in foreign policy that, for the most part, needed Republican support to succeed. Those who expected sparks to fly when the members of the Eightieth Congress took their seats in January were disappointed. The Republicans, for instance, demanded and received an increase in air force defense spending above what the president requested and with little objection from the White House. On other budget matters, Truman registered complaints with Congress for proposed cuts in reclamation, soil conservation, water resources, and a few other areas, but he steered clear of any major confrontations that might destroy the fragile bipartisan foreign policy coalition. On another issue, the Republicans (with help from their southern Democrat allies) passed a proposed constitutional amendment limiting the president to two terms in office. Again, Truman had little to say on the issue. When Congress passed a bill designed to curtail the rights of workers to be paid for time spent on the job location in preparation for work but not engaged in actual production, Truman signed the bill with only a few comments directed at the Supreme Court on how he believed the bill should be enacted. Several liberals in Congress, in addition to liberal members of the president's staff and even several cabinet members, opposed this portal-to-portal bill, as it was called, and were surprised at Truman's actions.[26]

Truman also made a series of appointments in the first months of 1947 that seemed designed to appease Republicans in Congress. In January, he pleased even the most conservative members of the Republican party by naming George Marshall as his new secretary of state. Marshall was praised by members of both parties during his confirmation hearings, and he was confirmed quickly and with no controversy. It was a brilliant appointment. Marshall became the new symbol of the bipartisan foreign policy—with the White House firmly in the lead of that policy and reaping all the political rewards over the next two years.[27] Truman also named Lewis W. Douglas as ambassador to Great Britain and A.L.M. Wiggins as under secretary of the treasury. Both men had been open critics of Roosevelt and the New Deal.

This period of conciliation was little more than a political phony war between the two sides as they prepared to do battle over the domestic issues that were sure to come up—specifically, labor reform. But the conflicts were also deferred because the Republicans at first had difficulty moving forward. The newness of the congressional leadership role flushed out too many Republican leaders, men who had spent their entire political careers serving as little more than obstructionists in opposition and now saw an opportunity to jump to the front of the party to conduct their own agendas. Added to this were those new, energetic faces such as Nixon and McCarthy, who wanted to rise quickly through the Republican ranks. And the Republicans were severely divided and fragmented on many issues. The result was slow movement in the first months of the Eightieth Congress.

Truman, however, needed Republican support for his foreign policy initiatives to succeed. This apparent lack of hostilities brought rave reviews for Truman from the people and the press, and his dismal ratings before the 1946 elections soared back up to 51 percent in a March Gallup Poll.[28]

The divisions inside the Republican party became most apparent in the debate over the confirmation of David Lilienthal to head the newly created Atomic Energy Commission. Lilienthal had served Roosevelt since 1933 as head of the Tennessee Valley Authority (TVA). By the late 1940s, the TVA was probably the most visible New Deal program; it was also considered by many Republicans to be one of the most radical because it was a government agency that manufactured a product, principally electricity, that competed directly with private businesses. Lilienthal had always been a favorite target of the Republican right, often accused of being soft on communism and tolerating communists in the TVA. He seemed to symbolize much of what the Republicans had been fighting since 1933. And now Lilienthal was being named to head the nation's Atomic Energy Commission, to be placed in charge of the country's most cherished secrets and its first line of defense.

The first attacks on Lilienthal came from the farthest right, from Kenneth Wherry of Nebraska, the onetime progressive senator and protégé of George Norris turned right-wing Republican. Joining him were E.H. Moore of Oklahoma and Kenneth McKeller of Tennessee. McKeller had held a personal grudge against Lilienthal for years over control of TVA patronage in his home state; to McKeller, Lilienthal was simply a communist. As president of the Senate and chairman of the Appropriations Committee, McKeller would be a formidable foe at the confirmation hearings. Ohio senator John Bricker joined others on the right in trying to stop the Lilienthal nomination. But the entire picture changed in mid-March when Taft threw his heavy political weight behind this group in opposition to Lilienthal.[29] As the hearings commenced before the Joint Committee on Atomic Energy, however, Senator Vandenberg announced that he would cast his vote to confirm. Over the next month the Republicans found themselves embarrassingly divided over the Lilienthal confirmation debate, with the Old Guard (led by the Ohio duo of Taft and Bricker) trying desperately to maintain a majority within their own party against Republican moderates led by Vandenberg. Generally, the debate focused on Lilienthal's New Deal background, his supposed ties to communism, and his belief that atomic energy should be controlled by international agreement. The attacks were strong, and at times Lilienthal considered withdrawing.[30] Vandenberg, however, quiet through most of the debate, stepped up as the committee's work was coming to a close and attacked Lilienthal's opponents, carefully refuting all the accusations and objections raised by the committee. He was, Vandenberg said, "no part of a communist by any stretch of the imagination." The Michigan senator then called for Lilienthal's confirmation as approval roared from the galleries. A motion by Bricker to have the nomination recommitted to committee was quickly defeated. On April 9, the full Senate voted to confirm Lilienthal, but the Republicans were badly divided. More important, Republican infighting had given Truman and the Democrats a victory over the Republican-controlled Congress.[31]

The period of conciliation came to an abrupt end by early summer. Tax cut legislation in early June put Truman on the defensive for the first time, and for the first time he openly criticized the Eightieth Congress for opposing the interests of the average American. The House Appropriations Committee proposed cutting the budget of the Department of Interior by nearly 50 percent, including most reclamation programs in the West. Oregon senator Wayne Morse responded by telling his fellow Republicans that they would suffer severe losses in the West in 1948 if reclamation programs were cut. The party would not be "entitled to the support of the West in a national campaign if this Congress and its leaders cut the heart out of the reclamation program."[32] In response, the Senate toned down the House cuts to about 27 percent. The House Appropriations Committee then attacked the administration's proposed budget for the Department of Agriculture. Conservation was cut, along with the school lunch program, farm tenant loans, crop insurance, and tenant mortgage insurance. Again the Senate moved to reinstate some of the House cuts. American farmers were conservative, but by 1947 they had come to depend on New Deal programs as a safety net that brought an end to the agony of the boom-and-bust economic cycles that always seemed to hurt farmers more than any other economic group. The Republicans were moving along with very little regard for how appropriations cuts might be translated directly into lost votes at the polls. Truman remained fairly quiet in response to all this furor until a press conference on June 5, when he lashed out at Taft for the first time for opposing foreign aid and domestic price reductions. The president called for full employment and full production, and he said that Taft and the Eightieth Congress were responsible for standing in the way of achieving those longtime Democratic party goals. He called Taft's initiatives "a defeatist economic policy" that followed "the old idea of boom and bust." The next day in Kansas City at a reunion for his old World War I division, Truman called for a raise in the minimum wage, an extension of Social

Security benefits, and provisions for adequate housing, and he criticized Congress for cutting reclamation and conservation programs and for cutting funds for public power projects.[33]

The first major conflict between the administration and Congress came over the question of labor reform. In the Seventy-ninth Congress a Republican–southern Democrat coalition had passed the Case bill, a mild labor reform act, that was vetoed by Truman in June 1946. The success of the Case bill and then the Republican victories in November ensured that the Eightieth Congress would pass a major piece of labor legislation. Also, the Republicans believed that they had been elected in November 1946 to achieve, among other things, major labor reform.[34] Fred Hartley, one of the chief spokesmen for antilabor legislation in the Republican party, stated in a press release that moving quickly to restrict the powers of labor "is our response to the mandate that the people of the United States gave to us last November."[35]

By the end of February, sixty-five bills restricting the powers of organized labor had been introduced in the two houses. Fearing the worst, CIO president Philip Murray warned workers that "nearly every form of union activity is attacked in one bill or another."[36] At the same time, antilabor legislation was making headway in several state legislatures.

The first major piece of labor reform legislation was reported from committee in the House on April 11. Its sponsor was Fred Hartley, the Republican chairman of the House Labor Committee. The bill had been inspired by the National Association of Manufacturers, then the most powerful organization representing management in the nation. It was approved in the House with the aid of seventy-nine southern Democrats.[37] The Republicans in the Senate moved to tone down the bill, with Taft leading the way as chairman of the Education and Labor Committee. Taft's committee included two liberal Republicans: Wayne Morse of Oregon and George Aiken of Vermont. Taft felt that a member of the Dewey camp should also be represented on the committee, and Irving Ives from New York was included to that end.[38] The Taft bill, moderate compared to the House bill, followed from a favorable Senate hearing on April 12, the day after the Hartley bill was approved.

The House-Senate conference committee, under Taft's leadership, produced the Taft-Hartley bill, the most wide-sweeping labor legislation since the Wagner Act. The Taft-Hartley bill would outlaw the closed shop, allow eighty-day injunctions when the vital interests of the nation were at stake, ban industry-wide bargaining and foremen's unions, deny collective bargaining rights to unions with communist officers, prohibit unions from making political contributions or endorsements, and forbid government employees to strike. The Hartley bill passed the House on April 17, only six days after it was introduced. Taft's versions passed the Senate on May 13. On June 4, the House passed the final version, and the next day the Senate followed suit.[39]

Without discussing the issue with his cabinet, Truman vetoed the bill on June 20. The House, in thundering defiance, overrode the veto the same day with a vote of 331 to 83. The Senate followed three days later, and Taft-Hartley became law. Organized labor pushed hard to stop the Senate override; Truman only tried to influence a few southern votes. Several in Truman's administration, including Clark Clifford and the other liberal advisers and aides, had advised the president to veto the bill. Undoubtedly their sights were set more on winning labor's support in 1948 than on effecting labor reform.[40]

The fight with Congress over Taft-Hartley proved to Truman that confrontation politics could be beneficial—an argument that several of his more liberal advisers were beginning to make. By September 1947 the president had begun attacking the Eightieth Congress for not doing enough. In his Labor Day speech he again called on Congress to increase the minimum wage, broaden the Social Security system, and establish a national health care system.[41] At about the same time, Taft seemed to realize that the Eightieth Congress was producing a record that Democrats could argue was opposing the needs of the average American, and he responded by asking Congress to enact several of his own initiatives, including a health care plan, housing and education bills, an extension of Social Security benefits, and an increase in unemployment benefits.[42] As Taft's candidacy for the 1948 nomination moved forward, he could not afford to be shackled with being labeled the leader of a Congress that was insensitive to the needs of the average American. But the Eightieth Congress refused to recognize the appeal of social welfare legislation, and it rejected Taft's initiatives.

In July, Truman vetoed the Eightieth Congress's second attempt to reduce taxes. In both veto messages he argued that tax reduction was inflationary and that a surplus was needed to retire the national debt. He also argued in both messages (as he would argue on the campaign trail the next year) that these tax reduction proposals were unfair to the average American because they reduced taxes primarily in the highest income brackets.[43]

Truman called a special session of Congress in November to deal with aid for Europe. The situation there was worsening rapidly, and many believed that communism was about to take over in Italy and several other countries. He used the time to introduce a ten-point anti-inflation program.[44] Food prices at home had jumped by 30 percent over the preceding year, and inflation was still the postwar economic bugaboo. Taft responded that the inflation was caused by too much government spending and high taxes.[45] Congress passed only a small part of what Truman wanted, including some consumer credit controls that focused primarily on voluntary participation. When Truman signed the bill just after Christmas, he chastised Congress for taking such "feeble steps toward the control of inflation. At a time when nearly everyone in this Nation is feeling the pressure of exorbitant prices, the Congress has enacted a bill that is pitifully inadequate."[46]

The special session was a big victory for Truman, although it seemed of little importance at the time. He got the aid he wanted for Europe, alleviating the crisis there, while adding to his growing prestige as the leader of the free world against the spread of international communism. He also forced the Republicans into a corner on the issue of inflation. Truman could easily pin the blame for any future inflation on the Republicans for their lack of action, while the public continued to see him as the man who was trying to aid the average American in dealing with the uncertainties of the volatile economy but being thwarted by a rich man's Congress. In addition, the bill that was finally passed succeeded in stabilizing the economy through 1948, and the president was able to run his campaign during fairly good economic times.

Going hand in hand with the president's loyalty program was the Truman Doctrine, one of the cornerstones of the administration's foreign policy. Delivered as a proposal to Congress just days before the president's loyalty program was enacted, the Truman Doctrine became the administration's attack on the forces of international communism. The election of 1946 had made it clear that voters wanted something done to stop the spread of communism, both foreign and domestic. The Truman Doctrine, together with the president's loyalty program, served to steal from the Republicans the thunder of anticommunism that they had used so successfully in 1946, and it placed the administration (and not the Republicans) at the forefront of the campaign to stop the spread of international communism. It also added fuel to the growing anticommunist hysteria that was sweeping the nation.

The situation that led to the Truman Doctrine developed in late February 1947, when the British minister in Washington told Secretary of State George Marshall that Britain could no longer support the government in Greece against a communist insurgency and that the Turkish government was under great pressure from Moscow. The news placed the United States in the awkward (and soon to be all-too-familiar) position of either giving support to Greece and Turkey or allowing, so it seemed, both nations to be swept away in a communist takeover. The situation offered an exceptional opportunity for Truman to show voters that he was not an appeaser, that he would stop the spread of communism, and that he was tough enough to stand up to aggressive dictators like Stalin.

Truman's speech before Congress requesting aid for Turkey and Greece was designed to "pull out all the stops," as then Undersecretary of State Dean Acheson remembered later. Vandenberg insisted that Truman would need to "scare hell" out of Congress if he expected support from large numbers of Republicans. Secretary of Defense James Forrestal also encouraged Truman to exaggerate the situation to win over Congress.[47] Written by Acheson and Clifford, Truman's speech essentially divided the world in two, one living in a free society, the other under the grinding thumb of totalitarian communism. It was a belligerent address that pitted the United States and its allies against the Soviet Union in an open Cold War for control of much of the rest of the world. Truman asked Congress for $400 million to deal with the problems that appeared to be developing in Greece and Turkey, and then he insisted that the United States must be prepared to give support to all free peoples of the world "who are resisting attempted subjugation by armed minorities or by outside pressures."[48] Largely because of the alarmist tone of the speech, Congress passed the president's plan with surprisingly little debate. The Truman Doctrine became the cornerstone of the bipartisan foreign policy of containment, and it had a major impact on the election of 1948.[49]

But Truman's fight against communism abroad did not end with aid to Greece and Turkey. War-torn Europe was in desperate need of financial assistance, and the situation seemed ripe for moves by the communists. Communist parties were gaining footholds in Italy and France as jobless rates climbed and people starved. At Harvard University's commencement in June 1947, Secretary of State George Marshall presented the administration's plan to rehabilitate Europe, a rehabilitation that, at first, was aimed at all of Europe—East and West. Within two weeks, however, the Soviets had rejected the proposal and the European Recovery Program (ERP) became a formula for stopping the spread of communism into Western Europe. It became the economic side of the Truman Doctrine and containment. Truman asked Congress to appropriate first $597 million as a stopgap measure for Italy, France, and Austria and then a whopping $17 billion over the next four years. Republicans in Congress balked. Isolationists Bricker, Jenner, Homer Capehart, and a few others met to try to head off the administration's program. Taft grumbled, calling it all "globaloney" and a "global WPA." It "goes far beyond any question of relief," he added, "and I do not think that the lavish distribution of dollars which is proposed will help these countries combat Communism in any greater degree than would a responsible willingness to help with goods that are particularly needed." Others in the party complained bitterly about subsidizing the socialized economies of Western Europe.[50] The fight over the Marshall Plan would further divide the Republicans between the isolationists and the internationalists, between those who wanted to aid Europe in its recovery and those who would stand in the way of a very popular program initiated and supported by the president.

The Truman Doctrine, the Marshall Plan, and the president's loyalty program kept the debilitating yoke of "soft on communism" from being placed on Truman, and the Republicans in Congress found themselves with few alternatives but to fall into line behind the president. Truman had forced them to make a difficult choice between two of the GOP's most sacred cows: lowering the deficit or supporting the forces of anticommunism on a global scale. For most Republicans in the Eightieth Congress, a vote against the president on the Truman Doctrine and the Marshall Plan might well cause their constituents to call their own anticommunism into question, and the Republicans were not about to allow the Democrats to abscond with the issue.

The Republican-dominated Eightieth Congress has gone into history as an example of a lost opportunity, a mandate misunderstood and mismanaged. Historians have argued that it accomplished much, particularly in foreign affairs. But the point is that the first session of the Eightieth Congress supplied Truman with an issue to take into the campaign the next year. The Eightieth Congress could not, or would not, enact laws to aid the average American in health care, housing, a raised minimum wage, or education, legislation that Truman repeatedly called for. It enacted labor legislation that allowed Truman to win labor's support. The Republicans made it clear that the Eightieth Congress would not aid farmers, whereas Truman (and, more important, FDR before him) had done a great deal to help farmers. Truman then shored up his flanks. He ended reconversion immediately and enacted anticommunist provisions to avoid the Republicans' charges of being soft on communism. Then, the Eightieth Congress collaborated with Truman in some of the most important and far-reaching foreign policy legislation and decisions of the twentieth century, allowing him to carry into the election the mantle of international statesman and leader of the free world. From the standpoint of politics and the next election, the first session of the Republican Eightieth Congress gave Truman exactly what he wanted.

4

Henry Wallace and the Split of the Democratic Left

In Philadelphia on July 24, 1948, Henry Wallace accepted the nomination of the Progressive party for the presidency of the United States. In his acceptance speech he told his supporters what they already knew, that in 1945 the war had ended and their leader, Franklin Roosevelt, was dead:

> And what followed was the great betrayal.
> Instead of the dream, we have inherited disillusion.
> Instead of the promised years of harvest, the years of the locust are upon us.
> In Hyde Park they buried our President and in Washington they buried our dreams.
> One day after Roosevelt died Harry Truman entered the White House.
> And 46 days later Herbert Hoover was there.
> It was a time of comings and goings.
> Into the Government came the ghosts of the great depression, the banking house boys and the oil well diplomats.
> In marched the generals—and out went the men who had built the TVA and the Grand Coulee, the men who had planned Social Security and built Federal housing, the men who had dug the farmer out of the dust bowl and the working men out of the sweatshop.
> A time of comings and goings . . . the shadows of the past coming in fast—and the lights going out slowly—the exodus of the torch bearers of the New Deal.[1]

Such was Henry Wallace's opinion of Harry Truman and his administration, and such was the opinion of many American liberals as the 1948 election approached. But by the time Wallace delivered this rousing speech in Philadelphia, much of liberal America had deserted Wallace's cause, and he was no longer the darling of American liberals as he had been a year earlier. By the November election, the promise of a liberal victory a year

Henry Wallace at the Progressive
party convention. From the collections of the University of Iowa.

before—a victory pushed on by a seemingly growing groundswell of liberalism—had died almost silently.

Many American liberals believed that Truman had turned his back on the
New Deal, on the Roosevelt legacy, and most of all on the New Dealers
themselves. The members of the left lamented that Wallace would have
become president in April 1945 had FDR not been persuaded to name
Truman as his vice-presidential candidate at the 1944 Democratic convention rather than keeping Wallace on for another term. They believed that
Wallace was the true New Deal standard-bearer, the real successor to the
New Deal coalition, the leader the Democrats needed to keep them together
in the face of a growing Republican resurgence. And Wallace understood
that. In 1943 Eleanor Roosevelt was not fully convinced that her husband
should run for a fourth term. She told Wallace that she wanted him to carry
on her husband's work, to be the successor to the Roosevelt legacy of liberalism. Wallace entered in his diary that Eleanor "and the President would
be for me as the logical one to carry out the policies of the President."[2]
    Wallace had won the hearts of American liberals while serving as FDR's
secretary of agriculture from 1933 to 1940 in the depths of the Depression.
In that role he was considered one of the primary innovators of New Deal
programs but also one who had the president's ear on more than just agricultural issues. It seemed clear that when he was tapped by Roosevelt to

run as vice-president in 1940 he became the heir apparent to whatever New Deal heritage there would be.

In 1942 Vice-President Wallace made a name for himself as an outspoken liberal when, in a speech entitled "A Century of the Common Man," he said: "Everywhere the common people are on the march. . . . The march of freedom of the last 150 years has been a long-drawn-out People's Revolution." He went on to recount the great liberal revolutions, beginning with the French in 1789 and ending with the Russian Revolution of 1917. And he made it clear that he was calling for an extension of that revolutionary period for America in the postwar period. It would be a revolution of the common man.[3]

By the 1944 presidential campaign, however, Wallace had become a liability to FDR because of his outspoken opinions that many moderates in the Democratic party considered flirted with the far left, even communism. Democratic leaders such as the big city bosses Edward J. Kelly of Chicago, Edward J. Flynn and Paul Fitzpatrick of New York, and Frank Hague of Jersey City worked to dump Wallace from the ticket. Democratic national treasurer Edwin Pauley, along with George Allen, Frank Walker, and Democratic National Committee chairman Robert E. Hannegan opposed Wallace's renomination. Among powerful southern conservatives in the party who also opposed Wallace were Senators Harry Byrd, James F. Byrnes, and John Bankhead. And there was another group of anti-Wallace liberals who were close to FDR and who saw Wallace as an idealist running against the pragmatic grain of the New Deal. That group included William O. Douglas, Tommy Corcoran, Harold Ickes, Estes Kefauver, and Alben Barkley. Altogether they were a powerful opposition force.

FDR was more than willing to drop a vice-president (he had done it twice) to promote party unity or increase his chances of winning. So, at the 1944 Democratic National Convention in Chicago, at the urging of these advisers and party leaders, FDR was persuaded to dump Wallace and accept Truman as his running mate. For many on the left, it was a monumental betrayal orchestrated by a coalition of the party's conservative forces. Even FDR, who was never one to shy away from political expediency, seemed to feel badly about the treatment Wallace had received. After all, Wallace had been one of the main shapers of the early New Deal, and at times he had been FDR's chief adviser on domestic policies. "I have been associated with Henry Wallace during the past four years as Vice President," FDR wrote the Democratic conventioneers in 1944, and "for eight years earlier while he was Secretary of Agriculture, and well before that. I like him and I respect him and he is my personal friend."[4] It was probably a sincere statement, but to the liberal Democrats in Chicago it was a surrender to the demands of the party leaders who did not want Wallace. One result was that Wallace immediately assumed the role of martyr among America's liberals, and the seeds of a new party were planted.

The split that originated at the 1944 Democratic convention turned into a chasm after the election when a fight broke out between liberals and conservatives in the party over returning Wallace to the cabinet. To compensate Wallace for being dumped in Chicago, FDR insisted that he remain at his side as secretary of commerce. Finally, in March 1945, after a two-month battle on Capitol Hill, Wallace's nomination to the cabinet post was hammered through the Senate, but only after a compromise was reached with several southern conservative Democrats who insisted that the Commerce Department under Wallace be stripped of its control over all lending agencies, including Reconstruction Finance Corporation funds. The result was a significant reduction in Wallace's power to influence government spending. When Truman took over in April 1945, one of the many problems he inherited from Roosevelt was a party that was hopelessly divided between Wallace and the liberals on the left and southern conservatives on the right.

Moreover, it quickly became clear that a break between Truman and Wallace was inevitable. Their power bases were different, their backgrounds were different, their political outlooks and attitudes toward government and foreign policy were different. They tolerated each other and tried to work together at first, but they remained two opposite poles waiting for the right moment to repel each other. Also, Truman was doing all he could to climb out from under the shadow of FDR; he was determined to be his own president, and that meant bringing in his own people and doing things his own way. He made it clear immediately that he was more conservative than Roosevelt, and that placed Wallace on the political fringes of the Democratic party as far as Truman was concerned. Despite their differences, the two men were able to coexist from April 1945 until September 1946.

At the same time, Truman and Wallace needed each other. Wallace's place in the minds of American liberals made him an important commodity to Truman. The president needed Wallace as a symbol of the New Deal to keep liberals and organized labor satisfied that their cause was being represented in the administration.[5] Truman realized that with Wallace in the cabinet the liberals might continue to criticize the administration, but they would not desert. In turn, Wallace felt he needed Truman. He hoped he could influence the president and pull him to the left on most issues, both foreign and domestic. Wallace might also have hoped that Truman would step aside in 1948, possibly even endorse him for the presidency. So it was to Wallace's advantage to remain in the administration for as long as possible. But Wallace always knew that his tenure would not last long, that he and the president would clash over some issue. "Ever since Morgenthau and Ickes had left," Wallace wrote, "I figured it was only a question of months until I'd be getting out."[6]

The break, however, came over foreign policy and not domestic issues. "I always had in my mind that if I were going to get out of the cabinet I should get out on the peace issue," Wallace wrote in his diary. "I wanted to dramatize peace."[7] Peace to Wallace, of course, meant an accommodation with the Soviet Union, a soft stance that was quickly becoming difficult to defend in the postwar years. Truman and his foreign policy advisers (principally James F. Byrnes, Dean Acheson, George Marshall, and James Forrestal) were moving in the exact opposite direction, toward a hard-line stance against Moscow. And it appeared that the administration's policy was what America wanted; just a year after the war ended, a poll showed that 62 percent of Americans distrusted the Soviets, and that number was growing fast.[8]

Wallace was well outside this get-tough-with-the-Russians philosophy of foreign affairs that permeated the Democratic administration and the Republican-controlled Congress. According to Wallace, what appeared to be Soviet expansion was simply a legitimate need for buffer zones and defendable perimeters in the wake of two disastrous invasions from the West in less than thirty years. But Wallace was not a communist. His plan was to deal with the Soviets, cooperate with them, and join them in a new world order to solve international conflicts and problems. But, it was a time when most Americans believed that Stalin was attempting to fulfill a longtime Soviet promise of world revolution through military force and intimidation. To a generation that had fought Nazi expansionism, Wallace's call for cooperation appeared to be little more than appeasement.

The final break between Wallace and Truman came on September 12, 1946, when Wallace criticized the administration's foreign policy in a speech at Madison Square Garden in New York. The rally was to be the opening volley of the 1946 New York gubernatorial campaign against the Republican candidate Tom Dewey. Wallace took the podium and made it clear that he represented the administration. He spoke against "British imperialism," and he called for a "soft" policy toward the Soviets. "We are reckoning with a force which cannot be handled successfully by a 'get tough with Russia' policy," he said. "The tougher we get the tougher the Russians will get.... We should recognize," he added, "that we have no more business in the political affairs of Eastern Europe than Russia has in the political affairs of Latin America, Western Europe and the United States."[9]

Wallace's speech was widely perceived in both the American and Eu-

ropean press as being in direct opposition to the policies of Secretary of State
Byrnes.[10] The next day telegrams arrived at the White House from several
U.S. ambassadors in Europe complaining to Truman that Wallace's speech
was causing confusion over American foreign policy. A State Department
communique claimed that Wallace's statements "would in large part repudiate the foreign policy which this country has been trying to establish for
the last year."[11] Arthur Vandenberg remarked to the press, with a heavy dose
of sarcasm, that he wanted to cooperate with the White House but that he
could work with only one secretary of state at a time.[12]

The incident placed Truman in the bad position of having to endorse
the policy of one secretary or the other. To make the situation worse, just
hours before Wallace was scheduled to speak, Truman told reporters that
he had read the speech, approved it, and did not see it as deviating from
the administration's foreign policy.[13]

The next day, Truman tried to cover up his carelessness by releasing a
statement that explained what he meant to say: "It was my intention to
express the thought that I approved the right of the Secretary of Commerce
to deliver the speech. I did not intend to indicate that I approved the speech
as constituting a statement of the foreign policy of this country." He then
went on to criticize Wallace for telling his audience that the speech had
been approved by the president.[14] Truman, however, later admitted in his
memoirs that he had not read Wallace's speech and that the speech was, in
fact, a direct attack on his foreign policy.[15]

Byrnes was attending the Paris Peace Conference and trying to make
American foreign policy clear to the rest of the world when he received word
of Wallace's speech. His reaction was exasperation: "If it is not possible for
you," he wrote Truman, "to keep Mr. Wallace . . . from speaking on foreign
affairs, it would be a grave mistake . . . for me to continue in office, even
temporarily. Therefore," he added, "if it is not completely clear . . . that Mr.
Wallace should be asked to refrain from criticizing the foreign policy of the
United States . . . I must ask you to accept my resignation immediately."
He said he would remain in Paris until his successor arrived. Byrnes's reaction was, of course, not released to the press, and the nation seemed to be
waiting for the other shoe to drop. *Time* reported: "Louder than a million
words, the overwhelming silence from Jimmy Byrnes echoed across the
Atlantic."[16]

Truman reacted quickly to Byrnes's threat by telephoning the secretary
in Paris. The telephone connection was poor so the two tried to make
amends over teletype. Again Byrnes growled at his boss for what seemed
to be a waver in American foreign policy at a crucial time in U.S.-Soviet
negotiations. He told Truman, "The world is today in doubt not only as to

American foreign policy, but as to your foreign policy."[17] Truman had to make a choice, and he chose Byrnes; Wallace resigned quietly on September 20.

Privately, Truman told his chief counsel, Clark Clifford, that he believed Wallace had set him up in an attempt to discredit his administration. Clifford himself came to believe that Wallace's removal from the cabinet "was one of the worst mistakes of the Truman Presidency."[18] The firing of Henry Wallace, however, would greatly aid Truman's 1948 campaign. It served to cast off all charges from the Republicans that Truman wanted to appease the Soviets, and it preserved Republican support for the bipartisan diplomatic strategy headed by Truman. Wallace's departure had much the same effect on domestic issues. During the 1948 campaign, the Republicans would not be able to attach the "soft on communism" label to Truman. That designation was reserved exclusively for Wallace. Truman was even able to move to the left on several domestic issues as the election approached and take votes from Wallace without being labeled a communist by the Republicans. In many ways, the firing of Wallace was one of the best parts of Truman's strategy for the 1948 campaign.

Again martyred, Wallace quickly emerged as the leader of the first faction of the Democratic party to spin off after FDR's death, the first faction that Truman was unable to control. Wallace's immediate response, however, was to oppose any plan for a direct third-party move, and he continued to maintain that posture through most of the summer of 1947 as he tested the waters for a possible Democratic nomination. He continued to believe that he was the choice of most Democrats, still the heir apparent, the true successor to the New Deal, and that Truman was the interloper, a temporary civil servant, holding down the office until 1948.

Now outside the constraints of the government, Wallace was free to oppose the administration and to seek the nomination openly. He accepted a position as editor of the *New Republic*, and from there be became the chief oracle of American liberalism and the chief critic of the Truman administration and the president's foreign policy of containment.

Through the summer of 1947 Wallace reached the height of his popularity. The possibility of a run for the Democratic nomination seemed real enough, and his rising stock put a scare into the White House.[19] Everywhere he stopped on his midsummer cross-country campaign trip, he drew tremendous crowds. Labor leaders openly supported him, middle-class liberals were coming to him in droves, and that meant financial support. Farmers supported him, as did the newest of political groups, African Americans in the northern cities. It looked as though Wallace might lead a liberal-labor coalition in 1948 that would make the New Deal coalition pale by comparison.

One group of Wallace's supporters, however, was the communists. They had supported FDR and worked within the Democratic party during the New Deal years, but they stayed quietly behind the scenes understanding full well that any open affiliation might run off moderates. After the war, however, their world changed. Their political actions became more aggressive and open, at least in part because there were several election victories and strong showings by communist-supported candidates around the country just after the war. In Chicago in November 1947, for instance, Communist party–supported candidates polled nearly 40 percent of the vote. In New York, in February 1948, Leo Isacson won a two-to-one victory in a special congressional election with strong Communist party support. And communists made impressive showings elsewhere. Also, the world communist information agency, the Cominform in Poland, had called for worldwide liberation movements to coincide with more active communist involvement in international politics. All of this was a signal for American communists to become vigorous in their political involvement.[20] So the communists jumped headlong into the Wallace movement and became its leading and most visible figures.

This active communist support for Wallace had a great impact on the politics of the postwar period and ultimately on the outcome of the 1948 election. Among other things, it went a long way toward changing the political character of the American labor movement. Wallace had been the defender of labor through the New Deal years, and he was considered a direct representative of organized labor among Roosevelt's advisers. In the summer of 1944, as Wallace's place on the Democratic ticket was being challenged, most of the nation's labor leaders made it abundantly clear that they wanted Wallace to remain on the ticket. At the 1944 Democratic convention in Chicago, Truman was making a bid for the vice-presidential nomination and paid a call on CIO president Philip Murray to solicit his support. Murray apparently showed Truman the door, not even giving the Missouri senator enough time to take a seat. Murray and the CIO had only one man, and that was Wallace.[21] When Truman became president, he did very little for the cause of organized labor, possibly as a result of the rebuff he received from labor leaders in the 1944 convention, but more likely because strikes disrupted Truman's reconversion plans. By mid-1947 America's important labor leaders began looking at the possibility of dumping Truman in favor of Wallace in 1948—or even supporting Wallace in a third-party move.

Several important labor leaders who supported Wallace between his dismissal from the Truman administration in September 1946 and December 1947, when he announced that he would run as a third-party candidate, included Jack Kroll, president of the CIO-PAC, A.F. Whitney of the Brotherhood of Railway Trainmen, and Murray. But by the time the campaign officially began in the summer of 1948, Wallace's labor support had fallen away. Communist support for Wallace together with his acceptance of the Soviet Union's foreign policies had alienated much of organized labor.

The communist-anticommunist fight inside big labor reached a high point in the early postwar years, and as communists became an increasingly vocal part of Wallace's support, anticommunist labor leaders (by then the most powerful of the nation's labor leaders) began looking for a new political home. Murray and Whitney, for instance, shifted their money and support to the liberal anticommunist group Americans for Democratic Action (ADA) after their formation in January 1947. Several other labor leaders moved back into the Democratic party in the summer of 1947 when Truman turned an about-face on labor issues and vetoed the Taft-Hartley Act. And still other labor leaders found it expedient to leave the communist-anticommunist choice to their rank-and-file members and avoid the highly divisive controversy. By the time Wallace made his speech in Philadelphia in the summer of 1948, the only labor unions supporting him were communist, and that support was clearly more detrimental to Wallace's campaign than helpful.

In late December 1946 in New York the Progressive Citizens of America (PCA) was formed out of ten major and minor left-wing groups. The most important were the National Citizens Political Action Committee (NCPAC) and the Independent Citizens Committee of the Arts, Sciences, and Professionals (ICCASP). NCPAC had originally been formed to promote a fourth term for Roosevelt and had then evolved into a powerful political organization made up of liberal businessmen, journalists, and politicians. ICCASP boasted many of the big names of the entertainment industry and the sciences, and it had a reputation for being communist-dominated. The PCA organized primarily in response to the Republican congressional victories the month before. And Wallace, as the press continually pointed out, was the organization's symbolic leader, speaking often at PCA meetings and rallies, including its founding convention in December. The PCA called for improved education, federally funded health care, better housing, civil rights for African Americans, increased veterans' benefits, and job training. They also wanted government ownership of the railroads, coal mines, and electric power facilities.[22]

Wallace and the PCA seemed to be made for each other: the new progressive political organization and the strong, experienced liberal leader. Wallace, however, never did join the PCA, insisting on maintaining his independence from such groups and claiming that leadership in any political organization would jeopardize his credibility as editor of the *New Republic*. Nevertheless, it was out of the PCA that Wallace's Progressive party would emerge.

In response to Wallace's foreign policy, the PCA called on all American liberals to support a working relationship between the United States and the Soviet Union and reject Truman's hard-line foreign policy. This demand effectively split the nation's liberals between those who wanted the United States to work with the Soviets and those who supported Truman's anti-Soviet line. This division came to a head in the summer of 1947 over the Truman Doctrine and the Marshall Plan. Wallace refused to support the Truman Doctrine, arguing that it would place the United States on the road to war, divide the world into spheres of influence, destroy any hope of reconciliation with the Soviets, and turn the United States into an international policeman. Truman, Wallace wrote, "proposes in effect that America police Russia's border. There is no regime too reactionary to us," he added, "provided it stands in Russia's path."[23] Wallace initially approved of the Marshall Plan, however, calling it "a great advance."[24] But he hoped that economic aid to Europe would be channeled through the United Nations and that the money would be used only to aid Europe's economic recovery, not for a military buildup. He also hoped that Eastern Europe would become part of the program and even that the Soviet Union would be a recipient. By the fall of 1947, however, Wallace began to see the Marshall Plan as leading to a further East-West division of the world, and he finally came out in opposition to it.[25] That stance further split the liberals between those who wanted to work with the Soviets in a postwar world and those who did not. As the Cold War hardened (and the Soviets became more aggressive and more strident in their anti-Americanism), Wallace's arguments became more and more untenable. His support weakened and then evaporated.

Well into the summer of 1947, Wallace continued to resist a third-party move. In those months he was at the height of his popularity while Truman seemed to be on a rapid downslide that threatened to eliminate him as a viable candidate for the Democratic nomination. On a cross-country speaking tour, Wallace drew thousands as he seemed to be testing the waters for a Democratic run. In his *New Republic* articles and editorials, however, he made it plain that a third-party bid was not in his plans. In June he wrote:

"Throughout this journey I have found sentiment for a third party strong among many groups, so strong I have tried to emphasize that the first problem now is to create, not a third, but a second party." But he also threw out hints that if the situation in Washington did not change, he would run as a third-party candidate. In Los Angeles in May 1947 he promised that "if the Democratic Party betrays its tradition by refusing to give expression to the liberal will of the people, the people will find expression in other ways." As late as September he insisted in a *New Republic* editorial that he intended to win "control of the Democratic convention."[26]

Finally, in a speech in Detroit on Labor Day (the same day the *New Republic* issue in which he stated his intentions to control the Democratic convention hit the stands), it seemed that Wallace was prepared to take the first steps toward forming a third party. "If we [cannot] make the Democratic Party into a party of peace and prosperity we shall build a new party." A week later, however, he went back on that statement, saying that he wanted to reform the Democratic party, not leave it.[27] Clearly, Wallace was facing a dilemma.

Through October and November, Wallace remained a Democrat and reticent about a third-party move mainly because of his eroding support from organized labor. But the mystery seemed to frustrate many liberals. Would Wallace run as a Democrat or as a third-party candidate? Freda Kirchwey, the influential editor at the *Nation*, seemed to speak for many on the left: "The time is rapidly approaching when Henry Wallace will have to fish or cut bait. Fifteen months is a long time to stand indecisively on the bank, rod over shoulder, and the fish are understandably beginning to lose interest."[28] Finally, on December 29, Wallace cast his line and declared himself a candidate of the Progressive party. At that point he believed he had some ten million supporters, more than enough to make a strong showing and build a foundation to run successfully in 1948.[29]

Wallace may have qualified as the leader of America's liberals, but a large number of those liberals believed his place was in the Democratic party, not on the political fringe as a third-party candidate who would certainly pull votes from the Democratic presidential candidate and possibly assist in the election of a Republican. Max Lerner wrote in *PM* that Wallace should return to the party and not allow "himself to become isolated from the large mass of independent American progressives."[30] Upton Sinclair begged Wallace to stay in the Democratic party and "help save us from another Republican regime."[31] In March 1948, Democratic party chairman J. Howard McGrath went on the radio to ask Wallace to come back into the fold, not to hurt the Democratic party by splitting its forces.[32] In the same month, Freda Kirchwey lambasted Wallace for splitting the Democrats in the face of a coming Republican assault on both the White House and Congress. Wallace should remove himself from the election and come back into the Democratic party, she wrote, because "his stature as a leader will be far greater than if he merely proves he can elect Mr. Taft or Mr. Dewey."[33] Several times during the 1948 campaign Democratic leaders and Truman operatives attempted to make a deal with Wallace that would bring him back into a united Democratic party.[34] Even Eleanor Roosevelt, by then the matriarch of American liberalism, was appalled at Wallace's defection and in her daily column compared him to Neville Chamberlain.[35] Among many leaders on the left, Wallace's decision was very unpopular and a big problem.

By December 1947 the left-wing split from the Democratic party was complete, and at that time it was a major predicament for the Truman administration. Truman, however, had an entire year to win back the hearts, votes, and considerable influence of those on the Democratic left who would support Henry Wallace.

5

Truman Versus Organized Labor: The Origins of Conflict

When conservative forces in the Democratic party convinced President Roosevelt in the summer of 1944 that it would be Truman and not Henry Wallace on the Democratic ticket in the coming election, FDR told an aide: "Clear it with Sidney." That was Sidney Hillman, one of the founders of the CIO in 1935 and since 1943 head of the CIO's Political Action Committee. For Roosevelt, Hillman was the spokesman for labor in the 1940s. Despite his clout with Roosevelt, however, Hillman did not speak for all of labor. Philip Murray, then the president of the CIO, was much less enamored with FDR's choice for vice-president; he was particularly annoyed that Wallace had been dumped from the ticket, and he made it clear that he did not like Truman. The relationship between Truman and organized labor over the next four years would be rocky at best.

Truman, of course, received the nomination in 1944. He may not have had the support of all the factions of organized labor that year, and he may not have measured up to Wallace's place in labor's heart of hearts, but by 1944 Truman had paid his dues to organized labor and he deserved its support. Throughout his career in public service he had always sat among the prolabor ranks. As a senator he had voted for the Wagner Act and supported the Social Security Act, the Guffey-Snyder Act, and the Fair Labor Standards Act. During the war, he voted for the Senate version of the Smith-Connally War Labor Disputes Act, but when Republicans in the House tacked on several antilabor provisions to the bill, Truman took labor's advice and voted against the House version, then voted to sustain FDR's veto of the bill. Five months after Truman became president, *New York Times* labor reporter Louis Stark wrote that organized labor had looked closely at the new president and concluded that he was "friendly and disposed to be reasonable."[1] For labor, he might not have measured up to Roosevelt and Wallace, but he was generally acceptable.

By 1946, however, President Truman, like many Americans, had concluded that organized labor had gone too far; it had misused its powers and disrupted the marketplace. Truman had come to see strikes as unpatriotic and an affront to his presidency, and he believed that the antics of some labor leaders (particularly John L. Lewis of the UMW and A.F. Whitney of the Brotherhood of Railroad Trainmen) were reprehensible, even treasonous, in the face of the nation's growing postwar economic problems.[2] To his wife, Truman wrote his opinion of big labor: "People are somewhat befuddled and want . . . a life guarantee of rest at government expense and some . . . just want to raise hell and hamper the return to peacetime production to obtain some political advantage." He added, "Big money has too much power and so have the unions—both are riding to a fall because I like neither."[3] Although he was a longtime supporter of its bargaining rights and of labor's right to organize, Truman was not willing to allow big labor to disrupt the American economy during his presidency.

The passage of the Wagner Act in 1935 and then World War II set the stage for the immense postwar conflicts between labor and management. The Wagner Act had been passed in response to public reaction to the poor treatment workers had received during the Depression. It guaranteed workers the right to bargain through unions of their own choice, and it prohibited employers from interfering with union activities. With this government assistance and recognition, unions were able to meet employers at the bargaining table on an equal basis. Through the 1930s and into the war years union membership increased rapidly because unions for the first time were able to aid and protect workers, and with those larger numbers and government support came a significant increase in power—particularly political power. By 1945, however, it had become apparent to many Americans that labor's power had increased too much, beyond that of employers, and that it might now be necessary to restrict the powers of labor. The American public made this clear in a variety ways. By 1946 several state legislatures had passed laws restricting the powers of unions. Some states demanded that labor deliver advance strike notices and agree to "cooling-off periods"; others outlawed secondary boycotts and restricted picketing. Six states allowed the use of court injunctions to settle disputes. But it was the enactment of right-to-work laws in several states that concerned the national offices of organized labor the most. These laws prohibited the practice of the closed shop that required all employees to join a union. The closed shop had been one of the keys to organized labor's success. State right-to-work laws threatened to undo much of that success.[4]

The public's discontent with the powers of labor was also reflected in the sheer volume of antilabor legislation proposed in Congress. During the Seventy-ninth Congress and then in the first four months of the Eightieth Congress, a total of seventy-three bills restricting the powers of organized labor were introduced in the House—most by Republicans. Between January 1946 and April 1947 some forty-five such bills were introduced in the Senate, most by Republicans.[5] In addition, public opinion polls taken in the three years after the war showed clearly that the vast majority of the public believed that some sort of federal restriction on organized labor should be imposed.[6]

The power of big labor in the postwar era was personified in John L. Lewis, the fearsome head of the United Mine Workers. Lewis, together with Hillman of the Amalgamated Clothing Workers and David Dubinsky of the International Ladies' Garment Workers Union, spearheaded the organization of the industrial workers in the late 1930s. By 1941 the CIO (under Lewis's leadership until 1940) had organized the auto industry, meatpacking, steel, oil, the electric industry, and a large part of the textile industry. But the CIO's organizing strategies led to huge, debilitating strikes that upset the economy and jeopardized the credibility of the federal government. In 1937 FDR was so annoyed by Lewis's fight with Tom Girdler of Republic Steel that he pronounced "a plague on both your houses." Lewis responded in his typically lyrical style: "It ill behooves one who has supped at labor's table and who has been sheltered in labor's house to curse with equal fervor and fine impartiality both labor and its adversaries when they become locked in a deadly embrace."[7] After the war Truman would find himself in a similarly frustrating position with Lewis.

In 1943 Lewis led the coal miners out on strike despite labor's promises not to strike during the war. Widespread discontent over the strike pushed Congress to pass the Smith-Connally War Labor Disputes Act, which gave the federal government the power to seize plants and mines necessary to the war effort. A year later Arkansas and Florida passed right-to-work laws. It was the first strong indication of a growing antilabor sentiment in the nation.

In the twelve months before America's entrance into World War II some twenty-three million man-days were lost to strikes. As a result of the war emergency and the no-strike pledge from labor, that number was reduced significantly in 1942 to just over four million man-days. By 1943, however, labor leaders such as Lewis and AFL head William Green began complaining that the workers' interests were being ignored as the government laid down wage and price controls necessary for wartime production. By then workers had become more restive and less willing to hold to their wartime no-strike pledge. They pressured their leaders to strike, and in that year the man-days lost increased to over thirteen million.[8]

To the average American who was making difficult sacrifices at every level for the war effort these strikes were unpatriotic, selfish, even treasonous. Strikes were condemned by the soldiers overseas and used as propaganda by the enemy as evidence of America's growing antiwar sentiments. "Speaking for the American soldier," *Stars and Stripes* wrote on its front page during the 1943 coal strike, "John L. Lewis, damn your coal black soul."[9] And the *Wall Street Journal* reported: "Workers, war-weary and fearful about their post-war future, seem to be grabbing almost any excuse for a strike these days."[10]

America's growing disaffection with its labor movement was deepened by the perception that communism was on the rise in the United States after World War II. That perception was, however, a fairly recent concern. With the exception of the brief post–World War I Red Scare, Americans had generally tolerated communists in their midst. During the Depression the nation came to accept that communists dominated the nation's industrial labor unions. During the war American communists joined the worldwide coalition against European fascism, and communists, both domestic and foreign, were accepted as allies. When the war ended, however, the situation changed dramatically. The nation began to fear the communist movement. American communists, in turn, became hostile to Washington's postwar foreign policy of containment that seemed directed at destroying Soviet communism. Then they added to the anticommunist sentiment by openly supporting Soviet aggressions, particularly in Eastern Europe, and setting themselves up as the most radical political group in America at a time when the country was becoming increasingly intolerant of radical groups of all kinds. All this resulted in the public distrust of the communists and their motives. For the future of the American labor movement, however, it was most important that Americans generally perceived that communism, in the postwar period, had taken refuge inside the nation's labor unions.[11]

The image of labor was also tarnished by a rash of blatant abuses in the postwar years, all of which received a great deal of press coverage. Unions, for instance, required that organization dues be withheld from paychecks, they often charged excessive initiation fees, and of course the closed shop system required all workers to join the union to hold a job in the industry. All this seemed unfair and undemocratic to the unorganized public. Unions were often accused of not bargaining in good faith, and frequently disputes (occasionally violent disputes covered by the press) would arise between unions over control of specific jurisdictions. Unions often employed secondary boycotts, shutting down entire sectors of the economy, which made life difficult for many Americans. Labor's image was damaged even further by specific examples of abuse that clearly annoyed the public.

In 1942, for example, Teamsters were stationed at the entrance of the Holland Tunnel in New York, where they stopped all trucks entering the city and gave the drivers three choices: pay a union driver to transport the cargo to its destination in the city, pay a fee to pass, or receive a beating on the spot. The Teamsters' actions led to the Hobbs Anti-Racketeering Act that failed in 1945 but passed Congress unanimously and without debate in the summer of 1946.[12]

In addition, organized labor steadfastly refused to compromise on any position in the face of growing public and congressional demands for restrictions. This came across as a defiant, stubborn resistance to the will of the nation's majority and an obnoxious selfishness. "For the moment, prices are none of my business," Murray stated at the beginning of the big postwar strikes. "We want substantial pay increases."[13] Labor's obstinate behavior, however, was a reaction to its own growing insecurity in the face of the new conservatism and the Republican party's promises to curb the power of the unions. But it further hurt labor's image and it made labor relations in the postwar years extremely volatile.

The insecurity that pushed labor into its uncompromising stance after the war was rooted in the immediate prewar years when the nation's economy was moving out of the Depression and into a higher gear. Wages were on the rise and jobs were again plentiful as America fed off the war and the anticipation of the nation's eventual involvement in the conflict. One result of this relative prosperity was increased friction between management and labor, and that culminated in the great strikes of 1941. In that year there were over four thousand strikes involving two million workers—twice as many strikes involving four times the number of workers as the year before. Also, a large number of these strikes were organized and conducted by unions that claimed significant communist affiliations. The backlash to this growth of labor power and activity was just beginning to be felt when the United States entered the war in December. The growing labor-management disputes were placed on hold temporarily in favor of the united war effort. But for the unions it was clear that the postwar period would bring increased conflict, accompanied by an increased public backlash. The result was insecurity about the future. In 1943 the CIO formed the CIO-PAC for the very purpose of undermining the antilabor sentiment that had gained strength before the war. It was also designed to make sure that labor's power was felt at all political levels and that labor's side of the impending conflicts would be correctly conveyed to the public. Labor was digging in and preparing for what would be the great propaganda and political fights of the postwar years.[14]

Labor's worst fears were realized. These incidents, situations, and abuses made organized labor a target of the postwar swing to the right and set the unions on a collision course with the American public. In a poll taken in 1946, 74 percent of those questioned agreed that the federal government should intervene and bring an end to the UMW coal strike that began in April and had nearly closed down the nation by late May.[15] Another poll taken the same year by Gallup showed that over 90 percent of those polled believed that some sort of federal restriction was needed to control the abuses of organized labor.[16]

In November 1946 the Republicans swept into Congress. Their victory was at least in part a reaction to the wave of strikes in that year and a cry from voters for some restrictions on labor's power to strike. It appeared that the conservative forces in Washington were forming against labor. The unions began to fear that all the gains that had been achieved during the 1930s would be erased by the new Republican Eightieth Congress. By that time even President Truman had proven himself to be hostile to labor's abuses and postwar strikes. Labor's insecurity redoubled in response.

The press played an important role in this growing conflict by supporting the antilabor forces and crying out with much of the rest of the nation for legislation to curtail labor's perceived abuses. *Life* was particularly antiunion, pointing out the ways the strikes had damaged the economy and hurt the American consumer, though it seldom took the time to explain the workers' need for increased wages.[17] During the big strikes of 1946, the *New York Times* called on Congress to act, to bring an end to the strikes by reducing labor's powers, which the newspaper believed had been allowed to increase beyond the powers of management.[18] The press would divide over the way the president finally dealt with labor, but generally the popular press believed (especially during the strikes of 1946) that organized labor was too powerful and needed to be restricted and regulated.

Lewis, of course, was the favorite goat of the press—no matter what actions the president took against him or his striking workers. He was always portrayed as a labor fat cat, obsessed more with his own power than with the welfare of the rank-and-file workers. *Life* called him an "absolute dictator" during the 1948 coal strike and accompanied the story with a photograph of the overweight Lewis smoking a big cigar in the back of a long black limousine.[19] A week later a *Life* editorial concluded that "the public must have protection from abuse and irresponsibility on the part of such labor czars as Lewis."[20]

But, in fact, American workers had a reasonable argument in this dispute. The war had hemmed them in. They had done their job; they had produced the material needed to win the war, but most American factory workers were actually better off before Pearl Harbor than after Hiroshima.

Everyone seemed to be profiting from the postwar expansion, especially industry and industry leaders, but not workers. In addition, there was a popular belief that the postwar period would bring on high unemployment, possibly even depression or inflation, or both. Most Americans had come to realize that the war, and not the New Deal, had brought the nation out of the Great Depression of the 1930s, and economists and pundits were predicting that the economy would slip naturally back into its prewar state of depression. Philip Murray wrote of his fears to the president: "There is not an economist in America who does not predict a bust to follow the present boom. It is purely a question of when the bust will occur."[21] In addition, twelve million Americans were in the armed forces and another eight million were directly engaged in war production. The impact of that many unemployed workers flooding into a soft labor market promised to have a catastrophic effect on the economy. Between V-E Day and V-J Day unemployment doubled; after V-J Day it tripled.[22] Along with these problems was the growing public discontent with the labor movement as a whole, the growth of communism within labor's ranks in a period of growing anticommunist sentiment, and the attempt by federal and state governments to restrict labor's powers. For organized labor it was an uncertain time.

As might be expected, much of labor's argument revolved around wages. When America abruptly converted to a peacetime economy after August 1945, the result was massive layoffs in the war production industries and a cutback of overtime pay for most everyone else. Organized labor had agreed to wage stabilization during the war under the so-called Little Steel formula, which froze basic wage rates. Consequently, when the war ended, the average American worker was taking home less money than during the war. Added to that problem was the slow but steady rise in consumer prices, and individual laborers argued convincingly that their situation was often far worse than it had been before the war. In 1941 the average American worker made $28.12 per week. In 1944 that figure was up to $36.72. But by war's end, the average weekly wage had fallen back to $32.27, and then it dropped over the next few months to a low of $31 per week. By July 1946 real wages had fallen even lower, to $30.72, and by the fall of that year the average worker's real wage increase through the war and postwar period had been wiped out by consumer price increases. By then the laborer's weekly wage was below the 1935-1939 level.[23]

The problems for labor might not have been so severe had Washington allowed wages to rise along with consumer prices. But to Truman and his economic advisers who were trying to manage the postwar reconversion, that was the first step toward runaway inflation and economic collapse. As labor leaders saw it, however, price controls were often relaxed (or removed altogether) while wage controls always remained firmly in place. It was a frustrating situation, at least partly because labor had helped elect the administration in Washington. In October 1946, Truman removed price controls on meat, prompting a heated response from United Auto Workers (UAW) chief Walter Reuther: "So far there has been no corresponding relaxation of wage controls, although their continuation is obviously intolerable if not impossible."[24] Another UAW official complained that the Truman administration "makes suggestions to industry while it gives orders to labor. We are *told* that we are not to ask for wage increases. Big Business is gently *urged* to re-examine its profit position and reduce prices wherever possible."[25]

Industry had made big profits during the war, and most industries were profiting from the peacetime reconversion programs as well. Corporate profits were soaring. In 1929 net corporate profits were at $8.4 billion. During the war, profits jumped to between $20 billion and $25 billion, but wartime taxes kept profit levels down to between $9 billion and $10.5 billion. By 1946 net corporate profits had risen to $12.5 billion, 20 percent above the best year of the war.[26] *CIO News* reported that U.S. Steel had an increase of after-tax profits of 113 percent between 1935 and 1944, from $576 million to $1.2 billion. During the war the assets of the steel companies increased from $4.86 billion to $6 billion, and dividends paid to stockholders amounted to over $700 million. "Contrast this with the financial position of America's 475,000 steel workers," Murray was quoted in the article. It was, he insisted, time for a wage increase.[27]

Management, of course, was not without its own arguments in these postwar labor disputes. Not surprisingly, American industry shared with labor many of the same uncertainties. When the war ended, the nation's largest industries lost their military contracts and faced an expensive and uncertain period of reconversion. General Motors lost $2 billion in defense contracts when peace came in August 1945, and it was faced with converting and retooling its 102 plants from military hardware, particularly tanks, back to automobiles. The day after V-J Day the federal government issued one hundred thousand orders canceling unnecessary war production. The federal government's reconversion plans produced other uncertainties. Stringent price controls continued after the war, often placing industry in a position of being forced to increase wages (as demanded by labor) without being compensated with comparable price increases. All this made management leery of locking itself into long-term wage contracts with labor. Consequently, management fought the strikes while demanding price increases from the federal government as their only bargaining position.

This situation was made worse by the uncertainty of the times. Would there be massive layoffs as the war industries ground to a halt? Would the loss of government contracts mean a drop in profits? What effect would the millions of discharged servicemen have on the work force? Would there be a new depression that would close factories or runaway inflation that would make salaries worthless? What would happen to prices once controls were lifted in an economy where goods were in demand? Would Truman's reconversion plans work?[28] Both American workers and employers believed they were in bad positions after the war. Salaries were low, profits were up for the moment but uncertain for the future, and the situation was volatile. To the worker, everyone else seemed to be profiting from a postwar prosperity that seemed to touch every sector of the economy except the factories. At the same time, a freeze on profits kept the hands of management tied. With few concessions from management and little assistance from Washington, labor and management became locked in a struggle that brought additional uncertainty to the nation's economic future. The postwar strikes were a reflection of a changing America. President Truman would have to deal with them in the nation's interest, and the coming 1948 campaign would play an important part in his decisions. The result would be that labor would play a significant role in his 1948 victory.

Truman was fully aware of the potential conflict that was brewing between labor and management through the summer of 1945. Between the two celebrations of V-E Day and V-J Day the country experienced forty-six hundred work stoppages, involving some five million workers with an industry loss of nearly 120 million,man-days. But Truman's reaction to the growing problem did not go far toward solving it. In mid-August he agreed to allow wage increases as long as there was no corresponding rise in prices. Such a plan of voluntarism was acceptable to labor, of course, but management had no incentive to raise wages while maintaining a price freeze.[29]

In September, forty-three hundred oil refinery workers went out on strike in twenty states, cutting off one-third of the nation's gasoline supply. Truman reacted by using his wartime powers that were still in effect and seized the refineries, but that action did not end the strike. He then called for a fact-finding board to deal with the refinery workers' strike and other strikes in progress or about to occur around the nation. The situation simply called for more action.[30]

In the hope of finding some solution to the general labor-management conflict, Truman convened the President's National Labor-Management Conference in Washington on November 5. Both sides of the conflict were represented. From labor, high-ranking officials attended from the American Federation of Labor (AFL), the CIO, UMW, and the railroad brotherhoods. From the other side came representatives from the National Association of Manufacturers and the Chamber of Commerce of the United States. The president called on the committee to recommend a mechanism he could use to keep the strikes from crippling the nation and hurting the economy while still treating labor fairly. But after three weeks the committee was deadlocked when the labor leaders (particularly Murray, Lewis, and Green) insisted that the committee recommend wage increases and the representatives from industry refused to agree to such a proposal.[31] The point was clear: conflict was coming, everyone knew it, and neither side was about to go into battle hampered by agreements made here. The committee was important because it was the first recognition that a conference might be used to advise the government on how to solve labor-management disputes, and it was of further significance because each group was forced to recognize the other as an equal. But more important, it tied the government's hands in this crucial period by leaving the president with no mechanism to deal with the massive labor disputes that were about to erupt. Truman's only method of ending a strike was to deal with each individual dispute through executive order. He would have to wade into the fracas himself.

While the conference was in session the UAW went out on strike against General Motors on November 22, idling some 325,000 autoworkers in more than ninety plants around the country. Truman responded by appointing another blue-ribbon committee to deal with the problem and make recommendations. The press pointed out the weakness of existing federal labor legislation, and the problem was made even more evident when the strike occurred only after several attempts at mediation failed miserably. The General Motors strike dragged on until March 1946, when it was finally settled with a raise to workers of 18.5 cents an hour.[32]

On December 3, just days after the National Labor-Management Conference admitted its failure, Truman sent a message to Congress asking for legislation to deal with strikes that he considered threatening to the national interest. Under Truman's proposed plan, the president could appoint fact-finding boards that would use broad subpoena powers to investigate strikes. The financial records of the industries involved also could be subpoenaed during a thirty-day investigation period—while workers remained on the job.[33] Organized labor, however, responded bitterly to Truman's plan. Labor leaders were particularly annoyed with the president's thirty-day "cooling-off" period, as they viewed Truman's plan for a thirty-day investigation. It is a "shameful betrayal of the public interest," Murray complained, "by an administration that labor's vote did much to elect." He added that Truman's policy "marks a very serious departure from the policies which the people of this country have repeatedly approved . . . under the leadership of President Roosevelt."[34] It was the beginning of a sharp break between organized labor and the president.

The response from industry was not much better. To industry leaders, fact-finding boards with the power to subpoena financial records meant that the federal government would be considering "ability to pay" as a factor in settling future strikes, something that industry leaders had, in the past, refused even to discuss. During the General Motors strike, management walked out of negotiations rather than allow the president's fact-finding board to subpoena its financial records or consider ability to pay as a collective bargaining issue.[35]

Truman had managed to offend both sides. In addition, his proposed plan did not give the mediation boards the powers necessary to end strikes; they could only recommend, mediate, and bring to the public's attention the ability of an industry to pay its workers higher wages. To the American people (who were being forced to endure the hardships of the strikes) and to the Seventy-ninth Congress (which was becoming more and more conservative on labor issues) Truman's plan did not go far enough toward solving the nation's labor relations problems.

Meanwhile, the country braced for a nationwide steel strike. The price of steel in the postwar period was regulated by the federal government, and the steel industry insisted that unless steel prices were allowed to rise, wages could not be increased. A strike was scheduled for mid-January. On December 30, Truman appointed another fact-finding board to deal with the problem. When that failed, the president himself stepped in to mediate the strike. The union accepted the president's offer, but the steel industry would not. On January 21, 750,000 steelworkers walked off the job. The week before, 200,000 electrical workers struck and another 200,000 packinghouse workers went out on strike. By the end of January 1946, America's basic industries sat idle, and the president's reconversion plans were in jeopardy. In addition, Truman had been forced to intervene in a failed mediation. He had also become an enemy of labor, a situation that he could not afford to endure in the political arena.

The steel strike was brought to an end in February when steel prices were allowed to rise to make way for a wage increase. But in the spring, 340,000 soft coal miners went out on strike from the first of April to the last of May. During that time Truman again intervened and failed to mediate an agreement between the union and the industry. On May 21 the president ordered the mines seized, although the mine workers did not return to work until May 29, after a complicated agreement was worked out between Lewis of the UMW and Secretary of the Interior Julius Krug that gave mine workers a wage increase in addition to health and welfare benefits. Again, the lack of collective bargaining legislation had forced the president to intervene. Again, his efforts failed, and a paralyzing strike occurred.

The real showdown came when the railroad engineers and trainmen threatened to strike in early 1946, pushing the coal and autoworker strikes onto the back burner. A railway strike would shut down the nation's commerce and much of its industry, and in this time of perceived economic crisis and escalating tensions overseas, it could not be tolerated. In April a Truman fact-finding board recommended a wage increase for the twenty railway unions, but the two largest unions, the Brotherhood of Locomotive Engineers headed by Alvanley Johnston and the Brotherhood of Railway Trainmen headed by A.F. Whitney, refused the offer and planned a strike for May 18. Again Truman intervened. He called Johnston and Whitney to the White House and in their presence signed an executive order giving him the power to take over the railroads if a strike occurred. On May 23, Johnston and Whitney sent Truman a note rejecting all compromises. The next day 250,000 railway workers went out on strike, creating the greatest transportation tie-up in the nation's history. Truman responded by comparing Whitney and Johnston to "the 'foreign enemy' of Pearl Harbor."[36]

At this point, after he had been in office just a year, Truman's ability to deal with any major crisis was coming into question. Just ten weeks earlier Winston Churchill had delivered his "Iron Curtain" speech at Fulton, Missouri, and Americans were beginning to see communism as a national threat. There was a growing perception that a president active in foreign affairs was needed to deal with the now aggressive Soviets. Clark Clifford and other presidential advisers and strategists in the White House had concluded that if Truman appeared incapable of dealing with labor, if he could not keep America's economy in check, American voters would begin wondering if their president could deal effectively with the growing communist menace that had been outlined by Churchill.[37]

It did seem in the early summer of 1946 that labor had forced Truman into a corner. He had lost a great deal of credibility in his failed attempts to mediate labor disputes in the absence of federal machinery to control such problems. Consequently, it is not surprising that Truman responded to the railway strike with Draconian measures in an attempt to boost his credibility and to win this fight against Whitney and Johnston—and what he had come to believe were the abuses of labor. Clifford recalled being witness at a cabinet meeting on May 24 to "Presidential anger I could not have previously imagined." In his rage Truman "demand[ed] the toughest labor law in history."[38]

That evening Truman delivered a strongly worded radio address to the nation. "This is no contest between labor and management," he said. "This is a contest between a small group of men and their Government."[39] The next day Truman went before a joint session of Congress while negotiations between his assistant John Steelman and labor leaders Whitney and Johnston continued at the Statler Hotel in Washington. Truman delayed his departure for Capitol Hill expecting a break in the negotiations before he delivered the speech, but none came. In his statement, which was written by Clifford, the president asked for emergency powers to end the railroad strike and future strikes that threatened the welfare of the nation. Under the president's plan, injunctions and contempt proceedings could be used against labor leaders, and strikers who refused to return to work under a presidential order would be subject to military draft.

In an incident that can only be described as dramatic, the strike was settled while Truman spoke. Clifford, in a handwritten note, informed the president that the strike had been averted. "He smiled silently," Clifford recalled, "and then read [the note] to Congress. The House chamber erupted in cheering—longer, louder, and more sustained than anything he had experienced before or was ever to experience again."[40]

Despite his victory over Johnston and Whitney, Truman did not back away from his legislative proposal; he completed his speech and asked Congress to enact his proposal promptly. Such an obstinate stance by the president following a mortifying defeat for labor was more than the nation's labor leaders could stand, and they marshaled their forces to do all they could to damage the president and his proposed antilabor legislation. Whitney vowed to use all of his union's $47 million to defeat Truman in 1948 and denounced the president as a "political accident." Bill Green of the AFL called Truman's plan "slave labor under fascism." Murray said that Truman's bill was born of "wild hysteria" and "constitute[s] a beachhead for those sinister forces in American life which seek to use the military power as a means of crushing labor." Clearly, the proposed legislation had hurt the president's chances of holding the labor vote in 1948. *Life* commented, "Observers thought that not in many years had any president of the U.S. done himself so much political damage in one speech."[41]

The House approved Truman's antilabor bill quickly, in fact, the same Saturday night that he delivered the speech. But the Senate was not so eager. After a few changes, including the removal of the provision to draft striking workers, the bill died as the emergency passed. It was Republican leader Robert Taft who placed the final death sentence on the president's bill when he told reporters that he believed it to be "farther toward Hitlerism, Stalinism, and totalitarianism than I have ever seen proposed in any strike."[42]

Truman settled the strike, but whatever mutual trust there had been between his administration and the unions was gone. At the same time he still had no mechanism to deal with the country's labor relations problems. With his bill dead in Congress (killed by liberals, labor, and even Republicans), the spotlight swung to the Case bill. In February 1946, with steelworkers and General Motors workers both out on strike and antilabor sentiment in the nation at a high point, the Case Bill passed the House by a substantial margin. It provided for presidential fact-finding boards and a permanent Labor-Management Mediation Board with the power to impose a sixty-day cooling-off period and injunctions against striking unions. The bill also prohibited secondary boycotts and made unions liable for damages incurred during a strike in breach of a union-management contract. The significance of the Case bill was that it was permanent; it was intended to replace all existing labor legislation and to change the current labor-management relationship for the future. On May 25, just a few hours after Truman asked for emergency measures to deal with the railway strike, the Senate passed the Case bill. A few days later the House accepted the Senate's version and sent the bill on to the president. It was the first postwar antilabor bill, and it was pushed rapidly through Congress on the backs of the two major strikes, one million idle workers, and the public's growing antilabor sentiments.

Labor pushed Truman hard to veto the bill, while representatives of industry insisted he sign it. Southern conservative Democrats had voted overwhelmingly with the Republicans, and they also pushed Truman to sign it. Congressman John Rankin of Mississippi argued that the Democrats would lose in November if Truman vetoed the bill.[43] Labor leaders insisted the bill was intolerable, particularly the antiunion injunction, a tactic used to break strikes before the Norris-LaGuardia Act outlawed the practice in 1932.[44] The president's cabinet members and advisers (with the exception of John Snyder) supported a veto of the bill; taking that advice, the president sent a veto to Congress on June 11. In his veto message he said he believed that the Case bill would not bring an end to labor strife and therefore it would be of little benefit to the public. It "strikes at the symptoms and ignores the underlying causes," he wrote.[45] The next day the House failed to override the veto by five votes.

Truman had not yet vindicated himself in the eyes of organized labor, but certainly he had hoped that a veto of the Case bill would go a long way toward vindication. By the summer of 1946 the major strikes were over. The threat of a railway strike was gone, the UAW was back to work, and the steel strike was resolved. Only Lewis and the coal miners remained restless. At the same time, Truman and his advisers had concluded that without labor there would be no Democratic victory in the 1948 presidential election. With the major strike threats gone, there was a need for reconciliation, and Truman's veto of the Case bill was a move in that direction. In a letter to the president, Oscar Ewing of the Democratic National Committee pointed out to Truman what had already become obvious to White House strategists: "The Democratic party must be the party of labor and the common people. Not only must it further their interests in the common good, but it must clearly appear to do so. On no other basis can we be successful at the polls."[46] Truman showed by his veto of the Case bill that he was not antilabor and that he would support organized labor in opposing permanent restrictions on its right to collective bargaining. The veto, however, did not bring labor back with open arms. In the 1946 midterm elections, labor showed its anger toward the administration for its handling of labor issues by simply staying away from the polls. Labor (at least the rank and file) would need more from the president of the United States in exchange for its votes.

One of the greatest labor-government showdowns of the postwar era was between Truman and Lewis. Lewis had accepted a strike settlement the day Truman became president. One year later, in April 1946, he called his miners out again, this time for over a month, causing brownouts in the East and railroad and autoworker layoffs all over the country. On May 29 Lewis and Secretary of the Interior Julius Krug came to an agreement that was a virtual capitulation by the government, and the strike ended. By fall, however, Lewis was no longer happy with the May agreements, and he demanded that Krug reopen negotiations, this time to discuss monthly vacation payments to miners. When Krug refused, Lewis complained to the press that Krug and the Truman administration had breached the contract and that on November 20 he would call his second strike of the year and bring the nation to its knees as he had done in April and May.[47]

The question of how to deal with Lewis was fought out among Truman's top advisers at the White House. Interestingly, it was the conservatives who most wanted to travel the path of conciliation and compromise with Lewis and the liberals who advocated breaking the strike and putting an end to Lewis's ability to shut down the nation's industries. Specifically, the conflict was between John Steelman, Truman's conservative assistant, and Clark Clifford, the president's special counsel. Both had allies. Supporting Steelman was a growing coalition of conservatives in the administration, including Secretary of Agriculture Clinton Anderson and Secretary of the Treasury John Snyder. Julius Krug (Lewis's nemesis) and Attorney General Tom Clark supported Clifford. On November 16, after refereeing an all-night debate between Krug, Clark, Steelman, and Clifford, Truman concluded that his only option was "a fight to the finish with John L. Lewis."[48] Clifford's winning argument was that "the majority of the people were opposed to Lewis's grandstanding, and if the President held his ground, Lewis would be beaten in the court of public opinion."[49]

On November 18 Truman ordered the Justice Department to seek an injunction forcing Lewis to call off the strike. When Lewis ignored the order and called his workers out two days later, Truman sought and received a contempt citation against Lewis. On December 3, a federal judge found Lewis and the UMW guilty of civil and criminal contempt for disregarding the original order and fined the union $3.5 million and Lewis an additional $10,000. It was the largest financial penalty ever imposed on a union by the federal courts. On December 7, Lewis called off the strike just before Truman planned to appear before the nation in a radio broadcast denouncing Lewis and the strike. Lewis extended his threat of a strike until March but withdrew his pledge after the Supreme Court upheld the contempt citation against the UMW (although the fine was reduced to $700,000) and the White House dropped all charges against Lewis.

Clifford's victory over Steelman and the conservative forces in the White House was the beginning of his political career and of a concerted effort by him (with others at his side) to develop a long-term strategy that would win the election for Truman in 1948. Clifford always called himself a liberal, and here he stood with the liberal forces against Steelman and the other conservatives in the administration. But Clifford, even at this early date, was showing himself to be the pragmatic political analyst who would orchestrate Truman's 1948 victory. "If [Truman] yielded to Lewis," Clifford recalled, "he would have great difficulty governing for the next two years . . . and surely would not be elected on his own in 1948."[50] As the situation stood in late 1945 and on through 1946, labor leaders Whitney, Johnston, and Lewis were clearly standing in the way of stable labor-management relations. Clifford knew in 1946 that the nation's volatile labor situation would have to be stabilized before Truman could again show himself as an advocate of labor and win labor votes in 1948.

This victory over Lewis was one of several successes that the Truman administration experienced in late 1946, and the public seemed satisfied for the first time that the president could deal with difficult situations. Consequently, his political capital began to rise in the polls.[51] Clifford recalled that the victory over Lewis even seemed to change Truman's attitude toward his job.[52] Lewis's defeat was also the beginning of the end of an era in American labor relations. Capped off by the Taft-Hartley Act the next year, labor unions would no longer wield the power they once had or had hoped to attain after the war.

The Republican Eightieth Congress came to Washington in a time of relative calm in the storm of the nation's postwar labor problems. But the members of the Eightieth Congress believed they had been given a mandate to bring an end to the New Deal, and for many in the Republican party that also meant bringing an end to the abuses of organized labor. It was also true that the election of many of these new congressmen was a direct reflection of their constituents' angry mood toward organized labor's actions since the end of the war.

Truman's response to the congressional state of mind was to ask Congress in his State of the Union message in January 1947 to avoid passing "punitive legislation" against the powers of labor. "Industrial peace," he said, "cannot be achieved merely by laws directed against labor unions." He agreed, however, that some labor legislation was necessary, and he asked Congress to pass a program that would stop jurisdictional disputes between competing unions and outlaw secondary boycotts. He also asked for an expansion of the Department of Labor to allow that body to make better use of voluntary arbitration. In addition, he proposed an expansion of social programs that would bring greater security to workers' lives, such as broader Social Security coverage, a national health insurance program, and a higher minimum wage. Last, he asked for a temporary committee to investigate the nation's labor relations problems.[53] These were mild requests in the face of almost rabid antilabor sentiment in the Eightieth Congress, and they clearly reflected Truman's belief that strong antilabor legislation would only cause further labor disputes.

But the Eightieth Congress had its own agenda. On June 4, 1947, Congress passed the Taft-Hartley Act, the most restrictive labor legislation since the Sherman Anti-Trust Act of 1890. The fate of the bill was then placed in Truman's hands. Mail to the White House favoring a veto outnumbered that in support of Truman's signature by 114,909 to 3,656.[54] Among those letters was one from AFL president William Green saying that the bill's "provisions are so patently and extravagantly unfair, unreasoned and unworkable as to make them thoroughly unacceptable."[55] Chester Bowles wrote that if Truman vetoed the bill, "you will do a great deal to unify the working people of the country generally behind the Democratic organization and to bring them to the polls in overwhelming numbers." If the bill was passed over his veto, Bowles continued, "I suggest that a vigorous effort be made to enforce the act so that working people in general will know in 1948 exactly what the Republican viewpoint means in terms of their daily life and their livelihood."[56] Wilson Wyatt of the liberal Americans for Democratic Action urged Truman to veto the bill. Many in the ADA believed that if Truman allowed the bill to become law a third party would form with organized labor as its guiding force.[57] In the *Washington Post*, Marquis Childs reported that Truman had hoped the Congress would make such a move: "That was the Administration's policy from top to bottom. The expectation was that, given enough rope, the extremist Republicans would write a bill so crudely restrictive that no President could sign it."[58]

Truman's decision to veto Taft-Hartley had three distinct sources. First, the president (as he had shown all his life) was prolabor; his veto of the Case bill the year before had made that clear. His tangles with the big unions in 1945 and 1946 reflected Truman's virtual hatred of John L. Lewis and of the powers of other big labor bosses like Lewis and a need to keep the economy in line in the face of a perceived economic disaster if inflation was allowed to spiral. Second, a veto would keep with Truman's long-held belief that repressive labor legislation would simply bring on additional strife and not solve the deep-seated problems that commonly bring labor and industry into conflict. Truman believed that labor conflicts could be settled through coolheaded voluntary arbitration, as long as egomaniacal bosses like Lewis were kept away from the bargaining table. Third, there were clear and present political considerations. Truman needed to hold the Democrats together to win in 1948. That need was reinforced by the 1946 defeats in Congress and was already an established policy among the White House strategists. The South would be the only major group in the party that would be offended by a veto of Taft-Hartley. Southerners in Congress had supported the bill from its inception, partly in response to the CIO's postwar "southern strategy" that sent labor organizers into the South in an attempt to organize industries there but also because the South was conservative and antiunion by nature. But the only southern response to a presidential veto of Taft-Hartley might possibly be a minor backlash from powerful southern congressmen, and even that was unlikely. Also, Truman's veto of Taft-Hartley would improve the president's standing as the rightful heir to Roosevelt and his policies, at least on labor issues. FDR's New Deal remained a very popular economic program among the American public, and it was still a political rallying point for Democrats of all shapes and sizes. The Wagner Act had been an important part of the New Deal, and for many, Taft-Hartley was the beginning of a methodical disassembling of the New Deal by Republicans. If Taft-Hartley succeeded, the Republicans might try to eliminate farm subsidies, loans for rural electrification, low-interest home loans, Social Security benefits, and a multitude of other programs directed at the average American. For those Americans who saw the New Deal as the savior of the nation's economy and for those who believed that New Deal policies should continue to be a part of the American economic system, Truman's veto of Taft-Hartley was a step in the right direction by heading off the Republican dismantling of at least one program. Had Truman chosen to sign the bill, labor might well have gone to the left and supported Henry Wallace in 1948. The result would have been a badly split Democratic ticket and an easy Republican victory. Thus Truman's veto went a long way toward uniting the liberal and moderate factions in the Democratic party behind the president as the 1948 election approached.

Truman's veto message, delivered on June 20, rang with New Deal rhetoric. The president made it clear again that he believed punitive legislation would do more to cause labor unrest than to solve the nation's labor problems. He wrote that the bill "would contribute neither to industrial peace nor to economic stability and progress. . . . It contains seeds of discord which would plague this nation for years to come." He added that the bill would weaken the unions and destroy national unity.[59] With very little fanfare or surprise the House voted 331 to 83 to override the veto that same day. The Senate waited three days to do the same by a vote of 68 to 25.[60] Taft-Hartley was law, and America's labor relations were changed for the future—but it also allowed Truman and the Democrats to keep labor in line and maintain control of the labor vote in the 1948 election.

6

The ADA and the Splintering of Postwar Liberalism

In February 1948 the Americans for Democratic Action met to discuss the divisive state of American liberalism. It was an important meeting for the ADA. The organization was preparing for the upcoming national election, and one objective of the meeting was to produce a political platform, a statement of objectives for the campaigns. "The election of 1948," the platform statement began, "will fix the course of history for decades."[1] The election came to fit that description, and the ADA had a great deal to do with making it one of the most important presidential elections of the twentieth century.

The members of the ADA were expressly liberal in the New Deal tradition, but at the heart of their ideology was the issue that divided American liberals in the postwar years: it was emphatically anticommunist. In fact, the ADA believed that the issue of anticommunism would replace the failed economy of the Great Depression era and the antifascism of World War II as the glue that would hold America's liberals together in the future.

The ADA was a very powerful political organization, but it hardly appeared so. In 1948, the ADA claimed only about twenty-five thousand members, located almost exclusively in the large northeastern cities and California. The organization spent most of its first few years swimming in a sea of red ink. In 1947, less than a year after its formation, the ADA was $20,000 in debt with no prospect of a bailout.[2] It was, however, the makeup of its membership rather than its financial status that made the ADA powerful. The liberals represented by the ADA were influential, and their support would be crucial to Truman's victory in November. James Rowe, in his memo to the president in the last months of 1947, made it clear that this group must somehow be placated. "They are," he wrote, "far more influential than their numbers entitle them to be."[3] Out front were such well-known names as Eleanor Roosevelt, Hubert Humphrey, the Alsop brothers, Melvyn Douglas, and even Ronald Reagan in his celebrated "liberal days." In addition, the ADA claimed the role of the New Deal in exile, the guardian of New Dealism and the legacy of FDR. With the exception of a few old New Dealers who supported Wallace's candidacy, most who had been in the Roosevelt administration were associated in some way with the ADA. So it was the ADA's place in the minds of most American liberals as the keeper of the New Deal flame that forced the Truman administration to seek some common ground with this group as the election date neared.

The ADA existed as a political force in postwar America almost entirely because of the course of wartime international affairs. In 1939 the Nazi-Soviet Non-Aggression Pact caused great consternation among liberals in the United States. A split developed between those liberals on the left who supported this agreement between Adolph Hitler and Joseph Stalin and more moderate liberals who would not. One result of this split was the emergence of a large group of anticommunist liberals, many of them middle class, who simply could not bear the Nazi-Soviet alliance. They began to operate independently, inside their own political organizations and outside the labor-liberal-communist-socialist coalition, better known then as the Popular Front.

Things changed in 1941, when Hitler invaded Russia. The liberal groups in America patched up their differences and came together in the face of the common enemy of fascism. The now united Popular Front supported the war effort, supported FDR as the nation's war leader, and even supported the wartime initiatives for industry, including labor's no-strike pledge. This wartime Popular Front was more of a loose coalition than an organization, and it included such diverse groups as the communists, socialists, progressives, liberals, labor leaders, and various other groups and individuals on the left and far left. Certainly there were dissenters, like John L. Lewis of the United Mine Workers, but for the most part, the Popular Front could claim a considerable degree of unity during the war because of its common link of antifascism.

In 1941 the ADA's predecessor, the Union for Democratic Action (UDA), was formed. This wartime liberal organization had split from the Socialist party of Norman Thomas after unsuccessfully opposing Thomas's isolationism in the face of the totalitarian aggressions in Europe and Asia. During the war other liberal organizations sprang up throughout the nation, each with a different agenda, including the CIO-Political Action Committee, the National Citizens Political Action Committee, and the Independent Citizens Committee of the Arts, Sciences, and Professions. The UDA had much in common with these groups, particularly support for the Roosevelt administration. But the UDA had the distinction of opposing both fascism and communism, and it refused to allow communists to join its organization. Several of the other Popular Front groups, however, were infiltrated with (and even controlled by) communists.

Along with antifascism, FDR himself was the singular symbol and driving force behind liberal identity and unity in wartime America. His death, coming at almost the exact moment that fascism was removed as a threat to liberal ideology, produced more strain than the tenuous liberal coalition could take. "From March, 1933 until mid-April, 1945," a prominent liberal wrote a year after FDR's death and in the midst of a liberal ideological war, "American liberals clung to the illusion that they had 'achieved power.' . . . However, there never existed an authentic liberal coalition which could survive the loss of Mr. Roosevelt."[4] It should not be surprising that after the war and after Roosevelt's death, American liberalism lost its center, reopened old wounds, and began to fragment.

The leading figures behind the UDA were James Loeb, the executive secretary, and Reinhold Niebuhr, the national chairman. Loeb was a rabid anticommunist who had fought the fascist menace in the Spanish Civil War but had returned home appalled by the actions of both the Spanish communists and the Spanish fascists.[5] Educated at Dartmouth and Northwestern Universities in the Romance languages, Loeb was teaching in the New York City public school system when the UDA was formed in the spring of 1941. He came to the office with an energy that carried the organization through several crises, the most serious of which was financial. He would be the strength and direction of the UDA and later the ADA, keeping both organizations in line in the fight against fascism and communism. Niebuhr had been a socialist in the 1930s. By the 1940s he was a well-known theologian and educator and one of the nation's leading anticommunist liberals.

The UDA, in its first meeting in May 1941, voted to abandon isolationism and support America's entrance into the war against fascism in Europe, a war that the United States had not yet entered. The UDA members made it clear, however, that they saw the USSR as no less threatening as a political, economic, and ideological menace to the world order, and they moved to exclude communists and all Communist party activity from their organization. On domestic issues, the UDA agenda reflected its socialist background. It called for socialization of the nation's banks and the great industries, a national planning board, government control of credit and investment, heavy income taxes, a full employment plan, fair employment policies, antidiscrimination measures, and a solution to world hunger.[6] These were popular issues in the New Deal years when liberal America looked forward to a peaceful, equitable postwar world fashioned in the New Deal image. But after the war, when the UDA would reorganize as the

ADA, this liberal domestic program would take a backseat to the near religion of anticommunism, a stance made necessary by the challenge from Henry Wallace and the Progressive Citizens of America for the heart of American liberalism.

During the war the UDA and Henry Wallace had maintained a close relationship. As did most liberals in this period, Loeb and other ADA leaders expected Wallace to carry on the mantle of the New Deal and American liberalism in the postwar, post-FDR world. After Wallace was bumped for Truman as the Democratic vice- presidential candidate in 1944, the UDA liked the idea of Wallace staying on in the cabinet as secretary of commerce under Roosevelt and then in the Truman administration. In that role, they believed, Wallace would move the country toward full employment after the war, a popular goal for liberals in this period and a vision that was often associated with Wallace and his followers. In December 1944, just four months before FDR's death, Loeb wrote glowingly to Wallace: "We are united in feeling that you have made yourself the leader of the American progressive movement and we, therefore, are convinced that no steps should be taken by any of us individually or collectively without seeking your advice."[7] That relationship began to sour, however, when, as a result of communist aggressions in parts of Eastern Europe in the summer of 1946, the anticommunist side of the UDA began to emerge as the dominant force in that organization.

In late September 1946, just after Wallace's Madison Square Garden speech that cost him his job in the Truman administration, Loeb began to show his disenchantment with Wallace. "I should welcome the opportunity to explain to you . . . my serious questions regarding this whole foreign policy problem," he wrote. "I am trying personally to reach some conclusions which will not be based either on the attacks made upon you by the extreme right nor on the clear support you are now receiving from the extreme left. I hope that a way can be found in which democratic liberals will be able to work side by side with you in pursuit of common aims."[8]

The war's end had a major impact on American liberals. Without the personality of FDR and the specter of fascism to unite them, liberal groups fell into disagreement again. For a few, fascism in Spain and Argentina filled the gap left by the demise of German and Italian fascism.[9] But for most on the left, a major postwar conflict developed over several issues, including the question of Soviet aggressions, the role of communism in American politics, and the foreign policy of the Truman administration. Through the summer of 1946, the UDA became increasingly anticommunist as the Soviet grip on Eastern Europe tightened and the first salvos of the Cold War were fired.

The Progressive Citizens of America was formed in Washington in the last days of 1946, just weeks after the Democrats were handed their embarrassing losses in the congressional elections. That disastrous defeat stirred American liberals nationwide with a shudder at the prospect of the first Republican Congress since 1930 and the dawning of what appeared to be a new age of national conservatism. The PCA was formed from a merger of several Popular Front groups, including the NCPAC and ICCASP, both with large communist memberships. Henry Wallace spoke at the PCA's first meeting and quickly emerged as the inspirational leader of the organization.

But Wallace's arguments were growing increasingly unpopular as the Cold War tightened. He maintained often that Stalin's actions in Eastern Europe and elsewhere were developed from legitimate security needs and that the Soviets were not a threat to any American interests. If only the United States and the Soviet Union could combine their industrial and military might, Wallace argued, the result would be world peace and prosperity. Consequently, Wallace and his supporters blamed Truman for starting the Cold War, for perpetuating a wartime mentality in America to win votes, and for ignoring the real enemy: fascism at home. On these issues, Wallace and the PCA placed themselves in direct conflict with the UDA.

In early January 1947, only a few days after the PCA was organized in New York, four hundred liberals met in Washington to form the ADA. Like the PCA, it was the Republican party victories in November and the fear of conservative dominance of America's immediate political future that led the UDA to move into a more aggressive stance. "The last illusion of progressive strength collapsed on November 5," Loeb wrote. "Out of that collapse has come the historic realignment of the potentially vast legions of American progressivism."[10] The 1946 defeats were devastating to the liberals and awakened them to the reality of a Republican resurgence of power. Loeb and his followers also felt that liberalism was being systematically purged from the Truman administration. For these men and women liberalism had been the political underpinning of the nation for sixteen years. They would not be relegated to a position outside the Truman administration, and they would not stand by while conservatives grabbed control of the government. The Washington meeting was, in part, an attempt to reassert a significant liberal power, first on Truman, then on the Democratic party, and finally on the nation.

The ADA leadership was made up of many of the big names of the New Deal era. Some had left the Truman administration in protest. Others were prominent liberals alienated by Truman's domestic policies that to them seemed contrary to the New Deal. Attending the Washington meeting were such liberal guiding lights as labor leaders Walter Reuther, David Dubinsky, Hugo Ernst, and James B. Carey. Eleanor Roosevelt and her son Franklin Jr. attended, as did John Kenneth Galbraith and Robert Nathan. Other important figures from the anticommunist left included Loeb and Niebuhr from the UDA, Leon Henderson, Chester Bowles, and David Porter of the wartime Office of Price Administration, Wilson Wyatt, boy wonder Arthur Schlesinger Jr., Joseph Rauh, columnist Marquis Childs, Robert Bendiner from *Nation,* Joseph P. Lash, Walter White of the NAACP, and soon-to-be historian William Leuchtenburg. James Rowe, the author of the strategy memo that would lead Truman to a victory in November, was also there. Several Hollywood types decorated the tree, including Ronald Reagan, who spent most of 1948 touring the country organizing for the ADA.[11] The co-chairmen named by the new group were Leon Henderson, chief of the wartime Office of Price Administration, and Wilson Wyatt from the Office of War Mobilization and Reconversion. Loeb was named secretary-treasurer and in that role remained the ADA's key figure.

Hubert Humphrey, the dynamic mayor of Minneapolis who had just burst onto the national political scene, was to have been the keynote speaker at the meeting, but he was unable to attend. Chester Bowles took his place. Bowles had recently gained notoriety by resigning from the Truman administration over a disagreement with the president's price control policies. In his speech, Bowles called for "liberal control of the Democratic party in 1948," and he voiced his hope that the new organization would resist the temptation to take a hard-line stance against communism and move toward an accommodation with the PCA. Eleanor Roosevelt, in the closing speech of the conference, asked the members to work within the Democratic party and ignore all third-party speculation.[12] In its final report, the ADA declared that it would work within the Democratic party as the party's left wing, attempt to bring its liberal opinions and ideas to bear on national and state politics, and not get entangled in any third-party moves.

In a press release following the January meeting, the new ADA (as had the old UDA) stated firmly its anticommunist, antitotalitarian stance. The organization rejected "any alliance with totalitarian forces on the Left or the Right." And on the domestic front they urged a "need for reconstruction of the U.S. liberal movement free of totalitarian influence." They also called for an expansion of New Deal programs to "insure decent levels of health, nutrition, shelter and education." They demanded an expansion of civil liberties "to all Americans regardless of race, color, creed or sex." They wanted a prosperous economy, support for the United Nations, and international control of atomic energy. But it was anticommunism that dominated the ADA's first policy paper: "America must furnish political and economic support to democratic and freedom-loving peoples the world over. ... We reject any association with Communists or sympathizers with Communists in the United States as completely as we reject any association with Fascists or their sympathizers. Both are hostile to the principles of freedom and democracy on which this republic has grown great."[13] The ADA constitution made many of the same statements, only more bluntly: "No person who is a member or follower of any totalitarian organization or who subscribes to totalitarian political beliefs may become a member of the Americans for Democratic Action."[14]

Funding for this new organization was to come from the only liberal organizations with money: the labor unions, particularly the International Ladies Garment Workers Union, the International Association of Machinists, the AFL, the Brotherhood of Railroad Trainmen, the CIO, Textile Workers Union of America, and the UAW. The early commitments of financial support were strong, and the money from these wealthy unions promised to keep the new ADA financially sound. But union support for the ADA never reached the amount pledged, and the new organization, much like its predecessor, ran from one financial crisis to another. The ADA expected most of its financial burden to be carried by the CIO, but CIO president Philip Murray feared that the ADA-PCA conflict would threaten longtime liberal-communist accommodation within the CIO, and in February 1947, just weeks after the formation of both the ADA and the PCA, he decided that the CIO should not join either group. Loeb and the ADA were devastated. For months Loeb and Wyatt tried desperately to bring labor back into the ADA orbit. Finally, in early 1948 labor agreed to support the ADA, but only after the PCA had emerged as a communist-dominated third party.[15]

What the PCA had in leadership the ADA lacked. It had no Henry Wallace to carry the standard of anticommunist liberalism into political battle, no dynamic, charismatic figure to rally the troops, to unite them and carry them on to political victory as a political party. The result was that the ADA was forced to remain in the role of a political action committee, destined only to influence the political process rather than to be the political base for a new postwar Democratic party, as its leaders had hoped.

The ADA may have lacked a charismatic leader, but it did not suffer from a shortage of political writers, and they became the organization's primary strength, as Rowe had pointed out in his memo to the president in September 1947. Writers such as Schlesinger, Niebuhr, and Joseph and

Stewart Alsop made it clear in their newspaper and magazine articles that there was an important minority on the American left that opposed both Soviet aggressions and communist organizations in America. They also made it clear that Truman was not their representative, that they believed he was doing a poor job in the White House, and that they wanted him out. ADA writers were published in many magazines, but the *Nation,* more than any other, provided an outlet for their opinions. Also the Luce press, particularly *Life* magazine, occasionally provided a place to air the ADA arguments of anticommunist liberalism in America. The *New Republic,* however, one of the traditional organs of American liberalism, effectively blackballed ADA writers and their anticommunist opinions during Wallace's tenure there as editor. Michael Straight, the publisher at *New Republic,* revered Wallace and let him have his way with the magazine.[16]

So within two months both the ADA and the PCA had formed. Both groups saw themselves as holding the legacy of the New Deal and FDR, a sort of New Deal in exile, and both believed that Truman was systematically and intentionally dismantling the New Deal programs and removing its leaders from his administration. On those points they were united; only the question of foreign affairs separated them. And they debated it in meetings and in the press.

The ADA-PCA split weakened the cause of liberalism at a time when a labor-liberal coalition might well have been an unstoppable political force in postwar America. Indeed, many ADA members, including Eleanor Roosevelt in the organization's early days, hoped that the groups would unite and that Wallace would come over to the ADA and bring with him the PCA liberals who were not communists. But Wallace believed that anticommunism was little more than Red-baiting, and he continued to maintain that the United States and the Soviet Union should work together to achieve world peace and prosperity. Like Eleanor Roosevelt, Wallace also hoped for unity of the two liberal political groups. In an article entitled "The Enemy Is Not Each Other" in *New Republic* in the month the ADA was formed, he wrote that most members of both groups believed that "liberals today in the so-called warring groups are about 90% in agreement."[17]

Possibly these two liberal organizations would have found some common ground on these issues and come together under Wallace's leadership had it not been for the Truman Doctrine and the Truman administration's Cold War foreign policy of containment. In March 1947, when Truman went before Congress to ask for aid to Turkey and Greece, Wallace and his supporters immediately opposed the plan as unnecessary and antagonistic, a policy that divided the world into East and West military camps. In a radio address on March 13 (the day before the president's message to Congress) Wallace said the doctrine was a commitment for the Truman administration to intervene against communism.[18] In a *New Republic* article just a few days later, Wallace called the Truman Doctrine a measure "advanced in the spirit of warfare against Russia."[19] Not surprisingly, the ADA responded, coming out in support of the Truman Doctrine, although with some reluctance, on March 27. The ADA's chief concern was that the Truman administration should go through the UN to resolve the situation in Greece and Turkey rather than initiate unilateral action. But the ADA endorsement set the foreign policy stage for the coming events between the two liberal groups.[20] From this point on, the ADA fell into line behind Truman's foreign policy, while the PCA and the extreme left continued to voice their criticisms from the diplomatic fringes.

The division between the two groups over the administration's foreign policy was reenacted three months later when the Marshall Plan was introduced as an economic companion to the Truman Doctrine. Again, the PCA voiced its opposition to the plan, while the ADA supported it. For those liberals who saw the Truman Doctrine as hard-line anticommunism—little more than supplying weapons to any group fighting communists—the Marshall Plan softened the administration's stance with the olive branch of economic aid, and it allowed many liberals who were not strongly anticommunist to accept the entire Truman foreign policy. This is "a new deal for the desperate, disillusioned and embittered peoples of war-ravaged Europe," Wilson Wyatt said. "We are for it."[21] Like the Truman Doctrine, the Marshall Plan drew a clearer dividing line between the two liberal groups. Throughout 1947 and into 1948 the foreign policy of the Truman administration and the ideas and opinions of the ADA leadership were drifting closer together, and that would have a major impact on the 1948 election.

The ADA-Truman amorous rendezvous on foreign policy carried over into domestic issues. Truman's anticommunist "loyalty" campaign—initiated through executive order in March 1947—was heralded by the ADA as one of several ways to rid the nation of the communist menace.[22] But Truman and the ADA found their real common ground when the president vetoed the Taft-Hartley bill in the summer of 1947. The ADA pushed the president hard to veto the measure, and when he did, most ADA members were pleasantly surprised. There was a general fear inside the ADA that if Truman had signed the bill, organized labor would have abandoned the Democratic party completely and thrown its support to Wallace and the PCA. Many ADA leaders had backgrounds in the labor movement of the 1930s, and the Taft-Hartley veto showed them that Truman was on the side of labor. But many still could not accept him as their political leader, and few believed he could win in 1948.[23]

Truman was not necessarily reacting to the ADA's anticommunist posture simply to win that group of liberals over for the Democratic party in 1948; his own anticommunist Cold Warrior stance in foreign affairs had been forming at least since the Potsdam conference, and the 1946 congressional defeats pushed him to set up the anticommunist loyalty program at home. Clearly, however, the ADA and the administration came together because the two sides had developed basically similar opinions separately, and the ADA members found themselves more and more in agreement with the president as the election neared. This relationship was enhanced further by their common fear of a Wallace run at the presidency. As that prospect became more apparent and more of a threat through 1947, Truman and the ADA became even closer, unfriendly allies against a common enemy. Both feared that a successful Wallace candidacy might push the Republican party far to the right. But probably more important, both believed that a Wallace third-party run in 1948 would split the Democratic ticket and put a Republican in the White House. It was that prospect, more than anything else, that thrust the ADA and the Truman administration into bed together in 1948.[24]

As late as the summer of 1948, however, the ADA still could not bring itself to support Truman. His anticommunist foreign policy was not enough to draw many ADA members back into the Democratic party, and his domestic policy remained inadequate to most liberals. Truman himself remained "That Little Man from Missouri" who seemed barely qualified to hold the door at the White House between presidents. As late as the spring of 1948, and despite the Taft-Hartley veto, the ADA had not wavered a bit in its opposition to Truman. "We cannot overlook the fact that poor appointments and faltering support of [Truman's] aides have resulted in a failure to rally the people behind the policies which in large measure we wholeheartedly support."[25] In June, just days before the Democratic convention, Leon Henderson said that if Truman were nominated, "Roaring reaction would ride the rails . . . leaving liberals helpless and underrepresented."[26] In March, Loeb circulated a memorandum to the ADA membership stating his fear that "a Truman nomination would be disastrous to the whole liberal-labor coalition."[27] But events would change quickly.

Just a few weeks after receiving Rowe's memo, which argued, among many other things, that to win in 1948 the president must move to the left and regain his base of support there, Truman delivered his State of the Union address calling for a liberalization of the American economy, including the expansion of several New Deal programs, plus inflation control, a high standard of living for all Americans, a stronger farm economy, and a tax reduction. He also hit on such liberal buzzwords as human rights, human resources, and conservation.[28] Truman went on to place several ADA members in important positions in his administration. It was a good political move, one that would pay off enormously in November. But the ADA remained independent, continuing its "anybody but Harry" (or Henry) stance and began looking for a champion it could support, someone who could unseat Truman at the Democratic convention in July and carry the party to victory in November.

7

The Loosening of Old Chains

By the time Harry Truman became president, the modern civil rights movement was already well under way. Much of the legal groundwork had been laid, protest tactics had been tested, and the economic and demographic forces were at work that would eventually remove many of the nation's old laws and attitudes. African Americans were also beginning to make headway in the political arena. During the New Deal years blacks received some concessions, even though Roosevelt almost always deferred to the demands of powerful southern congressmen over any appeals for civil rights for African Americans. For nearly thirteen years, FDR successfully walked a line between these two groups, but his political abilities always seemed to make enough room in the New Deal coalition for both African Americans and southerners. Truman inherited this conflict in the party, along with the fairly weak commitment to civil rights, when he came to office.

At this time there was an important distinction between African Americans who supported FDR and the New Deal and those who were actually Democrats. Abandoning the party of Lincoln was not easy for most African Americans in the 1930s and 1940s. They immediately found themselves uncomfortable as Democrats in a party that harbored outspoken racist demagogues such as Theodore Bilbo, John Rankin, Herman Talmadge, and others in the South. Through decades in Congress and in the statehouses, these men had come to wield such power that not even Roosevelt could influence the course of government without their support. Roosevelt's New Deal, however, aided African Americans through the Depression and gave black workers jobs during the war. It was surely a dilemma, but despite the southern racist element among FDR's supporters, African Americans voted in large numbers for Roosevelt—the leader of the party that seemed to be doing the most to alleviate their plight. Like black leader Channing H. Tobias, many African Americans felt confident voting for Roosevelt, but they still could not bear to leave their beloved Republican party. In 1940, 67 percent of America's blacks supported FDR, but only 42 percent considered themselves Democrats.[1] As the 1948 election approached, there was a great fear among Truman's advisers that without the Roosevelt magic, African Americans might revert back to voting Republican. Truman would have to convince African Americans that it was the convictions of the Democratic party, and not simply those of the dead Roosevelt, that would lead them on to future civil rights advances, and he would have to show them that he carried those convictions.

In 1932, only 21 percent of the African-American vote went to Roosevelt. But in 1936 that figure jumped to 75 percent in one of the most dramatic voter shifts in American history. Blacks turned to Roosevelt because New Deal programs offered them some relief from the depths of the Depression—because of their condition of poverty, not their race. In fact, most New Deal programs continued to impose segregation and discrimination as government policy. Civilian Conservation Corps (CCC) camps, for instance, were strictly segregated, as were most Tennessee Valley Authority (TVA) projects. The National Recovery Administration (NRA), dubbed "Negroes Ruined Again" by some African-American leaders, authorized lower pay scales for African Americans. And the Federal Housing Authority (FHA) upheld race-based restrictive covenants in housing. Despite the segregation and discrimination, however, African Americans did receive TVA jobs and were welcomed into CCC camps; they also received an increased working wage as a result of the NRA, and they were able to buy houses under FHA programs, opportunities they had not had before. Clearly, African Americans were denied their fair share of what the New Deal had to offer, but their condition improved considerably as a result of the programs.[2]

The New Deal went a long way toward bringing African Americans into the Democratic party in the Roosevelt era, but there were other reasons why blacks supported FDR. Roosevelt often showed sympathy for African Americans by naming black leaders to federal posts, and many of his appointments to New Deal agencies were sensitive to African-American issues. In 1935 the African-American educator Mary McLeod Bethune was named by FDR as his special adviser on minority affairs. A year later she was appointed director of the Division of Negro Affairs of the National Youth Administration (NYA). Through her efforts, African Americans received a fair share of NYA funds. The Interior Department, under its secretary Harold Ickes, became the home of the much publicized "Black Kitchen Cabinet." Ickes, a strong supporter of civil rights, appointed several African-American leaders to important positions in his department, including Clark Foreman, Robert C. Weaver, and William H. Hastie.[3] Throughout the 1930s and 1940s, this assemblage formed a pressure group that pushed the administration to end various aspects of segregation. Ickes also poured federal money into black schools and hospitals in the South. For the first time in American history, African-American leaders had at least some input into the federal governmental process.[4]

Roosevelt also worked to liberalize the Supreme Court, and, as black Americans saw it, that served the cause of civil rights and further endeared FDR to the African-American community. Before 1937 the Court was primarily conservative, reflecting appointments made by Republican presidents in the 1920s. It blocked civil rights initiatives by finding almost exclusively for states' rights in civil rights matters. In 1935, for instance, the Court, in *Grovey v. Townsend*, affirmed the legality of the white primary. After 1937, however, FDR was able to appoint five justices to the Court, including liberals Hugo Black and William O. Douglas. The result was a more liberal Court and positive decisions on civil rights. In 1944, the Court overturned *Grovey v. Townsend*, and in the case of *Smith v. Allright* that same year it concluded that African Americans could not be excluded from voting in state primaries. *Smith v. Allright* was a major success for the NAACP, and it paved the way for the civil rights court battles of the 1950s.

Another reason African-Americans supported the New Deal was the actions and attitude of the president's wife. Eleanor Roosevelt was in the unique position of being able to give significant support to the civil rights movement without subjecting her husband to the political liabilities that would have come had he supported that cause. Throughout her husband's tenure in Washington, Mrs. Roosevelt played the role of official ombudsman for African Americans and associated herself often and openly with African-American leaders and associations. Her personal friendships with Walter White of the NAACP and Mary McLeod Bethune of the National Council of Negro Women were well known. In addition, she often brought her influence to bear on her husband and other New Dealers on civil rights issues. Her openness and visibility as a supporter of civil rights causes brought further significant African-American support to the Democratic party during the Roosevelt years.

The migration of African Americans into the North during the Depression and war years also brought large numbers of black votes to the Democratic party. These African Americans found jobs in the factories of Detroit, Chicago, and the other industrial centers of the urban Northeast, Midwest, and in California. During the 1940s alone, more than two million African Americans had moved to the North for better jobs, doubling their numbers in that period. Between 1940 and 1947, the number of African Americans in New York City grew from 100,000 to over 800,000; in Chicago the number increased from 300,000 to 420,000; in Philadelphia from 300,000 to 415,000; and in Los Angeles from 100,000 to 210,000.

These new factory workers joined unions, thus becoming increasingly proletarian in their social, economic, and political outlook. They came to associate their situation more with the American factory worker than with the ancient problems of Jim Crow and the Old South. By 1948, the vast majority of northern urban African Americans no longer associated with the party of Lincoln; they saw their future in the party of American labor and American liberalism, the Democrats.[5]

African Americans may have been moving into the Democratic party in large numbers during the Roosevelt years, and Roosevelt may have done more than any other president to aid the cause of civil rights, but many blacks, particularly those in the growing middle class, were not satisfied that FDR had done all he could. They made their opinions known as the election of 1940 approached, an election that proved to be crucial in the political history of the modern civil rights movement.[6]

Despite all their bluster and programs, the Democrats had failed to deliver on several of their promises to African Americans. They still had not passed an antilynching law or an anti–poll tax law, and they had not acted to end disfranchisement of blacks in the South. Democrats continued to accept discrimination and segregation in New Deal programs, and they failed to desegregate the armed services. Possibly most important, the Democratic party continued to harbor southern racists.

The Republicans in 1940 made a valiant attempt to bring blacks back into the GOP. The Republican candidate, Wendell Willkie, made promise after promise to blacks, and the party platform called for significant concessions to African Americans. The Democratic party platform, in contrast, reflected the power of the party's southern wing and thus was weak on civil rights. By late summer of 1940 several members inside the Roosevelt administration began to fear a loss of black support unless concessions were made to African Americans.

Black leaders such as Walter White of the NAACP and A. Philip Randolph of the Brotherhood of Sleeping Car Porters began to push Roosevelt on a variety of issues, particularly on the desegregation of the armed forces. In the days just before the 1940 election, however, the Roosevelt administration responded that any such initiative was impossible, and FDR even extended segregation of the armed forces in an obvious attempt to keep the South in line. Black leaders were outraged. On October 11, just three weeks before the election, the NAACP announced: "We are expressly shocked that a President of the United States at a time of national peril should surrender so completely to enemies of Democracy who would destroy national unity by advocating segregation."[7] The Roosevelt administration was caught off guard by the dissension and, facing what might be a significant loss of black votes, responded with a flurry of symbolic gestures to appease black leaders and keep African-American voters from deserting the party at the last minute. On October 25, the president announced the promotion of Colonel Benjamin O. Davis to brigadier general, the first African American to hold that rank. In addition, he appointed William Hastie to be the civilian aide to the secretary of war and Campbell Johnson to be the aide to the director of the Selective Service. He also added an antidiscrimination clause to the Selective Service Act and approved the establishment of an army air corps training school for African-American pilots at Tuskegee Institute in Alabama.[8]

These concessions amounted to little more than thinly veiled political expediency only days before the election, and they made no significant inroads into Jim Crowism in the military. In fact, the military remained segregated throughout the war, the Tuskegee Airmen flew as a segregated unit, and General Davis did not command troops—black or white. Roosevelt, however, won the election, taking large percentages of black votes in nearly every major city in the North.[9]

The election of 1940 was a foreshadowing of the political events to come. Civil rights was about to become a problem for the Democratic party, and the 1940 election was the first whiff of how difficult that problem might become. In 1940 Roosevelt was able to straddle the civil rights issue, either using his own political abilities or, more likely, because civil rights was not yet a terribly volatile issue. Roosevelt was able to keep both the South and African Americans in line in 1940 by pitching only a few fairly insignificant gestures to each side. After the war, as Truman began to try to tackle civil rights, the issue would be much more volatile, and the two sides—African Americans and white southerners—would not be so easily appeased. The 1940 election also made it clear to African Americans for the first time that they were a potentially powerful voting bloc, that they could make demands and receive concessions. And finally, the civil rights concessions made by FDR just before the election laid the foundations for a series of concessions that Truman would make as the 1948 election approached.

After the election, Philip Randolph concluded that Roosevelt's preelection concessions had not gone very far toward helping African Americans although they had done a great deal to help the president in the election. And in the summer of the next year he threatened the administration with a march on Washington of as many as one hundred thousand angry African-American protesters if FDR did not end segregation in both the armed forces and in employment by government contractors. This was a new militant strategy that quickly got the administration's attention. The federal government was now, for the first time, forced to deal with African Americans as a singular (and possibly even dangerous) pressure group and to accept their threat of direct action as a potential political liability. African Americans were thought to be generally apathetic toward politics, disorganized, and uncontrollable in any modern political sense. But Randolph had promised that up to one hundred thousand African-American citizens could be collected in the same place to make the same demands of the government. FDR would have to listen.[10]

The president tried to convince Randolph to call off his march, but when Randolph refused, Roosevelt agreed to meet some of Randolph's demands. On June 12, FDR issued a press release that would become the basis of Executive Order 8802. It was hardly a demand for action: "Complaints have repeatedly been brought to my attention that available and much-needed workers are being barred from defense production solely because of race, religion, or national origin. . . . Also that discrimination against Negro workers has been nation-wide. . . . All holders of defense contracts are urged to examine their employment and training policies at once to determine whether or not these policies make ample provision for the full utilization of available and competent Negro workers."[11] Two weeks later, the president issued his executive order which banned racial discrimination in government-contracted war production industries. It also created the Fair Employment Practices Commission for the purpose of investigating and publicizing cases of discrimination.

Randolph responded by agreeing to call off the march. He described his deal with the administration as "the most significant and meaningful United States declaration affecting Negroes since the Emancipation Proclamation."[12] It was, however, much less than that. In fact, the new FEPC had no authority, relying mostly on moral suasion to urge government-contracted industries to hire African Americans, and ultimately with little success.[13]

Despite the demographic shifts that placed African Americans in a position of potential political power and despite the concessions made by the Roosevelt administration, blacks generally received little during the war. They had hoped that good jobs in the war industries would allow them to make a place for themselves in the national economy, a place that would be maintained in the postwar period. But they held only the most menial jobs, and they were the last hired and first fired. Despite the enactment of the FEPC, the federal government continued to allow discrimination in hiring practices when it was demanded by government-contracted employers. In the electrical industry, for instance, African Americans held only about 1 percent of the jobs and in the rubber industry only 3 percent. Both industries were almost totally mobilized for war and under government contracts, and no amount of pressure from the FEPC could force either industry to hire African Americans in large numbers.[14] The military remained segregated during the war, and with the exception of the Tuskegee Airmen, who saw significant action in North Africa and Italy, African-American soldiers spent most of the war away from the action on the docks as Service of Supply laborers or in the navy belowdecks in the ships' kitchens and laundry rooms.

It was clear, however, that after the war African Americans would be making demands. Membership in the NAACP increased dramatically during the war years, showing an interest among African Americans in the civil rights movement. By 1946 the organization had ballooned to 450,000 members from just 50,000 in 1940. Its membership jumped to 600,000 within two years after the end of the war, with 1,500 NAACP branches throughout the country.[15] When the war ended, African-American leaders began a major push to make their demands heard. First on the agenda was full employment. The NAACP feared that peace would send the American economy spiraling into another depression, and a congressional promise of full employment seemed to be a hedge for African Americans against such a possibility. African Americans also wanted a permanent FEPC, and they continued to push for an end to segregation in the armed forces. In addition, they renewed their longtime demands for an antilynching bill and for federal legislation to end the poll tax.

Such was the state of the African-American movement for civil rights on April 13, 1945, when Harry Truman took over the presidency. African Americans were not yet sold on the Democratic party; they had embraced only FDR and his programs. To keep those votes in the Democratic corner, Truman would have to prove his worthiness to black voters, show that he would do more than the Republicans or Henry Wallace, that he would advance the cause of civil rights in America. The war had been the seedtime for change in the civil rights movement; African Americans now had new political and economic opportunities at hand, but they also had new political and economic power. They knew that demographic changes demanded that Washington act on their behalf. At the same time, postwar America was now the beacon for world democracy, independence, liberty, and human rights. Could the United States, in a postwar world of decolonization that brought self-government to millions of people of dark skin on two continents, afford to maintain a system of segregation and discrimination based on race? Such were the problems facing President Truman in April 1945.

One year before the 1948 election, Walter White, president of the NAACP, wrote in *Colliers* magazine that the coming election "is certain to be the most crucial election in the history of the United States."[16] White realized that African Americans had arrived on the political scene and for the first time in American history both major political parties would have to make concessions to the African-American voter. He was correct, and the result was a new chapter in the civil rights movement.

Before 1947 Truman's gestures toward civil rights had been halfhearted at best. In 1945 he supported a permanent FEPC, but he failed to lead the battle for appropriations against a southern filibuster, and the bill died. While the bill was being considered on Capitol Hill, a prominent African-American member of the FEPC resigned in protest over the administration's failure to end discriminatory hiring practices in the District of Columbia. Similarly, the president backed away from supporting an anti-poll-tax bill, citing his fears that a second southern filibuster would bottle up more important legislation and stall his Cold War initiatives. When the Daughters of the American Revolution (DAR) refused to rent Constitution Hall to African-American pianist Hazel Scott (the wife of Congressman Adam Clayton Powell), the president refused to take a stand on the issue, and Mrs. Truman likewise seemed to condone the action by refusing to sever her relationship with the DAR. The African-American press hit the Trumans hard for this indiscretion, often recalling what they considered to be better times when Eleanor Roosevelt publicly resigned from the DAR in 1939 when Marian Anderson was refused use of Constitution Hall.[17] In January 1947 Truman further insulted African Americans by crossing a picket line set up by the Congress of Racial Equality (CORE), which was protesting the refusal of Washington's National Theater to admit African Americans to performances.[18] By early 1947, after nearly two years in office, President Truman was hardly the civil rights leader that African Americans felt they needed in the White House.

The African-American vote was crucial to the Democratic campaign strategy, but the Republicans also realized the importance of black voter support in 1948. Thomas Dewey had built a strong record on race issues. He had put in place a state FEPC in New York, had named African Americans to prominent state administrative positions, and had worked hard to bring African Americans into his New York State Republican political coalition. In the 1942 and 1946 gubernatorial campaigns Dewey had even carried Harlem. In his 1944 presidential campaign against Roosevelt, Dewey inherited much of the support African Americans had given Wendell Willkie in 1940, although FDR was still the major recipient of African-American votes in that election. The 1944 Republican platform called for an end to segregation and discrimination in the military, the establishment of a permanent FEPC, a constitutional amendment to abolish the poll tax, and antilynching legislation. Results of the 1944 election showed that Dewey might have won had he been able to carry the African-American vote in the northern urban industrial states. As the 1948 election approached, the Republicans and Dewey again came out in support of the most popular civil rights measures. Dewey often told audiences on the campaign trail: "No man should be deprived of the right to earn his bread by reason of his race, his religion, or national origin. This is simple justice."[19] It was a clear challenge to the Democrats.

In his campaign strategy memo to the president in September 1947, James Rowe predicted that the African-American vote would be a deciding factor in the 1948 election. Rowe went on to explain that black leaders such as Walter White would willingly throw African-American support to the Republicans if they offered a significant civil rights agenda and that the Republicans were willing to deliver the necessary concessions if that would bring them black votes. "To counteract this trend," Rowe continued, "the Democratic party can point only to the obvious—that the really great improvement in the economic lot of the Negro of the North has come in the last sixteen years only because of the sympathy and policies of the Democratic administration." Rowe warned, however, "Unless there are new and real efforts . . . the Negro bloc, which . . . *does* hold the balance of power, will go Republican."[20]

Some of Truman's advisers, however, thought the problem was not the Republicans but Wallace and the Progressives. Reports from William Batt's research division of the Democratic National Committee estimated that as much as 75 percent of the vote in Harlem and other African-American urban areas in the North and Northeast would go to Wallace and that 20 to 30 percent of the country's remaining African Americans would vote for Wallace.[21] These figures finally forced the Truman administration to see the importance of the nation's black voters. Early in the campaign Wallace had denounced all forms of race segregation and discrimination, and polls showed that northern African-American voters were responding to his messages.[22] In addition, Wallace gained the endorsement of several prominent African-American leaders, including the venerable W.E.B. Du Bois and actor-singer-political activist Paul Robeson. Many African Americans believed that Henry Wallace held the key to the future of civil rights in America.

The strategy in the Truman camp to stop Wallace's encroachment on African-American votes was to initiate an aggressive civil rights stance that would show black voters that it was the Democrats who held the future for civil rights in America, that Wallace's campaign was communist-influenced, and that the promises from the Republicans were empty and insincere. By the first of April 1948 Truman's advisers and strategists had established an informal advisory group to deal specifically with African-American issues.[23] The group insisted that "proper handling of the Civil Rights issue is of crucial importance. It can virtually assure the re-election of the President by cutting the ground out from under Wallace and gaining the enthusiastic support of liberal and labor groups."[24] Other advisers suggested that Truman arrange to be photographed with African-American congressman William Dawson, that Secretary of Defense James Forrestal meet with black soldiers, that William Hastie be appointed to a prominent post in the administration and be seen often in the president's company, and that the president work toward desegregating the armed forces.[25]

Of course, the problem in initiating these reforms was the South. Could Truman support civil rights and still keep the party together, as Roosevelt had done so successfully? Could he give the northern African-American voting bloc what they demanded without alienating the South? These seemed to be important questions, but Truman's advisers told him that such concerns were not necessary, that the South would hold. Even if it did not, even if southern voters bolted the party or stayed home on election day, it would not significantly affect the election's outcome.[26] An important strategy memo on the subject (this one from Oscar Ewing's office at the Democratic National Committee, probably in the spring of 1948, and possibly from the Wardman Park group) offered the following advice on the South: "There is no danger of losing the South. It will neither go Republican nor vote for Wallace. In any event, however, it takes a considerable number of southern States to equal the importance of such States as New York, Pennsylvania, and Illinois. . . . A split with the southern wing of the Party will do no harm politically. . . . It is not going to make a great deal of difference on this score whether certain Democrats bolt [because of] this issue or not." It concluded: "There is, therefore, everything to be gained and nothing tangible to be lost by making the most forthright and dramatic statement on this issue and backing it up with equally dramatic and forthright action. Every attempt to compromise loses the votes which count." Then the memo's author added a cynical postscript: "This issue is of such importance that its handling should be properly staged to give the firm impression that the President really means business and that he is vigorously following through on it."[27] Through 1947 and 1948 Truman's advisers would counsel the president to move more aggressively in the civil rights arena.

Historians most often cite changing demographics as the primary reason politicians finally began to pay attention to the civil rights movement in the postwar period. But there were other reasons. The end of World War II brought with it the knowledge of the horrors of the Holocaust, and Americans for the first time saw at least one manifestation of the evils of race prejudice. Race also became an important factor in the growing Cold War. In the last phases of World War II, Roosevelt became the chief proponent of ending the decaying European colonial system. As colonies gained their freedom after the war and in the midst of the beginnings of the Cold War, the Soviet Union often pointed to America's system of racism to counter the American promises of liberty, freedom, equality, and independence under a capitalist-democratic government.[28] By 1947 American racism had become a yoke around the neck of the country's foreign policy. At the same time, anticommunists at home (both conservatives and liberals) began to see the nation's system of racism as a tactical advantage for the forces of worldwide communism, and they tried to convince the government to force an end to many of the most blatant and horrific aspects of racism. Civil rights leaders, of course, made good use of this point. African Americans often complained bitterly that racial groups in other parts of the world were being treated better by the U.S. government than African Americans. In *To Secure These Rights*, the report from the President's Committee on Civil Rights published in 1947, the committee pointed out: "An American diplomat cannot argue for free elections in foreign lands without meeting the challenge that in sections of America qualified voters do not have free access to the polls."[29] This statement was apparently in response to Truman's demands that the Soviet Union conduct free elections in Poland.

By the summer of 1947 Truman seemed to come around to this way of thinking. He told an NAACP rally, "Putting our house in order [would gain the] support of desperate populations of battle ravaged countries who must be won for the free way of life."[30] In his civil rights speech of February 2, 1948, the president said: "If we are to inspire the peoples of the world whose freedom is in jeopardy, if we wish to restore hope to those who have already lost their civil liberties, if we wish to fulfill the promise that is ours, we must correct the remaining imperfections in our practice of democracy."[31]

As the Cold War intensified and the United States became more involved in world affairs while representing itself as an example of moral justice and equality, it became imperative that America's racial situation must change.

As these political, demographic, social, and even diplomatic changes in attitudes toward race were emerging in the postwar period, economic forces were also at work. The American economy had grown tremendously through the 1940s from a gross national product of just over $200 billion to about $320 billion as the decade closed; at the same time, the average weekly pay of wage earners increased by over 50 percent, climbing from about $25 in 1940 to nearly $57 in 1950.[32] African Americans shared in this growth—although certainly not as extensively as did whites—making possible increasing incomes for African Americans and better job opportunities. The median income of African-American wage and salary earners rose from 41 percent of the white median in 1939 to 60 percent in 1950. The percentage of African-American male workers in white-collar jobs rose from 5.6 percent in 1940 to 7.2 percent in 1950. The number of African-American craftsmen increased from 16.6 percent of the work force in 1940 to 28.8 percent in 1950. As rosy as these statistics might look, African Americans were still being discriminated against in both the public and private sectors. Whereas white males after the war earned about $2,400 a year, African-American males averaged only about $1,300.[33] In addition, as defense plants reconverted to peacetime production and began laying off unneeded laborers, the African Americans were laid off first. There were, of course, advances, but they were well below any standard level of equality with whites. The nation's economic growth in the postwar period pulled a large number of African Americans out of the Depression-era realm of abject poverty, but that may have resulted in little more than a menial job and an apartment in a northern urban ghetto. Nevertheless, economic advancement (despite its inequality) helped push African Americans into the political arena after the war.

In addition, the representation of African Americans in labor unions increased significantly in the postwar period, resulting in better jobs, better working conditions, and better wages for many African-American industrial workers. Gunnar Myrdal, in his *American Dilemma*, wrote in 1944 that the labor unions would take the lead in promoting civil rights for African Americans. Certainly, African Americans who joined unions were better off than if they had not, but after the war, labor leaders backtracked on most wartime commitments to African-American workers. In 1946, the AFL decided to continue its old ways of using segregated auxiliary locals, and the CIO under Walter Reuther's leadership in the years after the war did nothing to change the discriminatory hiring practices of industries unionized by CIO workers. But again, the result was that gains were made for African-American workers even though those gains were minimal compared to those made by white workers under the same conditions. After the war African Americans became a significant minority in some of the nation's largest and strongest unions. In 1946 there were fifty thousand African Americans registered with the AFL. In the CIO there were over ninety-five thousand African-American workers in the Steelworkers of America; ninety thousand members of the Automobile, Aircraft, Agricultural Implement Workers of America were black; and another forty thousand African Americans had joined the Marine and Shipbuilding Workers.[34]

The vibrant postreconversion economy created a labor shortage in most industries that allowed many African Americans to move into the labor force without taking white jobs. This had been a serious problem after World War I in several northern cities where African Americans were harassed for taking wartime jobs now "needed" by whites. The result was violence. But after World War II African-American economic progress seldom threatened white advances or the white economic structure in any way. Consequently, the postreconversion boom removed one of the most important sources of white anxiety about the advancement of African Americans.

Economic advancement also meant political affluence. During the war and then in the postwar years, membership in civil rights organizations skyrocketed, bringing a corresponding growth in financial contributions to those organizations. The NAACP was growing rapidly, and organizations such as CORE, the National Urban League, and the March on Washington Movement had a corresponding growth.[35] The result, of course, was money to fight expensive court battles, lobby Congress and state legislatures, even grease the gears of government when necessary. By 1945, the nation's civil rights organizations had arrived; they were prepared to do business in the political arena on the same level as any other powerful political action group.

There were other factors that set the stage for postwar civil rights advances. One was the dispelling of the old notions used to justify segregation and discrimination. Ever since the nativist era of the first decades of the twentieth century produced such books as Madison Grant's *Passing of the Great Race* (1916) and Lothrop Stoddard's *Rising Tide of Color* (1920) racism had been, at least, pseudoscientific and acceptable to most of white America as the natural order of things. But in the 1930s, advanced scholarship in the fields of anthropology, psychology, and biology began to turn those old

myths around. Works such as Otto Klineberg's *Negro Intelligence and Selective Migration* (1935) and J.B.S. Haldane's *Heredity and Politics* (1938)
brought much needed new light to the old beliefs, and many educated
Americans came to understand that environmental factors, and not race,
determined such traits as intelligence, personality, and character. Among
these works, Gunnar Myrdal's monumental *American Dilemma* was probably the most important. Myrdal wrote that "the popular theory behind race
prejudice" in the United States "has gradually decayed." "America can never
more regard" its black population "as a patient, submissive minority."[36]

At the same time, symbols of the erosion of racism seemed ever-present
in the postwar period. One of the most poignant symbols was the success
of a bipartisan coalition of Republicans and northern Democrats in deny-
ing Theodore Bilbo his seat in the Senate in January 1947. Bilbo was an
outspoken Mississippi bigot, a representative of the old-style southern racism that existed behind the Magnolia Curtain in Mississippi. He had once
proclaimed, "You and I know what's the best way to keep the nigger from
voting. You do it the night before the election. I don't have to tell you more
than that. Red-blooded men know what I mean."[37] His terrorism kept African Americans out of the voting process in Mississippi and kept him in
the governor's chair between 1916 and the mid-1930s and then in the Senate until 1946. He often boasted that there were only 1,500 African-American voters out of a potential black electorate of 500,000 in Mississippi.[38]
Bilbo's racist activities and remarks in winning the 1946 election came under question by a Senate investigative committee in December 1946 and
again in January 1947. Meeting in an open hearing in December in Mississippi, 102 African Americans testified that they were subjected to the
intimidation and terrorism of "Bilboism" and that under Bilbo's leadership,
Mississippi was far outside the American democratic process.[39] Bilbo was
exonerated of all wrongdoing by a committee led by sympathetic southern
senators, but he was refused his seat on the first day of the Eightieth Congress because his credentials were, as recorded, "tainted with fraud and corruption." Bilbo was excluded from Senate proceedings until further
investigations could be conducted. He died of cancer later that summer
before he could return to the Senate.[40] Bilbo's ejection was the official repudiation of the rotten southern political system based on racial hatred, the
system that had kept southern congressmen in Washington for decades.
Bilbo was a symbol of the past.

On August 14, 1946, the body of a twenty-eight-year-old African-American war veteran, John C. Jones, was found near Dorcheat Bayou, three miles
from Minden, Louisiana, in Webster Parish. Jones, obviously murdered, had

been dead for at least six days. Reports later stated that Jones's arms had been burned off by an acetylene torch, probably before he died. Walter White of the NAACP wrote that "a blowtorch so charred his flesh that the undertaker described him to us later as having been jet black in color though his skin had been light yellow."[41] Beaten badly and left for dead with Jones was Albert Harris. Harris claimed he could identify the murderers (all of whom were prominent citizens of Webster Parish), and consequently he became a hunted man on the run, reported first in Texarkana, Texas, and then headed for California. The story hit the national press that Harris was willing to testify and that a mob was hunting him down.[42]

The NAACP became involved in the case in an attempt to keep Harris alive so that he could testify against the murderers. Walter White, through the NAACP's network of local organizations, finally located Harris, on the run with his father in Muskegon, Michigan. The NAACP investigated the case and aided in the courtroom prosecution. Finally, on March 1, 1947, after months of wrangling, the five men indicted for the murder of Jones were acquitted—despite Harris's eyewitness testimony—in federal district court in Shreveport, Louisiana.[43] In a press release, the NAACP warned African Americans in the South: "Acquittal of the five alleged lynchers of a Negro war Veteran . . . serves as a declaration to every Negro in the South and particularly those who fought for their country in the last war, that they are now entirely at the mercy of white supremacist lynchers."[44]

At about the same time there were six other lynchings in what Walter White called "that terrible summer of 1946." In July two black former GIs were lynched in Marshall, Texas. In Walton County, Georgia, two black men (one a recently discharged soldier) and their wives were shot. In Batesburg, South Carolina, Isaac Woodward was on his way home after three years of military service in the South Pacific when he was beaten severely and blinded by a mob led by the local chief of police. There was a lynching in Lexington, Mississippi, on July 22. In Columbia, Tennessee, a riot at the county jail left two African-American men dead with no explanation or prosecution.[45] Added to these atrocities was the old system as usual in the South. Bilbo had called openly for intimidation of black voters in his Senate reelection campaign in 1946, and in Georgia in that same election Eugene Talmadge evoked racist tactics to win the gubernatorial race. There was a postwar resurgence in the activities of the Ku Klux Klan, apparently brought back to deal with the African-American men returning to the South from the war and to keep Bourbons like Bilbo and Talmadge in power. Southern spokesmen continued to jump to the defense of the region, claiming that the South was a victim of interference from Washington, of meddling northern liberal groups, and of "Negro uplift societies." All this received a great deal of attention in the national press, usually with an antisouthern bias that showed the plight of southern blacks in a fairly favorable light. To many Americans the situation in the South at the end of 1946 had become intolerable.

It was these incidents, particularly the murder of Jones and the blinding of Woodward, that drove Walter White to request a meeting with President Truman to ask his support for an antilynching bill then before Congress.[46] White had met with presidents from Calvin Coolidge to Roosevelt and had, for the most part, failed to receive their cooperation against mob violence or even the broader cause of civil rights. "I frankly doubted," White later wrote, "that our efforts on this occasion would be any more rewarding than had been those we had made with any of Truman's predecessors."[47] He expected little.

White brought a distinguished group of civil rights leaders with him to the meeting. For the occasion, the group formed the National Emergency Committee Against Mob Violence. Along with White were African-American community leader Channing Tobias, James Carey of the CIO, Boris Shiskin of the AFL, NAACP administrative assistant Leslie Perry, and religious leader Frederick E. Reissig. The primary topic of the meeting was lynchings and mob violence in the South. "The president sat quietly," White recalled, "elbows resting on the arms of his chair and his fingers interlocked against his stomach as he listened with a grim face to the story of lynchings in Georgia and Louisiana. . . . When I had finished, the President exclaimed in his flat, Midwestern accent, 'My God! I had no idea it was as terrible as that! We've got to do something!'"[48] White recalled that presidential assistant David Niles suggested that the president appoint a committee to look into the problems.[49] "My first reaction," White remembered, "which was shared by other members of the delegation was skepticism. President Roosevelt had made a somewhat similar suggestion several times to me but I had invariably gained the impression that he had made such proposals as a means of postponing decisions on issues which would bring him into conflict with belligerent anti-Negro southern congressmen and Senators." Tobias was also doubtful that anything would come of the meeting. He accused the president of setting up a committee that would take months, even years, to come to any useful conclusions. Truman responded that he would establish the committee by executive order and ask for its findings quickly, possibly within twelve months.[50]

Truman issued the executive order on December 5, creating the President's Committee on Civil Rights (PCCR). In his speech to the committee, Truman said, "In some places from time to time the local enforcement of law and order has broken down and individuals, sometimes ex-servicemen and even women, have been killed, maimed or intimidated." He then called on the committee members to recommend the action necessary to protect the civil rights of the nation's minorities.[51]

For the next month Niles and another White House assistant with an interest in civil rights, Philleo Nash, worked quietly to select committee members. The chairman of the committee would be Charles E. Wilson, the president of General Electric and a Republican who would later serve as Dwight Eisenhower's secretary of defense. Franklin D. Roosevelt Jr. lent his name as the committee's vice-chairman. Others named included three of the six members of White's original National Emergency Committee Against Mob Violence that met the president in September: Tobias, Shiskin, and Carey. Others came from the ranks of labor, education, and religion. The executive secretary of the committee was to be Robert K. Carr, a political scientist from Dartmouth and a passionate liberal. It became Carr's job to supply information to the PCCR, and as a result he exerted a major influence over the committee.[52]

White was not named to the committee, but he worked hard to dominate its daily workings by feeding the members large amounts of NAACP-compiled information. "We must move fast," White told Thurgood Marshall, "because this Committee is an NAACP creation . . . we must not let anybody else steal the show from us."[53] White's strategy was successful. "It goes without saying," Carr wrote White in March, "that the President's Committee is counting heavily upon your Association for advice and help."[54] In many ways, the PCCR became an arm of the NAACP.

Truman did little for the civil rights movement while the PCCR deliberated through the spring, summer, and fall of 1947. In June, however, he addressed ten thousand people at an NAACP rally at the Lincoln Memorial. Rejecting his more cautious aides' advice to keep his remarks short, Truman spoke at length.[55] He told the crowd: "Every man should have the right to a decent home, the right to an education, the right to an equal share in making the public decisions through the ballot, and the right to a fair trial in a fair court. . . . We cannot, any longer await the growth of a will to action in the slowest State or the most backward community. . . . We cannot wait another decade or another generation to remedy these evils. We must work, as never before to cure them now."[56] The night before he delivered the message, Truman wrote his sister that his attitude on race was changing with the times: "Mrs. Roosevelt has spent her entire life stirring up trouble between whites and black[s]—and I'm in the middle. Mamma won't like what I say because I wind up by quoting old Abe. But I believe what I say and I'm hopeful we may implement it."[57] After the speech he made a similar statement to Walter White: "I said what I did because I mean every word of it—and I am going to prove that I do mean it."[58]

On October 29, the PCCR published its report, *To Secure These Rights*, a document that ranks as one of the milestones of the modern civil rights movement. This controversial and farsighted report examined the general problems of racism, discrimination, and segregation in America, but it focused mainly on the plight of black Americans. It blamed segregation for many of the problems African Americans faced, and it placed the responsibility for solving those problems squarely on the federal government. Washington, the committee reported, must be a friend and not an enemy of civil rights. Specifically, the committee members proposed that the civil rights section of the Department of Justice be reorganized and strengthened and that each state create its own agency to deal with local civil rights violations. They asked for a permanent commission on civil rights to be established in the executive department, plus federal legislation to outlaw police brutality, poll taxes, and lynchings. They called for a permanent FEPC, the desegregation of the armed forces by executive order, and the immediate revocation of all federal and state Jim Crow laws. They also proposed that all federal grants-in-aid be withheld from both public and private agencies that practiced segregation and discrimination in the workplace.[59]

The response was immediate. White wrote Truman, "May I on behalf of the National Association of Colored People express to you our profound admiration for the report of the President's Committee on Civil Rights. It is beyond all question the most forthright government pronouncement of a practical program for assurance of civil rights not only to minorities but to all Americans which has yet been drafted."[60] Mary McLeod Bethune pronounced it "a document which will forever live in the hearts of all liberty loving people."[61] By February 1948, over one million copies of the report had been sold or distributed by the U.S. Government Printing Office and by private publishers.[62] There was little reaction from the South.

In response to the appeals of the PCCR, Truman, on February 2, 1948, delivered a civil rights message to the nation. It was the first time in the twentieth century that a president had sent a message to Congress dealing solely with the issue of civil rights, and it was the beginning of the Democratic party's commitment to that cause. In his message, Truman gave enthusiastic support to many of the PCCR's proposals. He asked Congress to establish a commission on civil rights, a joint congressional committee on civil rights, and a permanent Civil Rights Division in the Department of Justice. He called for the strengthening of existing civil rights statutes, enactment of an antilynching law, protection for the right to vote, and the creation of a permanent FEPC. He also proposed a bill that would end discrimination in interstate transportation. He asked Congress for a comprehensive civil rights bill and called that initiative his "first goal. . . . We cannot be satisfied," Truman continued, "until all our people have equal opportunities for jobs, for homes, for education, for health, and for political expression, and until all our people have equal protection under the law." He then tied the South's overt racism to America's role in the growing Cold War, arguing that the system had to be changed if the United States were to triumph over the evils of communism: "If we are to inspire the peoples of the world whose freedom is in jeopardy, if we wish to restore hope to those who have already lost their civil liberties, if we wish to fulfill the promise that is ours, we must correct the remaining imperfections in our practice of democracy." He then added that he would issue executive orders ending discrimination in federal hiring practices and end segregation in the U.S. military.[63] But Truman remained a long way from supporting all of the recommendations of the PCCR. He did not, for instance, claim segregation had caused socioeconomic problems for the nation's African-American population, and he ignored totally the committee's proposal to withdraw federal aid to public and private groups that engaged in segregation and discrimination.

The president's message was generally received well outside the South, but an editorial in the *Washington Post* predicted that Truman would not follow through with his proposals. The paper implied that the president's only purpose was to embarrass the Republican Eightieth Congress and to win black votes by showing African Americans that the Republicans had no civil rights agenda.[64] Generally, the *Post* was right. Truman's February 2 message was clearly political, and the president did not intend to deliver substantially on his civil rights proposals before the election. To carry the big industrial states, he needed African-American votes in November, and he needed an issue for the campaign that he knew would place him in the liberal column and on the side of civil rights.

Truman's speech also helped define another important issue in the coming campaign: the Republican-dominated Eightieth Congress. In February 1948 there were already bills before the Congress to establish most of what Truman and the PCCR had called for. There were bills to establish a permanent FEPC and to abolish the poll tax. There were several bills to outlaw lynchings, a bill to prohibit segregation in interstate travel, and one to abolish discrimination and segregation in all public establishments in the District of Columbia. Truman's civil rights message was a challenge to the Republican Congress to pass those measures or stand aside when it came to black votes. The Republicans in Congress, overconfident about their political future, accommodated Truman by killing every civil rights bill placed before it. For Truman the challenge to Congress on civil rights was an important move. He had forced the Republicans to admit that they would not support civil rights.

Truman believed that African Americans were being treated unfairly by the Jim Crow laws in the South. He also believed, as he stated in his February 2 speech, that the United States should be the leader of the free world and that such a role was inconsistent with the South's overt racism. The PCCR was a result of those concerns, and his February 2 civil rights message was an outgrowth of the committee's proposals. But clearly, the February 2 message was also steeped in the political necessities of the election of 1948, and it had little to do with the president's personal commitment to civil rights. It reflected the campaign strategy of the Wardman Park group, the Rowe memo, and a growing fear among administrative operatives that Henry Wallace's popularity among liberals, African Americans, and organized labor in the industrial regions of the Midwest, Northeast, and California might divide the liberal votes there and throw the large electoral votes of those states to the Republicans. Truman's civil rights message was principally an appeal for support from the growing coalition of northern liberals, African Americans, and organized labor. "With the civil rights program," *U.S. News* concluded, "Mr. Truman now has a fighting chance to win the electoral votes of such big States as New York, Illinois, Pennsylvania, and Ohio, where the Negro vote can be the balance of power."[65]

In early 1948, however, Wallace's strength still threatened to split the liberal vote in such important states as New York, Pennsylvania, California, Illinois, and Michigan, with the potential result of throwing the electors from those states to the Republicans. On February 17 Leo Isacson, a Wallace-supported candidate running for the Twenty-fourth Congressional District seat in the Bronx, defeated a mainline Democratic party candidate by a thumping two-to-one margin. Isacson's victory stunned the Truman administration. The Democrat had enjoyed all the support and trappings of the Democratic party, including an appearance from Eleanor Roosevelt—which was more than Truman was receiving at that point in the campaign. *Newsweek* reported that Isacson's victory might be an omen for what was to come in November: "If the special election in the Bronx can be taken as a test-tube event, then it is evident that President Truman will perform a miracle if he carries New York State next November."[66] A *New York Times* survey, conducted just after Isacson's victory, showed that Wallace's political weight was gaining in the nation's key industrial areas and that Truman would have difficulty carrying Michigan, Pennsylvania, Illinois, New York, and New Jersey. Other polls showed that Wallace could receive as much as

30 percent of the African-American vote in 1948.[67] The response in the White House was to push Truman farther to the left on civil rights and other liberal issues in an effort to plunder Wallace's liberal support.

Truman found himself caught squarely between his party's left wing, led by Wallace, and the conservative South. Southern Democrats were not willing to accept the argument (being made by some in the administration) that Truman's civil rights message was merely a plea for votes from the party's left wing and that the president had no intention of making sincere concessions on civil rights. Southerners chose instead to believe that the president's appeal was the beginning of an infringement on the conservative southern wing of the Democratic party, an attack on their long-waning political power and ultimately on the southern way of life. The president's civil rights message was one of several strong signals coming from the Democratic party in the postwar period that it was changing its direction, that the northern liberal coalition was about to jump into the leadership position of the party, mostly at the expense of the conservative southern wing. Many leaders in the South, such as South Carolina governor Strom Thurmond and Mississippi senator James Eastland, saw the president's civil rights message as an indicator for the future. There did not seem to be enough room in the Democratic party for both the southern conservatives and the new liberal coalition of northern liberals, African Americans, and organized labor. Truman's "popularity with Negro voters in the North has risen," reported *U.S. News*, "in about the same proportion as it has dropped among white voters in the South. . . . A Truman victory in a big State like Pennsylvania, with thirty-five electoral votes, would almost offset the loss of Alabama, Arkansas, Mississippi and South Carolina." And since a victory for the Democrats in Pennsylvania would pull that state away from the Republicans, the article concluded, "the swap might be a good one."[68] It was definitely the direction Truman and his political strategists were headed.

8

The End of Southern Dominance in the Democratic Party

It was understood well in the White House that the cause of the Democrats' humiliating defeat in the 1946 congressional elections was the loss of millions of votes from the left, particularly from organized labor, from African Americans in the northern cities, and from traditional liberals. Most of these voters had stayed away from the polls out of sheer indifference toward the administration and its policies. As Henry Wallace began to move toward dividing the party from the left, the administration saw immediately that the threat he presented was crucial and countered with a liberal agenda designed to bring the left wing of the party back into the Democratic camp. But the problem with indulging the left was that it would alienate the right, and in the postwar Democratic party that meant the South. As the 1948 election approached and the administration stepped up its courtship of the left, southern conservatives became more and more rebellious. By the summer of 1948 another split in the party, this time from the right, seemed inevitable.

Southerners had always believed that Truman was one of them, a southerner with a southern background in tune with southern values and ways. In 1944 a strong conservative coalition that included southerners had pushed Wallace off the ticket and replaced him with Truman, and many of these politicos felt that Truman owed his job to the South.[1] Southerners also considered Truman a party conservative because of his handling of labor during the railway workers' strike of 1946, and they did not expect him to continue FDR's liberal policies. Truman had made a major gesture toward the South by appointing a southern favorite, James Byrnes, as secretary of state. Just one month before the 1946 elections, South Carolina governor Strom Thurmond offered his complete support to the president. "The Democratic Party already has its candidate for 1948," he told a crowd in his home state.[2] Truman and the South, it seemed, would get along.

After the 1946 elections, however, Truman realized that at some time before the 1948 election he would have to choose between the two divergent wings of the party. His decision, as spelled out in James Rowe's memo, was to cater to the liberals and hope that the South would do as it had always done: stay put. Truman and the South may have had a great deal in common between April 1945 and November 1946, but all that fellowship evaporated when Truman began moving to the left, particularly in the area of civil rights.

Since Reconstruction, the South had always made up the most conservative wing of the Democratic party. But by the 1920s the party had become increasingly more urban in its makeup, and by the 1930s, the powerful forces of organized labor had begun turning many of the party's gears. During the war years, southern African Americans moved north to work in the war industries, and the vast majority (unable to vote before in the South) began voting the liberal-labor Democratic party line. At the 1936 Democratic convention, the South was forced to give up the two-thirds rule, the party balancing act that had given the South a near veto over its party's nominating process since the age of Andrew Jackson.[3] By the beginning of the postwar years, the South had lost considerable influence in the party, yet its vote could be counted safely Democratic in any election.

As the party became more and more urban and more and more under the control of liberals and labor, southern conservatives began making their dissatisfaction known. In 1928, a group of southern dissidents known as "Hoovercrats" rebelled against the urban, wet, Catholic coterie of Al Smith and made a significant break in the Solid South for the first time since Reconstruction. The Hoovercrats gave Florida, Texas, North Carolina, Tennessee, Virginia, Kentucky, Missouri, and Maryland to Hoover in that election. In addition, following the beginning of Roosevelt's second term, southern congressmen often voted a conservative domestic line, and that meant voting with the Republicans on several key issues. This southern-Republican conservative coalition continued its alliance through the remainder of Roosevelt's administrations and then into the postwar years, often making the passage of a liberal agenda very difficult.

Voters in the South, however, had generally supported Roosevelt and the New Deal. As FDR pulled together the various groups to build his coalition, he was usually able to keep the southern conservatives in line. With the exceptions of his prolabor agenda, the establishment of the wartime FEPC, and an occasional antisegregationist statement by his wife, FDR was generally successful in mollifying and appeasing the South throughout most of his thirteen years in office. He kept the South accommodated through such popular grass-roots projects as the Tennessee Valley Authority, the Rural Electrification Administration, farm credit plans, and the establishment of military bases and wartime industries in the South.

There were always some defectors, mostly powerful southern senators who saw the New Deal as an abusive federal program that cut deeply into the southern political religion of states' rights. These "irreconcilables," as they were called, occasionally voted against New Deal proposals in Congress, stopped antilynching bills, and helped kill FDR's Court-packing plan. Prominent among this group were Carter Glass and Harry Byrd of Virginia, Josiah Bailey of North Carolina, Ellison D. (Cotton Ed) Smith of South Carolina, Walter F. George of Georgia, Thomas P. Gore of Oklahoma, and Millard Tydings of Maryland. Despite these disaffections, when FDR died, the South remained an important part of the fragile New Deal coalition.

In the volatile Democratic party politics of the postwar years, however, an FDR-style balancing act between opposing groups within the party had become exceedingly more difficult. In addition, Truman lacked FDR's ability as a political leader to keep these groups in line. His attempt to ride the fence between southern conservatives and northern liberals was almost always a dismal failure.

After only two months in office, Truman began pushing for a permanent FEPC to replace FDR's wartime emergency program. This was to be Truman's first testimony that he intended to be FDR's successor as the captain of New Deal legislation. The FEPC had been established during the war to prohibit discrimination in factories that were under government contracts, and it had been sold to southerners by the Roosevelt administration as an efficient way to make use of the labor force during wartime. The FEPC did little to aid blacks or the cause of civil rights during the war, but most southern political leaders nevertheless wanted the agency abolished as soon as the war ended. Truman's plan, however, was to give the FEPC a permanent place in the American system, and the South saw this as the beginning of a call for civil rights, something that liberals had been demanding since before World War I. Liberals like Henry Wallace were still in positions of leadership in the Democratic party, and African Americans were beginning to make themselves felt as a political force in the nation. Truman's proposal for a permanent FEPC made southerners nervous.

The southern-Republican conservative alliance in Congress worked effectively to hamper liberal domestic legislation, including civil rights initiatives. Consequently, the power of that alliance was brought to bear to kill Truman's FEPC plan, and the bill died in a House committee. Then, to assure that the FEPC wartime emergency measure was also removed, Mississippi senator Theodore Bilbo filibustered until he was granted a measure that effectively emasculated the entire program. In January 1946 liberal Democrats in Congress tried again to pass a statutory FEPC, but southerners sustained another filibuster for three weeks and finally killed that bill as well. The FEPC was dead, and at least for the moment, civil rights as legislative action came to an end. The bill had been supported by northern urban blacks, northern liberals, and organized labor.

In September, Truman's 21-Point speech set the administration's agenda for a significant expansion of the New Deal. Liberals applauded it as a logical plan for the future, a continuation of the spirit of New Deal liberalism. But southern Democrats were not so hopeful. They responded by joining again with Republicans in Congress to kill most of the president's domestic agenda. This southern-Republican conservative coalition defeated an unemployment compensation bill, a full employment bill, and a plan to extend Truman's reconversion agency, the Office of Price Administration. Clearly, southern Democrats in Congress did not support the president's extension of New Deal liberalism.[4]

The 1946 defeats convinced Truman that he had to win back the loyalty (and the votes) of organized labor. But such a policy again brought him into conflict with the South. As soon as the war ended, the CIO initiated "Operation Dixie," a well-publicized plan to organize workers in the South. Southerners hated this invasion by northern liberals who seemed bent on subverting southern institutions by altering a significant portion of the economic base. In nearly every local election in the South in 1946 organized labor became the issue, and in many parts of the South any association with organized labor, specifically the hated CIO-PAC, replaced race as the primary political issue. A candidate who could effectively pin the badge of organized labor on his opponent usually carried the election. This southern hatred for organized labor placed Truman in a dilemma. He needed labor support to win in 1948, but to concede to labor would obviously alienate the South. For instance, he ruffled southern feathers by vetoing the Case bill, the antiunion legislation passed in 1946 by the southern-Republican conservative coalition.[5] His veto of Taft-Hartley would do the same. Not surprisingly, southerners wondered where Truman would take the party as the nation moved toward the 1948 general election.

In December 1946, just a month after the election, the southerners got their answer when Truman issued the executive order establishing the President's Committee on Civil Rights. Certainly, Truman's establishment of the PCCR was motivated by a need for black votes in 1948, but he might also have wanted to punish the South. By this time he had few reasons to support southern demands. By the end of 1946 southern politicians had turned against Truman on nearly every domestic issue he had proposed since he took office. Consequently, he owed nothing to the South and certainly he owed nothing to southern politicians in Congress. In June 1947, with no apologies to the South, he vetoed the southern-supported Taft-Hartley bill and moved to appease labor, African Americans, and northern liberals on other fronts. Truman had concluded what James Rowe had outlined on paper: "The *only* pragmatic reason for conciliating the South . . . is its tremendous strength in Congress. Since Congress is Republican and the Democratic President has therefore no real chance to get his own programs approved by it . . . he has no real necessity for 'getting along' with Southern conservatives. He *must*, however, get along with . . . labor if he is to be reelected."[6] Other Truman operatives arrived at the same conclusion. George Elsey, Truman's administrative assistant, wrote to Clifford that "proper handling" of the civil rights issue would cut the ground from under Wallace and win votes from liberals and organized labor. But, he continued, "It takes a considerable number of Southern states to equal the importance of such states as New York, Pennsylvania, and Illinois."[7] In October, when Robert Hannegan resigned as chairman of the Democratic National Committee, Truman overlooked demands by southern leaders for a southern chairman and recommended instead J. Howard McGrath, a loyal senator from Rhode Island, as the new DNC chairman. Clearly, Truman had come to see the obvious: to satisfy southern demands would bring no more electoral votes for 1948.

In October, Truman's Committee on Civil Rights published its findings in *To Secure These Rights*, and southerners responded by promising to fight any attempt by the administration to push for legislation on any of the issues called for by the committee. In his State of the Union address in January, Truman announced that he would send to Congress a civil rights legislative package, and on February 2, he delivered on that promise.[8] Again, the South registered its disgust with the federal government. Within hours the Ku Klux Klan was marching in Swainsboro, Georgia.[9] Senator James Eastland of Mississippi responded to Truman's message by telling a crowd that "this proves that organized mongrel minorities control the government."[10] In Congress, Louisiana representative Overton Brooks charged that war had "been openly declared by the chieftain of the National Democratic party against the traditions and Caucasianism of the South."[11] A southern journalist wrote, "The South has been kicked in the pants," and they "turned around and kicked us in the stomach."[12] At a press conference following the speech Truman let it be known that he had little concern for the South's anxieties. When asked if he had a plan to appease the South, he responded that he had not given it much thought.[13] Several southern leaders immediately called for a revolt against the party.

Later in February, the South's governors held their previously scheduled Southern Governors' Conference in Wakulla Springs, Florida, near

Tallahassee. In response to Truman's civil rights speech earlier in the month, the planned agenda was scrapped and the governors took up the now pressing topics of civil rights, the hapless Truman administration, alienation from the party, and states' rights. The conference accomplished little, but it did result in the emergence of two leaders: South Carolina governor Strom Thurmond and Mississippi governor Fielding Wright. Both men opposed the administration's new antisouthern stance on civil rights, but they could not agree on a course of action. Wright, the more radical of the two, proposed that the southern states immediately secede from the Democratic party. The moderate Thurmond proposed a cooling-off period while he and a few associates approached the party leadership in Washington in an attempt to get some answers. He was supported by the vast majority of the governors, including M.E. Thompson of Georgia, James McCord of Tennessee, and Millard Caldwell of Florida.[14]

To that end, Thurmond and an entourage of southern governors headed directly to Washington, where they met with J. Howard McGrath, the new Democratic National Committee chairman. It was unfortunate for Thurmond and his group that just at that moment the Wallace-supported candidate Leo Isacson showed surprising strength in the special congressional election in New York, and the significance of the left (which included African Americans) had just become much clearer to White House political strategists. Consequently, arguments from southern conservatives were not being entertained by the White House with much enthusiasm. The meeting was abrupt. McGrath refused to soften any statements made by the president, and he made it clear that he would not use his influence to persuade Truman to change his stance on civil rights. The southern governors pushed McGrath hard, but he stood firm. On states' rights, McGrath told the group, "It is constitutional for the federal government to legislate in states' rights matters." On segregation, he said, "The president has called attention of the Congress to the fact that segregation has been declared unconstitutional . . . thereby indicating that Congress has the right to legislate in this field." He said he would support a permanent FEPC and a strengthened Division of Civil Rights in the Department of Justice, and he would oppose the poll tax. McGrath, however, was willing to give some ground. He agreed that education and intrastate transportation were within the legislative realm of the states, and he said he would oppose a strong civil rights plank in the 1948 Democratic party platform—but nothing more. At the meeting's end, McGrath held out an olive branch to the southern governors and to the South: "Personally[,] and speaking for the Democratic National Committee, we appreciate the great loyalty our Party has had from the Southern States through the years." He then added a hint of the chang-

South Carolina governor Strom Thurmond. From the archives of the Clemson University Libraries Special Collections Unit.

ing wind in the party's balance of power: "I don't take the attitude that they are with us anyway so the 'H' with them. . . . I just hope," he added, that "we will have a happy reunion in the not too distant future. . . . I think the South has much to gain in playing along with the Party and in fighting our battles out within the Congress."[15] The meeting was not friendly, and despite McGrath's various attempts to mend fences, he seemed to give the South few choices. Thurmond's moderation evaporated immediately. In an announcement following the meeting, he suggested that the southern states move to block Truman's nomination and election. The Democratic party, he added, "will soon realize that the South is no longer in the bag."[16]

McGrath's brush-off convinced several other southern governors to join Thurmond and Wright in their retreat from moderation. Governors William Tuck of Virginia and Ben Laney of Arkansas joined the revolt, along with several important local leaders, including Birmingham's police commissioner Eugene "Bull" Conner and the Alabama state Democratic party chairman Gassner T. McCorvey.

The rebels considered several plans to put pressure on the Democratic party at the national convention in July and then in the general election in November. One was to elect only delegates to the convention who would agree not to vote for any candidate supporting civil rights. If Truman were nominated, they would walk out. In the national election, the plan was to withhold southern votes from both major party candidates in the electoral college. If the election were close and a majority of electoral votes were not won by either major party candidate, the electoral votes controlled by the South would become the balance of power. The southern electors might then throw their support to either candidate based on concessions received in exchange, or they could simply withhold their electoral votes altogether and throw the election into the House of Representatives and wield their power there. In any case, it was necessary for the entire South to stick together and vote as a solid bloc. By late spring Thurmond was certain that Truman could not win the election in November without southern support and that the president would soon come to that same conclusion and reject his civil rights program. The conflict would then come to an end and the Democratic party would go into the election united.

One problem for Thurmond and the other less radical leaders was that the repugnant issue of white supremacy might dominate this southern movement. He realized that many prominent southern moderates saw racism as a hindrance to the future of the New South and that to them the image of the South as a racist backwater was intolerable. Thurmond's hope was to build a party around a large voting bloc of conservative southerners who were longtime Democrats but who had opposed the New Deal, opposed organized labor, and opposed the Truman administration—but whose political beliefs often were not related to the doctrines of white supremacy. Thurmond also realized that the southern principle of states' rights was an appealing concept to southern moderates. To bring in this larger sweep of southern voters Thurmond attacked lynching and the poll tax in hopes of removing the racist stigma that was already being planted on the movement by the northern press. All remnants of the race issue were dropped from the agenda. Racists such as Gerald L.K. Smith were denounced, and states' rights became the primary issue.[17] Thurmond also made it clear often that these states'-rights Democrats believed that they were the real Democrats; it was Truman who had strayed from the center and swayed to the left. This, of course, was mostly ideological rhetoric, but it allowed the states' righters to purge the white supremacists from their midst and to associate themselves with the familiar ideology of the Democratic party of the past.

On March 13, the southern governors met in Washington to decide their fate following Thurmond's fruitless meeting with McGrath. The governors of Maryland, Mississippi, Texas, Alabama, Georgia, South Carolina, and Arkansas attended. The governors of Louisiana, Kentucky, Tennessee, North Carolina, Florida, and West Virginia were absent. Senator Harry Byrd of Virginia sat in the absence of Governor Tuck. McGrath's antisouthern attitude had pushed several members of this group to rebellion by this time, although some governors still believed that secession from the Democratic party could only hurt the South, and their influence at the meeting temporarily placed a general tone of moderation over the movement. This moderate faction was led by Governors William Lane of Maryland, R. Gregg Cherry of North Carolina (who did not attend the Washington meeting), Thompson of Georgia, and James Folsom of Alabama. As a result of the moderate influence of these voices, the declaration issued from the Washington meeting called for a controlled rebellion within the Democratic party structure, not a bolt from the party. But it also called for a repudiation of Truman and the Democratic leadership and southern opposition to all civil rights proposals. The group also agreed to oppose Truman's nomination at the Democratic party convention in July and the nomination of any other candidate who supported civil rights. The governors added to their declaration that their ideological differences with the Democratic leadership were based solely on the question of states' rights versus federal authority, and they stated their intention to have a statement of states' right placed in the Democratic party platform at the convention. They also added that they would demand that the party reinstate the two-thirds rule that had, until 1936, given the South a veto over the party's nominating process. These pronouncements were not new and they surprised no one, but the governors added that if Truman (or anyone else who supported civil rights) received the Democratic party's nomination, the South would withhold its electoral votes from that candidate in the November election. That pronouncement was new, and it was the first statement from the southern governors that constituted a real rebellion against the party. Thurmond, however, had laid another plan before the governors, one much more radical. He wanted the southern states' electors to be chosen by state conventions after the November election, which would allow the states more control over the electors and their votes. But that plan was rejected.[18]

On May 10, the southern governors met again in Jackson, Mississippi. But this time, under Mississippi governor Field Wright's leadership, the conference took on a more radical tone. Some fifteen hundred delegates and another two thousand spectators crowded into the Jackson city auditorium to hear the new prophets of southern rebellion. The attendees were mostly boisterous locals who espoused white supremacy, some disgruntled Mississippi businessmen, and a few unreconstructed rebels. Arkansas's Ben

Laney was voted chairman of the group, and Thurmond was the keynote speaker. In a fiery speech, Thurmond told the crowd what they wanted to hear: the "leaders of both political parties will realize we no longer intend to be a doormat on which Presidential candidates may wipe their political shoes every time they want to appeal to minority groups in doubtful states. . . . So far as I am concerned," he added, "the die is cast and the Rubicon is crossed. As a governor of a sovereign state, I do not intend that the rights of my people shall be sacrificed on the block of blind party loyalty." And in his final statement he professed to foretell the future: "Harry Truman has never been elected President of the United States and he never will be." Thurmond was interrupted with applause thirty-one times during his forty-five-minute speech.[19]

The only new notion to come from this meeting was an important one: if Truman and civil rights emerged victorious at the Democratic convention, these southern dissidents would meet again in Birmingham on July 17 to select alternative candidates for president and vice-president. They added that they were the true Democrats and that it was Truman and his supporters who had chosen to leave the party.[20]

Truman began to back away from his civil rights initiative immediately following his February 2 speech. He probably did not yet fear a southern rebellion, but he did fear losing the votes (and significant financial support) of southern moderates who had no intention of leaving the Democratic party but who opposed civil rights. A Gallup Poll in April showed Truman losing southern support at an astonishing rate, with 82 percent of those southerners polled claiming to oppose his domestic program.[21] He also feared the wrath of southern congressmen and senators, whose support he needed to pass his initiatives, both foreign and domestic. So, through a policy of inaction in the summer of 1948, Truman moved to quiet the fervor that was welling up in the South. And as the convention approached, he moved farther and farther away from the issue of civil rights. He had said in February that he would issue orders to desegregate the armed forces and the federal government. By mid-July he had done neither. At a press conference on May 13, he denied that he had ever said he would abolish segregation among federal workers.[22] Truman, who had taken a giant step forward into the new politics of the postwar period and had left behind the old-time politics of sectionalism, was having second thoughts; his prewar political instincts of trying to satisfy all sides had taken hold again. But by the late summer of 1948 the president's advisers (with Clifford in the lead) were fully committed to the strategy spelled out in Rowe's memo of pushing for support from the liberal-labor-African-American coalition while generally ignoring southern interests. Also, at this point in the spring and summer of 1948, Truman still lacked the labor vote (a crucial part of his coalition) despite the Taft-Hartley veto.[23] Consequently, most of Truman's campaign advisers continued to push him toward the left as the election approached.

9

The Eisenhower Phenomenon

The Republicans in 1948 were prepared to field several good candidates for president. Party leaders Taft, Dewey, and Vandenberg were joined by California governor Earl Warren and Minnesota governor Harold Stassen, plus several favorite sons. Despite the Republican party's infighting, it was the conventional wisdom that the Republican nominee, to be chosen in Philadelphia in late June, would be the next president. While the Republicans sorted out their differences in several primary campaigns around the country, the Democrats seemed to divide their forces, and then divide again, as it became even clearer that Truman could not win the election—and they searched desperately for some way to keep the White House from falling into Republican hands. For the Republicans, 1948 promised to be a good year.

Before the Republican campaign could begin, however, some problems had to be resolved. One problem was Dwight Eisenhower. Would he run? And if he did, would he run as a Republican or a Democrat? This wild card factor that entered the political landscape from well outside the nominating structure of both parties caused all candidates to balk, but it particularly affected the Republican hopefuls. Eisenhower was a genuine American hero, a natural vote-getter, a sure thing for the White House if he chose to run in 1948, as the polls confirmed.[1] He had not been dirtied by politics, but seemed above politics, giving the appearance of a true candidate of the people. He would be a strong candidate, so his intentions would have to be known before the Republicans could move forward.

Ike fueled the draft-Eisenhower movement by refusing to make a simple definitive statement of his intentions. Instead, he responded by saying he did not want the job as many ways as he could without actually saying no, always leaving a small crack in the door. He was often asked simply to quote William T. Sherman: he would not run and would not serve if elected. But he would not. So his refusal to reject meant acceptance, or at least some consideration of acceptance.

During the war, even before Eisenhower's successes at Normandy, he

Gen. Dwight D. Eisenhower refused to comment on the
campaign to draft him for the Democratic presidential
nomination. Courtesy of AP/World Wide Photos.

was mentioned as a possible candidate for president. When the general returned home in 1945, he answered inquiries about his presidential aspirations with unequivocal statements. "It is silly to talk about me in politics,"
he told an audience in Abilene in 1945, "and so for once I'll talk about it,
but only to settle this thing once [and] for all. I should like to make this as
emphatic as possible. . . . In the strongest language you can command, you
can state that I have no political ambitions at all, make it even stronger than
that if you can. I'd like to go even further than Sherman in expressing myself on this subject."[2] That statement was definitive enough, but the election was three years away, and during that time Eisenhower at least toyed
with the idea of running for president.

After the 1946 Republican victory, Eisenhower's name came up repeatedly as a Republican candidate for president in 1948. At the same time, Ike
seemed to awaken as a possible presidential candidate—or at least so the
press saw it. *Time* referred to his "tremendous reputation, unencumbered
by political liabilities, his wonderful name, his poise, tact, and amazing

popularity. . . . Ike might find it hard to slap down the presidential bee," the article concluded. *Life* reported that Ike was on the stump, discussing labor issues and other nonmilitary subjects, "thereby starting a big boom to make him a presidential candidate." Another *Life* article announced that a "boom for 'Ike'" was on and included a full-page photograph of a pretty girl wearing a "Draft Ike" button as a monocle.[3]

That Eisenhower had no apparent political leanings had much to do with the scope of the draft-Eisenhower movement. Eisenhower worked hard to sustain this view, mostly by representing himself to the public as an apolitical soldier. He spoke often, but he discussed few of the issues that might have pinpointed his political affiliation. In a 1947 poll, 22 percent believed Eisenhower was a Republican and 20 percent thought he was a Democrat. The largest group, 58 percent, responded that they did not know his affiliation. As early as 1946, *Time* reported that he might make a successful run on either ticket.[4]

In this noncandidate role, Eisenhower was able to acquire a candidate's visibility without any of the responsibilities. As a potential candidate for either party, he was able to avoid criticism from both parties, which otherwise would have been ruthless before the election. With his intentions unknown, no one dared criticize his policies, and he made no enemies. Nor was he responsible to the press or the public for possessing policies on specific issues. All of this added to his growing popularity.

In June 1947 Eisenhower announced that he would leave his position as chief of staff at the Pentagon and take over as president of Columbia University. There he expected some relief from those who were pushing him to run for president. He wrote a friend in August 1947 that the position should give "some shelter from the constant political darts that are launched in my direction by well-meaning, but I fear short sighted, friends."[5] But the public and the press saw the general as university president differently. For some, his acceptance of the Columbia position was an affirmation that Eisenhower wanted to remain in the public eye and in public service. John Gunther wrote that Eisenhower's announcement that he would go to Columbia caused "the movement to make him President to spread like fire through dry wheat."[6]

Eisenhower was undecided about running for president. To friends he spoke of a need to serve his nation and of his distaste for politics. To Walter Bedell Smith, his friend and wartime chief of staff, he wrote in the late summer of 1947: "I do not believe that you or I or anyone else has the right to state categorically, that he will *not* perform *any* duty that his country might demand of him. . . . There is no question in my mind that Nathan Hale accepted the order to serve as a spy with extreme reluctance and distaste. Nevertheless, he did so serve." To refuse to run, he told Smith, "would be almost the same thing as a soldier refusing to carry out the desires of his commander." Eisenhower added that he had no taste for political life, but possibly under the right circumstances his mind could be changed. "On the other hand, if you should assume the occurrence of an American miracle of a nature that has never heretofore occurred, at least since Washington, you might have the spectacle of someone being named by common consent rather than by the voice of manipulations of the voters."[7] Apparently, under the right circumstances he would consider running.

Ike often referred to his fantasy of being drafted by acclamation. To another friend he wrote: "Since no man—at least since Washington's day—has ever gone into high political office except with his own consent, indeed with his own connivance, I feel perfectly secure in my position" of rejecting a candidacy.[8] In September 1947, an editorial in the *Kansas City Star* explained the type of draft Eisenhower might accept, describing it, as Eisenhower might have, as an "absolutely honest" draft, "an honest-to-God draft that came from the people without conniving and intrigue." Eisenhower responded to the editorial by arguing that such a draft "is not possible in this country."[9] To his brother Milton in October Ike expressed the same thoughts: "No man since Washington has been drafted, yet the principle remains valid."[10]

He also felt that the politicians wanted only to use his popularity and name to win election, and he found that idea repugnant. He told Milton that he did not feel any sense of duty to a party that would, "in desperation, turn to some name that might be a bit popular around the country, in the effort to drag a political . . . organization out of a hole." He added that under the present political system it would be a miracle if a majority of delegates at a convention, spurred on by popular pressure, would draft a candidate of the people. Since those were the only circumstances "that I believe could impart a sense of duty to a normal human being, I come around again to the conclusion that by deciding . . . to use words similar to Sherman's, I am merely punishing myself for adhering to a principle."[11]

In addition, if Eisenhower chose to run as a Republican he would have to fight several primary battles, and since primary victories in 1948 garnered less than half the delegates needed to win at the Republican convention, he could then surely look forward to a bloody convention fight as well. Dewey and Taft were not likely to give up without a battle, and their combined forces might well have foiled any Eisenhower bid in 1948. The polls may have shown that Eisenhower was the most popular of the potential candidates in 1948, but convention delegates would be hard to come by in a political system that still chose delegates mostly through state legislative caucuses and pandered to political insiders and the wishes of local political machines. Rather than risk his reputation in a bloody battle that he might well lose, Eisenhower would decline.

All this came to a head in January 1948. Early that month a group of Eisenhower supporters entered the general's name in the March primary in New Hampshire. Their action was apparently unknown to Eisenhower until Leonard Finder, the publisher of the Manchester, New Hampshire, *Union Leader*, sent him a copy of the newspaper's endorsement. In a letter to Eisenhower, Finder wrote: "While we appreciate that you are not anxious for political aspirations, we are equally confident that you will not resist or resent a genuine grass-roots movement. That is exactly what we have here in New Hampshire." As Eisenhower once said, Finder concluded, "no man should deny the will of the people in a matter such as this. All that we are attempting is to have the will of the people made so clear that it cannot be obviated by the usual politicians assembled in convention."[12]

Eisenhower was forced to respond. He immediately issued a statement through the army's Public Information Division maintaining that he had no desire to enter politics. Nine days later, on January 23, he issued a more formal response in a letter to Finder that was released to the press.[13] It was as close to Sherman's statement as Eisenhower would get. Eisenhower wrote that he was not surprised that some had misinterpreted or found hidden meaning in his statements, "but my failure to convince thoughtful and earnest men . . . proves that I must make some amplification. I am not available and could not accept nomination to high political office." He then gave his reasons for not running, emphasizing that he did not feel he had the right to "violate that concept of duty to country which calls upon every good citizen to place no limitations upon his readiness to serve in any designated capacity." He continued, arguing that soldiers should not become politicians; he apologized to those who might have worked on his behalf; and he concluded with a pivotal statement: "My decision to remove myself completely from the political scene is definite and positive [and] I could not accept nomination even under the remote circumstances that it were tendered me."[14] Eisenhower believed he had brought an end to the speculation and the pressure. To a friend he wrote, "I feel as if I've had an abscessed tooth pulled."[15] But the letter to Finder did not kill the draft-Eisenhower movement. It quieted the Republicans but it awakened the Democrats, who seemed to interpret the Finder letter as Eisenhower's disavowal of his Republican affiliation. Thus, they concluded, he must be a Democrat.

Besides the Eisenhower noncandidacy, the Republicans in 1948 fielded three major and several minor candidates for their party's nomination.

Harold Stassen, the governor of Minnesota, announced his availability early—in December 1946. Taft entered the race officially in late October 1947. Dewey, the governor of New York and the party's unsuccessful candidate in 1944, announced in January 1948. The three were from very different backgrounds and political philosophies, thus they offered clear choices. And it seemed that everyone believed that either Taft, Dewey, or Stassen would win the Republican nomination in Philadelphia in June and then be swept into the White House in November.

Stassen was a strong contender in 1948. Only forty years old, he represented youth, vigor, and action in the Republican party—a fresh face. He presented the image of a man in a hurry, a political star on the rise. Elected governor of Minnesota at age thirty-one and then reelected twice before resigning to serve in the military during the war, Stassen already had a long and successful career behind him when he declared his candidacy. But Stassen had actually accomplished little as a public servant. His only real claims were the passage of a fairly stringent labor law in Minnesota and a short stint as a delegate to the San Francisco conference that led to the formation of the United Nations.

Stassen's greatest attribute was his campaign organization, which was staffed with mostly young volunteers, many of whom were students at the University of Minnesota. Called the Paul Revere Riders, these workers were known for their willingness to go anywhere and do anything for their candidate, which usually meant shoe-leather canvassing. They gave an even more youthful appearance to Stassen's campaign, which was running against the old stodgy Republican image represented by such men as Taft and Vandenberg. Stassen also insisted on running outside the Republican party structure, which was under the control of the Old Guard leaders in Washington. Thus, Stassen had something of a grass-roots appeal as an outsider running against the Democrats but also against the excesses and problems of his own party, including the less-than-stellar record of the Eightieth Congress.

In his announcement speech, Stassen called himself a liberal.[16] He was, in fact, as much a conservative as his Old Guard confederates in Congress. In a campaign publication titled *Where I Stand*, Stassen wrote that he opposed federal aid to housing, supported a cap on federal income taxes, and opposed the Marshall Plan on the grounds that the Western European governments were socialist. But still Stassen was often described in the press as a liberal Republican in the Wendell Willkie mold, and for Taft and others on the right who were crushed in Willkie's surprising ascension in 1940, Stassen seemed a real threat.

Taft waited until fall 1947 to declare his candidacy, but his campaign planning had been in full swing for months with the establishment of Taft Clubs around the nation, along with a long-term plan to set up campaign headquarters in the states that promised to be crucial in the primaries.[17] But Taft had problems. His lack of public appeal throughout his career had translated into a popularly perceived notion that he could not be elected to the presidency. Despite his own resistance to being "humanized," as he called it, Taft allowed his election committee to hire a public relations firm. Headed by General Oscar Solbert (who had been chief of the nation's psychological warfare strategy during the war), this organization was given the task of pumping up Taft's image from a stale legislator to a bright, vibrant, electable political candidate with a forward-looking agenda. The result was the predictable campaign literature filled with the beaming smiles and the slap-on-the-back personal life of a very human figure: "Bob Taft is by no means an austere or aloof person." He was described as a man who played with his grandchildren, did not smoke (but ate candy). "He plays golf (as his father had) and he fishes." But (it seemed important) "he does not hunt." Some of Taft's campaign material seemed an almost desperate attempt to put the best face on the candidate. "It is claimed that Taft is cold. . . . Actually Bob Taft is a poised and genial man, [who] enjoys life . . . and gets along well with people. . . . When Taft gets out among people some of them are visibly shocked at [his] affability." Taft replaced his old rimless glasses with modern horn rims.[18] Despite all the efforts, Taft's campaign committee, and even Taft himself, considered the plan a dismal failure. And in the end, when the campaign was lost, Taft confided to Solbert that the task had been nearly insurmountable, but, he made it clear, he believed it never would have mattered anyway: "I really doubt if there was anything we could have done that would have changed the result."[19]

Dewey jumped into the fray in January 1948, behind the other candidates.[20] The Rowe strategy memo compiled for Truman just a few months before predicted that Dewey would win the Republican nomination, but in early 1948 it was not at all apparent that the 1944 loser could win another nomination. He was, however, still the best known of the Republican candidates and the most successful of the four Republican losers to run against Roosevelt. But he was still a loser, and as Alice Roosevelt Longworth had quipped, "You can't make a souffle rise twice." Yet Dewey had bounced back from his 1944 defeat by winning reelection as New York's governor by the largest margin in the state's history and by keeping his name in the national press and maintaining his popular image.

Dewey had built his image as a "gangbuster," a term at the time for a prosecuting attorney who sent organized crime bosses to jail. In a number of high-profile cases, he had busted rackets led by Dutch Schultz and Lucky

New York governor and Presidential candidate Thomas E. Dewey built his reputation as a gangbuster. Courtesy of the University of Kentucky Special Collections and Archives.

Luciano. He also successfully prosecuted several Tammany machine crooks, and he broke up the infamous murder ring known as Murder Incorporated. Ideologically, his place in the Republican party was somewhere to the left of center. He won praise from party liberals and moderates for supporting a state FEPC that outlawed racial discrimination in the workplace, a measure that the Democrats in Washington could not get through the peacetime Congress, mostly because of southern resistance in their own party. Dewey appealed to progressive urban voters, but he had also compiled a record as a conservative by balancing his state budget and cutting taxes.

In 1940 Dewey made a run for the presidency but was crushed in the Willkie onslaught. Four years later he lost to FDR, but party operatives believed he made a good showing. In fact, he appeared very strong in 1944 until he went on the offensive and began attacking Roosevelt, and only then did his popularity fall in the polls. Dewey was definitely one of the big three Republican leaders at the beginning of 1948, but he was running behind in the polls. Everyone knew, however, that he would finish the primary season as a power to be reckoned with, and that he would be hard to beat in Philadelphia in June.

Dewey, not unlike Taft, had something of an image problem. Taft appeared grim to the average voter; Dewey's problem was that he was intensely disliked by those around him. "You have to know Dewey really well to dislike him" was a common refrain.[21] A Republican party conservative had commented that the haughty Tom Dewey was a self-made man who worshiped his creator.[22] And John Gunther wrote: "A blunt fact about Mr. Dewey should be faced. It is that many people do not like him."[23] Whatever unappealing characteristics were apparent to those close to Dewey, his flaws had to fall second to his popularity with the voters. He won elections. Voters saw him as youthful, progressive, a proven administrator, an internationalist, and an avid anticommunist. To party decision makers he was a strong campaigner, an effective vote-getter.

Stassen, Taft, and Dewey led the Republican field, but a group of lesser lights and favorite sons sat on the sidelines threatening to be spoilers in a convention deadlock. The prize might be to grab the vice-presidential spot or to find some momentum in the primaries that would carry into the convention and on to the nomination. Chief among these characters was Arthur Vandenberg. Running as Michigan's favorite son, Vandenberg stayed out of the primary process but went to the convention with enough delegate strength to be a factor in the nomination. General Douglas MacArthur was riding a wave of support during the summer of 1947. He had strong ties to wealthy businessmen and old isolationist organizations in the Midwest. He would allow his name to be entered in a few primaries, but he refused to return from Japan to campaign actively. Early on, John Bricker promised to be a major candidate. As a presidential aspirant in 1944 who had to settle for the number two spot on the losing ticket, Bricker was a GOP heavyweight. But his election to the Senate in 1946—after four two-year terms as Ohio's governor—placed him in Taft's giant shadow as the freshman senator from Ohio. Consequently, he threw his support to Taft early. Other contenders included Governor Earl Warren of California, House Speaker Joseph Martin, and Pennsylvania senator Edward Martin.

Taft tried to get a feel for what was ahead and to generate some publicity by traveling on what was billed as a "nonpolitical" trip to the West in the late summer of 1947. The entire trip backfired, however, as Taft fell into one ridiculous gaffe after another, and the press made all it could of the situations. The first day out, he inadvertently crossed a picket line to make a speech. The press was relentless in its attack, describing Taft as the antiunion author of Taft-Hartley. Several days later, in Los Angeles, he said that welfare legislation should not be enacted until the Republicans came into the White House. That, by most accounts, was some sixteen months away. How long were America's poor expected to wait? In Santa Cruz, California, in mid-September he said that high demand had caused food prices to rise. He was asked if he meant that people should eat less. Taft answered, "Yes. Eat less meat and eat less extravagantly." The press responded by portraying Taft as the coldhearted defender of the wealthy—those who could afford to eat meat. His car was egged in Seattle. Signs popped up at his speeches: "Taft says: 'tighten your belt—eat less meat.'" In San Francisco fifteen hundred pickets heckled him. The press kept the story in the papers for nearly a month, and Taft returned to Ohio in October to declare his candidacy, but he was way down in the polls and much the worse for wear.[24]

The first real test for the candidates was the Wisconsin primary in April. Wisconsin was important because Stassen maintained great strength there and MacArthur called it his home state, although he had never actually lived there. MacArthur had jumped into the Wisconsin primary in 1944, but he lost to both Dewey and Stassen and dropped out of the race. It was characteristic of MacArthur to announce that he would not run, and he did so in 1947.[25] But he made it clear to American visitors to Japan that he was interested in the 1948 race, and in the fall he apparently told Eisenhower that he would run.[26] MacArthur-for-President committees sprang up throughout the nation, and the general became the candidate most touted by the Hearst newspapers.[27] By April he had made it clear that he would run, but he refused to return from Japan to campaign, and that soured several of his chief supporters. He left his primary campaign in Wisconsin to Phillip La Follette, but La Follette was well outside the Wisconsin political machine, by then under the control of Senator Joseph McCarthy and state boss Tom Coleman, both of whom had thrown their support to Stassen. In a major attack against MacArthur, McCarthy wrote what he called a "Dear Folks" letter to thousands of Wisconsin voters describing MacArthur as twice divorced, too old, out of touch with civilian life in the United States, and not a resident of Wisconsin beyond establishing legal residency for the purpose of running for office.[28] With the machine's support, Stassen upset MacArthur, pulling an impressive 40 percent of the popular vote to MacArthur's 36 percent. Dewey, who willingly let Stassen and MacArthur fight it out on their own turf, pulled 24 percent of the vote after spending only forty-eight hours in the state. Taft stayed away.

Several things were sorted out in Wisconsin. Primarily, it effectively removed MacArthur from the campaign. His popularity, his war hero status, and his proclamation that he was a Wisconsin favorite son all demanded a strong showing in Wisconsin, which he failed to get. The primary also showed the strength of Stassen's organization, his indefatigable Paul Revere Riders, who virtually blanketed the state with leaflets and pamphlets.

The Wisconsin primary also made it clear that Dewey, in only a halfhearted effort, was going to be a formidable candidate and that he and Stassen differed on important issues. In several major speeches on foreign policy, Dewey attacked Stassen's call to outlaw the Communist party, and he endorsed the Marshall Plan, which Stassen opposed, insisting that the primary allies of communism were hunger and fear. He called for a united states of Europe and U.S. involvement on all levels of world diplomacy.[29] These were bold statements of internationalism and a moderate approach to communism at home at a time when rabid anticommunism and old-time isolationism seemed to be the foundation of postwar Republicanism.

The next big primary for the Republicans was in Nebraska, a state that had much in common with the Stassen strongholds of Wisconsin and Minnesota. Consequently, Stassen was expected to win. He had, in fact, won the Nebraska primary in 1944. An upset victory (or near victory) for Dewey or Taft might destroy Stassen's campaign and start a bandwagon rolling for the spoiler. Taft had wanted to avoid Nebraska, but he jumped in at the last minute when he was offered the use of a major Republican political organization in the state. He mounted a strenuous campaign, but he probably destroyed any chance he had of showing well when he told a crowd in Omaha that he opposed farm supports. Stassen, as expected, won in Nebraska by polling seventy-nine thousand votes. Dewey finished a strong second with sixty-three thousand, and Taft trailed with twenty-one thousand votes. MacArthur limped in a dismal fifth behind Vandenberg. At first glance, Stassen seemed to be picking up momentum, but in fact it was Dewey who had crept up on Stassen and maintained a strong showing in Stassen's own backyard—and without much effort.[30]

The real news from Nebraska was that Taft was mortally wounded. After a strenuous campaign in a conservative state with an isolationist history, Taft had failed to win any delegates. He would stick it out, entering and even pushing hard in Oregon and in his home state of Ohio, and he would maintain enough strength to be a major player at the convention. But his candidacy for president was by all accounts ended in Nebraska. It was apparently true: Taft could not win.[31]

The Republican primary battle then shifted to Taft's own turf in Ohio. On January 26 Stassen had announced that he would challenge Taft in Ohio in an attempt to show his liberal-internationalist side against the leader of the Old Guard conservative isolationists.[32] Stassen may, however, have been retaliating for Taft's "nonpolitical" trip to the Northwest in the summer of 1947. As one of Taft's advisers noted, Stassen considered the Northwest "his private hunting preserve," and he was annoyed by Taft's intrusion into the area.[33] Stassen may also have hoped to pull a strong vote among industrial workers in Ohio against the author of the now much hated Taft-Hartley Act, or he may have hoped to render one final blow that would eliminate the wounded Taft from the campaign field. Nevertheless, the prospect of Stassen, on a roll fresh from victories in Wisconsin and Nebraska, entering the Ohio primary head-on against Taft brought on new fears of opening the old party wounds just a few months before the election. Stassen and Taft met to try to work out the problem, but Stassen insisted on making the run.[34] "If a primary battleground must be chosen," Taft told the press, "I am delighted he has selected Ohio where he has no chance of success."[35]

In the end, the Ohio primary hurt both men. Taft failed to sweep his home state, but he did take fourteen of the twenty-three contested delegates. It proved once again that Taft was not a big vote-getter, and for Republican party operatives that was becoming more and more clear as the convention approached. Stassen won nine delegates in Ohio, but, more important, he received the antipathy of the Republican Old Guard for what seemed to be an intentional effort to split the party. From then on in the campaign Stassen was marked as a sort of pariah, working outside the Republican party's acknowledged system, a candidate fighting both the Democrats and the Republicans. For Taft and Stassen, delegates would be hard to come by after Ohio.

Dewey had yet to make a strong showing. His second place to Stassen in Nebraska had kept him in the fight, but the press was beginning to write him off as the Stassen bandwagon appeared to be rolling, and polls showed that he would probably lose to Stassen in Oregon, the next big Republican face-off.[36] For Dewey, Oregon was a must-win. It was much the same for Stassen. Taft stayed away.

Dewey's main attribute so far in the campaign had been his directness. He said he opposed universal military training, the peacetime draft, and a nationalized health care system. On foreign policy he offered a seven-point plan that included sending advisers to aid Nationalist China and a continuation of the bipartisan foreign policy. He continued to complain bitterly about Stassen's plans to outlaw the Communist party in the United States, and he opposed slashing the budget. To an Oregon newspaper he outlined his plans to stop the inflation spiral: "We must reduce Government spending, restrain any further expansion of bank credit for speculative or nonproductive purposes; expand the sale of Government Savings bonds; sharply restrict consumer credit; encourage other savings by both business and individuals; maintain a Government surplus and use it to retire bank-held Government debt; and revise taxes to provide increased incentives for production and thrift while maintaining penalties upon luxury spending."[37] In the campaign against Truman, Dewey's remarks would become vague, even obscure. But against Stassen in the Oregon primary, Dewey was direct, specific, even bold.

Dewey pushed hard in Oregon. After making an early obligatory statement that he was much too busy as governor of New York to campaign actively in Oregon, he dumped everything he had into the state, including some $150,000, three times the record for any campaign ever financed there.[38] *Newsweek* characterized Dewey's campaign as "barnstorming through Oregon. . . . He spoke at places that were little more than a cluster of service stations and crossroad stores. He strode into greasy hamburger stands to shake hands all around." He delivered more than two hundred speeches, used a direct mail campaign, and took on Stassen directly in a nationally broadcast debate on the highly controversial issue of outlawing the Communist party.[39]

Dewey swept the state, winning 53 percent of the vote and twelve delegates. Stassen was stopped cold, and Dewey went to the top of the list of Republican contenders. He was now by all accounts the party's best campaigner and biggest vote-getter. For Stassen, Taft, Vandenberg, Warren, and the other Republican hopefuls, the only logical prospect now was a deadlocked convention. Dewey held only 300 of the 548 delegates needed to win in Philadelphia, which meant he would need the support of several of the other candidates to receive the nomination. As the convention approached, deals were in the works—several to stop the Dewey steamroller.

10

The Democrats and the Eisenhower Diversion

The Republican plan to draft Eisenhower in 1948 had fizzled when the general made it clear in January that he had no intention of running for president. But Ike's appeal as a possible presidential candidate sent the Democrats panting after him in the mistaken belief that he had turned down the Republicans because he was, in fact, a Democrat.

Like the Republicans, the Democrats had been trying for some time to persuade Eisenhower to cast his lot with them, and he had refused just as he had refused the Republicans. But the Democrats had a bigger problem, or at least they thought they did. They believed that Truman was certain to lose the election in November, and that defeat would bring an end to the fifteen years of Democratic dominance in the nation. Possibly worst of all, a Truman defeat at the head of the ticket would drag down local Democratic politicians who were standing for election in 1948. One Democratic leader insisted that Adlai Stevenson and Paul Douglas would both lose in Illinois if Truman ran, that Hubert Humphrey would lose in Minnesota, Helen Douglas in California, Chester Bowles in Connecticut, Henry "Scoop" Jackson in Washington, James Murray in Montana, and the list continued.[1] The polls showed that such predictions were probably true. The polls also showed that Eisenhower as Democrat pitted against any Republican had an excellent chance to win.[2] So, to save their party from certain defeat, the Democrats continued to pursue Eisenhower on through the winter and spring of 1948, well after the Republicans had given up the chase. For the Democrats the immediate future of their party seemed to hang on whether Eisenhower would run as a Democrat.

The Democratic draft-Eisenhower movement was made up of a remarkably diverse group of party leaders. But it was the ADA more than any other group or faction that led the way in trying to convince Eisenhower to run. The ADA was desperate to throw its support to anyone except the doomed Truman. At its national convention in Philadelphia in February 1948, the six hundred delegates in attendance were restless over being bound to Truman. One participant wrote that they "almost erupted in an anti-Truman explosion," and several delegates proposed that they attempt to persuade Truman not to run.[3]

In the two months between the ADA convention in February and the ADA's next national meeting, James Loeb came to the conclusion that not only would Truman lose in November and take a large number of liberals down to defeat with him but that a Truman nomination might lead to the unraveling of the fragile labor-liberal coalition, and that could lead to the untimely death of the ADA. It also might lead, he believed, to a mass defection of liberals to Wallace's standard, something Loeb and other ADA operatives greatly feared. Anyone could see that massive liberal support for Wallace meant a certain Republican victory. For Loeb, the answer to the dilemma was clear. He began looking for a popular figure, an effective campaigner, and an anticommunist to replace Truman as the Democratic party's 1948 candidate. In the spring of 1948 Loeb began sounding out sentiment among the ADA rank and file for pushing Truman out and drafting Eisenhower.[4]

In mid-April Loeb and several members of the ADA board met in closed session in Pittsburgh to discuss an endorsement of Eisenhower. They issued a statement designed to pull directly on the strings of Eisenhower's sense of responsibility to his nation: "This Nation has a right to call upon men like Dwight D. Eisenhower . . . if the people so choose. . . . No one . . . can enjoy the privilege of declaring himself unavailable in this hour of the nation's need." Eisenhower, they added, "would stir the popular enthusiasm which will sweep progressive candidates across the country into Congress."[5] The ADA finally had someone to promote for president. ADA founding member Reinhold Niebuhr wrote, "We are sunk now [with Truman] and Eisenhower is the only possible candidate who [can] defeat the Republicans. I would support almost any decent man to avoid four years of Republican rule."[6] These words seemed to reflect the attitude of the ADA: anyone but Truman, anyone but Wallace, anyone but the Republicans. At best, the Eisenhower distraction was an expedient, an act of desperation, simply someone the ADA thought could win—and defeat the others.

The ADA did not stand alone among Democrats in this scheme to draft Eisenhower. Others included a group of big city bosses consisting of Cook County (Chicago) boss Jacob Arvey, New York City mayor Bill O'Dwyer, and mayor-boss Frank Hague of Jersey City. All were powerful in their districts and in the Democratic party structure; they were men who could deliver votes and sway conventions. From the South, the players occupied the extremes. The liberals included John Sparkman and Lister Hill from Alabama and Claude Pepper from Florida. All three had been party loyalists and active New Dealers, supporters of the TVA, federal farm programs, and Social Security. Conservative southern Democrats who wanted Eisenhower were generally those who would soon pull together the Dixiecrat movement. They included Governors Strom Thurmond of South Carolina, Ben Laney of Arkansas, Herman Talmadge of Georgia, and William Tuck of Virginia. Powerful southern senators who supported the move included John Stennis of Mississippi and Harry Byrd of Virginia. These southerners were prepared to desert Truman because of his newfound civil rights posture and give their support to Eisenhower, a believer (so they had convinced themselves) in states' rights.

Despite Truman's Taft-Hartley veto, some of labor's most important leaders remained disenchanted with the president and wanted to dump him for Eisenhower. Much of this disenchantment came from the CIO, the labor organization that had received the most battering by the president's labor policies since the war. By 1948 CIO president Philip Murray, secretary-treasurer James Carey, and Jack Kroll of the CIO-PAC were all prepared to accept anyone but Truman, and each tried to persuade Truman to step down in favor of Eisenhower. Walter Reuther of the UAW and David Dubinsky of International Ladies Garment Workers Union also supported drafting Eisenhower.[7]

By early spring the leadership role in the draft-Eisenhower movement had come to revolve around FDR's three sons: Franklin Jr. in New York, James in California, and Elliot in Texas. Their leadership was unofficial, but their heritage and name brought legitimacy to the movement. Their father had kept the Democrats together since 1933, and they believed that Eisenhower's popularity would continue that unity into the 1950s. Their mother, Eleanor, was by this time the unofficial leader of American liberalism and a member of the ADA, but she had no interest in her sons' notions of drafting Eisenhower.

James Roosevelt wrote in his memoirs that he believed the prevailing attitude in America after his father's death was for change, Truman had very little chance to win in 1948, and his defeat would end the New Deal era. A Truman victory, he wrote, was a long shot at best. "It seemed so clearly time for a change that only an unusually attractive campaigner could keep our party in power. I was not alone in thinking Truman was not that man. . . . I just did not think he could be elected, so I looked for someone who could."[8]

On March 10, Franklin Jr., who was serving as the vice-president of the ADA, called on the Democratic convention to draft Eisenhower. "Circumstances require a man who will convince the Russian leaders that the constant aim of our policy is to secure . . . lasting peace . . . and who, at the same time, will take all necessary steps to stop further aggression. . . . The American people have such a man in General Eisenhower."[9] Throughout March and April, Franklin Jr. and Elliot made several statements and speeches asking Eisenhower to run and insisting that the American people had a right to call the general back into public service as president of the United States. The Roosevelt brothers made particular use of the Soviet invasion of Czechoslovakia in February to appeal to the nation that a strong military leader like Eisenhower was a necessity in the face of such continued Soviet aggressions.[10]

Eisenhower had kept his distance from much of this Democratic party activity as it developed during the early spring of 1948. By March, however, local Democratic Eisenhower-for-president organizations were popping up throughout the country and many were raising money to further the cause. By April, Eisenhower came to realize that he would again have to surface and make another Shermanesque statement, this time for the benefit of the Democrats.

He wrote his friend and confidant Walter Bedell Smith on April 12, the day the ADA board endorsed him for president: "Recently the Democrats have taken the attitude that Mr. Truman cannot be re-elected; therefore they do not want to renominate him. In this situation they are turning desperately to anyone that might give them a chance of winning, and they have the cockeyed notion that I might be tempted to make the effort."[11] To another friend he wrote that the Democrats are "desperately searching around for someone to save their skins." He added that his friends in the Midwest "would be shocked and chagrined at the very idea of my running on a Democratic ticket for anything."[12]

The endorsement by the ADA board was reported in *Time* on April 19. In that same issue, Eisenhower was asked to respond. "I wrote a letter," he said, referring to the Finder letter of four months earlier. "And I meant every word of it." Still, Claude Pepper was quoted in the same article: "He may be pulling the door a little closer to him, but I didn't hear the lock click."[13] It would take more than Eisenhower's aloofness to stop the desperate Democrats.

Truman later wrote in his memoirs that the draft-Eisenhower movement "threatened to develop at any time during the spring into a full-fledged boom for General Eisenhower."[14] On June 13, the president met with his campaign advisers to discuss the growing interest in the general. On July 3, the *New York Times* reported that the president would send George Allen (a friend of both the general and the president) to ask Eisenhower to end the speculation and issue a statement for the Democrats similar to the one he had issued for the Republicans in January.

This story has been told in several different ways by various participants. According to Peter Lyon, in his *Eisenhower: Portrait of a Hero*, Allen felt he could not carry out Truman's wishes, and the job fell to Secretary of the Army Kenneth Royall. According to Cabell Phillips, in his *The Truman Presidency*, Truman was not simply asking Eisenhower to withdraw from the race but offering to run with Eisenhower on the same ticket—with the general at the top of the ticket and Truman in second place. Truman made the offer, according to Phillips, because he did not believe he could win reelection or even the Democratic nomination. In an attempt to corroborate his story, Phillips contacted the other parties involved in this deal. Royall responded that Phillips's story was "substantially correct. . . . Mr. Truman was a realist and from time to time doubted whether he could win in 1948. But he never gave up trying." Eisenhower refused to comment on the incident. According to Phillips, Eisenhower refused Truman's offer to run.[15]

Truman always denied that he made such an offer to Eisenhower: "That story . . . has been going around and around. I never agreed to help Ike get the Democratic nomination," he wrote Phillips in the 1960s. "There is nothing to that story." In his memoirs, Truman wrote that he and Eisenhower met to discuss the situation just before the Democratic convention. After a discussion of politics and military heroes, "I asked him if he intended to run for President. He told me that he had no intention of running for office and cited [the Finder letter] in which he had given reasons for his decision not to run. . . . Eisenhower showed me this letter," Truman continued, "and I told him that I thought he was using good judgement." A few years later, Truman told Merle Miller: "He said I offered him the Presidency, which I didn't. In the first place it wasn't mine to offer. What happened [was] . . . we had a talk, and *again* he assured me he had no political intentions whatsoever of going into politics. I told him that was the right decision. And it was."[16]

There seems no certain way of knowing whether Truman asked Eisenhower to withdraw from the campaign or whether he wanted Eisenhower to join him on the ticket. At Potsdam in 1945, Truman apparently made a similar gesture to Eisenhower, and in that case it appears that Truman actually agreed to step down if Eisenhower decided to run in 1948.[17] But by the summer of the nominating convention, the political climate had changed considerably from 1945. At Potsdam, Truman did not see himself as a future candidate for president. He had even written his wife that he hoped Eisenhower would run as a Democrat in 1948.[18] But by the time of the party convention, Truman had made it abundantly clear that he would pursue the Democratic nomination, and by then only Eisenhower appeared to stand in his way. Rather than accept Phillips's argument that Truman was prepared to offer an Eisenhower-Truman ticket, it seems more likely that on the eve of the Democratic convention, with Eisenhower's popularity running at nearly fever pitch, the president asked the general to step aside—which he did the next day, July 5. It is difficult to imagine Truman, the consummate lifelong politician with an incumbency and much of the Democratic party machinery in his hands, giving up the nomination just days before the convention, even to the likes of Eisenhower, even in the face of discouraging public opinion polls. Clearly, he was on his way to an easy first ballot win. Truman wrote in his memoirs that those who were pushing Eisenhower to run did not realize that an incumbent president was simply too powerful to unseat. Truman pointed out that it had never happened before. Not even the immensely popular Theodore Roosevelt could remove his own chosen successor in 1912. "The convention will operate," Truman wrote, "in the manner in which the chairman and the President want it to. . . . In 1948 I was in a position to control the nomination."[19] In such an advantageous position, why should he offer the nomination to someone else? Clark Clifford, Truman's special counsel, recalled the situation in an interview years later. He found it hard to believe that after months of coordinating strategy in preparation for the convention Truman could have made any serious offer to Eisenhower to run on the Democratic ticket at that late date. Clifford seemed to believe that if Truman made such a statement it was not in a serious vein; by that time in the campaign the president was fully committed to running for a second term and would not have stepped aside voluntarily for any candidate.[20]

No matter what the message was to Eisenhower, Truman simply may have been looking for the answer to the question that everyone else was asking: would Ike run? He sent Royall to get the answer, and he got it. It gave Truman the inside information he wanted, that the general had no intention of running as a Democrat.

In the weeks before the Democratic convention James Roosevelt arranged to have telegrams sent to all 1,592 delegates inviting them to a caucus in the days just before the convention to select "the ablest and strongest man available. . . . It is our belief," his message continued, "that no man in these critical days can refuse the call to duty and leadership implicit in the nomination and virtual election to the Presidency of the United States." The signers of the telegram read like a strange brew of Democratic politicians of every configuration. Among them were Mayor O'Dwyer of New York, Alabama senator Lister Hill, Arkansas governor Ben T. Laney, Chester Bowles of Connecticut, Jacob Arvey of Chicago, Hubert Humphrey, Strom

Thurmond, Texas governor Beauford H. Lester, and Governor William Tuck of Virginia.[21]

All of this activity finally forced Eisenhower to act again. He would have to speak out or, by keeping silent, lend his consent. On July 5, the day after he met with Royall, Eisenhower issued a statement through the Columbia University public relations office: "I will not, at this time, identify myself with any political party, and could not accept nomination for any public office or participate in partisan political contest."[22] The next day, the *New York Times* headline read, "Eisenhower Says He Couldn't Accept Nomination for Any Public Office; Gives Answer to 'Draft' Campaign."[23] But because the general used the phrase "at this time," the fires continued to burn. In fact, Eisenhower's use of that phrase provoked John M. Bailey, the Democratic state chairman from Connecticut, to suggest that Eisenhower's name be placed into nomination at the convention. On that same day, July 6, Claude Pepper announced that he would be the one to carry out that mission on the convention floor. Pepper's plan was to draft Eisenhower as a nonpartisan candidate and give him the power to write his own platform and to choose his own vice-presidential candidate. This, thought Pepper, would turn the draft-Eisenhower campaign into a national movement.[24] Pepper's scheme was obviously meant to meet what appeared to be Eisenhower's demands for a draft: that the general would be nominated by acclamation and not have to become involved in the muck of partisan politics. Pepper proposed his plan in a letter to Eisenhower: "I neither expect nor desire either an acknowledgment or reply," he concluded.[25]

Pepper's scheme forced Eisenhower to disavow his political ambitions one more time. On July 8 and 9, he wrote letters to Pepper, James Roosevelt, and Mayor Frank Hague of Jersey City. Each letter was different, but each contained the following phrase: "No matter under what terms, conditions, or premises a proposal might be couched, I would refuse to accept the nomination." Pepper's office released the letter, and it appeared on the front page of the *New York Times* on July 10.[26] With that, the draft-Eisenhower movement finally died.

A group of Democrats, finally accepting defeat, issued a statement saying that "the Democratic party has been strengthened, rather than weakened, by the movement to draft Eisenhower. A political party never errs when it earnestly strives to serve the majority's will."[27] On July 9, James Roosevelt relented: "Because of the personal and confidential telegram I have just received from General Eisenhower, I am now convinced he would not serve if nominated by the Democratic Party."[28] He called off his preconvention meeting. Pepper wrote back to Eisenhower: "I reluctantly bow to your determination."[29] O'Dwyer of New York and Arvey of Chicago capitulated and came out for Truman. A party emissary was sent to New York in one last attempt to bring Eisenhower around, but the general apparently did not even feel a need to meet with the group.

By the time the convention began, many liberal Democrats who had supported Eisenhower found themselves without a home. They felt that leaving the Democratic party to support Wallace would simply add to the liberal division that had already threatened to turn over the election to the Republicans. But supporting Truman was still out of the question. To return to Truman's camp now after having just led a highly visible, highly critical rebellion against him would be a humiliation that few were prepared to endure. Consequently, in an eleventh-hour hope of recouping their losses and saving their faces, a group of liberals led by the ADA came out for Supreme Court justice William O. Douglas. "The Democrats must choose Douglas," Leon Henderson said, "or invite a disaster that will imperil the future of progressivism in America."[30] As ADA leader Carl Auerbach of Wisconsin added, "We would rather lose with Douglas than lose with Truman."[31] But Douglas was not interested either, and for him there would be none of Eisenhower's "I may run under the right conditions." On July 10, he issued a statement that left nothing to the imagination: "I am not a candidate, have never been a candidate, and don't plan to be a candidate."[32]

Two days after Douglas's statement, in a nearly comic conclusion to the draft-Eisenhower movement, Claude Pepper announced he would run for the Democratic nomination. At least he wanted the job. He made his announcement at the abandoned Eisenhower headquarters across from the Bellevue-Stratford Hotel in Washington where obviously he hoped somehow to associate himself with the general who had all the right qualities but none of the inclination. "This is no time for politics as usual," Pepper said, "for this nation is trembling on the brink of war and our national economy is threatened by an economic depression. . . . Only a liberal candidate has the opportunity to win," he concluded. He called himself a "practical" southern liberal and said that he opposed Truman's civil rights program, calling it a "snare and a delusion."[33] The ADA was not interested. Henderson's response to Pepper's candidacy was, "We have already had two dark horses shot from under us. Why the hell should we get up and ride a red roan?"[34] Two days later, Pepper withdrew for lack of support.

For most of these Eisenhower supporters in the Democratic party, the general was little more than an expedient, someone who could win the White House and keep the Republicans out of office for another four years. He was expected to bring in a liberal Democratic Congress. But few liberals harbored any notion that Eisenhower was any sort of a liberal. In fact, he had made it clear during the spring of 1948 that he opposed desegregation in the armed forces, a policy that even Truman had come to support. "I think he will run," Chester Bowles told an ADA operative in June, "and in spite of our reservations about him we would certainly be a lot better off with him and a Democratic Congress than with any of the other alternatives."[35] Loeb wrote in the same month that Eisenhower as Democrat in the White House "would be preferable to a Republican sweep, which would mean a Congress way beyond the control of such [Republican] moderates as Vandenberg."[36] Liberals in 1948 were willing to accept Eisenhower no matter what unliberal attitudes he might hold in order to stay in office, to stay in control of the government.

The Republicans were less affected by the draft-Eisenhower movement than the Democrats. The Finder letter ended all speculation for them in January, six months before their convention and more than enough time for party members to choose from among the crowd of Republicans with presidential aspirations. But for the Democrats, their answer did not come until July, just a few days before their convention began. The move to draft Eisenhower by the Democrats may appear to have split further the already badly fragmented Democratic party, but in fact it served to force the party's center back into the fold. As the Progressives and the Dixiecrats went off in opposite directions, the vital center coalesced around Eisenhower. When the general declined, this group, which included the ADA and a large portion of the urban-labor coalition, was left leaderless, twisting in the wind. With no place else to go and with Truman insisting on the nomination, those who had supported Eisenhower fell in line behind the president. The result was an unhappy unification of the party's central forces. With the ADA conspicuously in the lead, figures such as Pepper, Humphrey, Sparkman, the Roosevelt brothers, Murray, and Reuther made their way into Truman's camp—by default. It was not a happy coalition, and many of these figures never warmed up to Truman (and the feelings were mutual), but they played an important part in bringing votes to Truman and the Democrats in the November election.[37]

11

The Do-Nothing Eightieth Congress's Second Session

By the time the second session of the Eightieth Congress met, it was clear to the Republicans that Truman was more intent on building a record against Congress than actually achieving any legislative results. The president's State of the Union address in January 1948 was a primary indication of that strategy; it was also the first salvo launched by the administration in the 1948 presidential contest, and it was the president's first move to put into action the strategy devised by Clifford, Rowe, and the Wardman Park group. The speech was a definite shift to the left by Truman, a direct appeal to the needs of the average American. Gone was all tone of conciliation. One of the occasional members of the Wardman Park group, presidential aide George Elsey, told Truman that his State of the Union message "must be controversial as hell, must state the issues of the election, must draw the line sharply between the Republicans and the Democrats. The Democratic platform will stem from it," he added, "and the election will be fought on the issues it presents."[1]

In his address Truman outlined a bold plan that both Democratic and Republican leaders knew would not be passed by the Eightieth Congress. He called for a broadening of Social Security, a national health insurance program, federal aid to education, a long-range housing program, an increase in the minimum wage, an expansion of soil conservation and reclamation programs, the establishment of more TVA-like projects, farm price supports, crop insurance, and legislation for the establishment of marketing cooperatives for farmers. In addition, he asked that Congress adopt his long-range anti-inflation program and refrain from cutting taxes except in the lower income brackets. A month later, in another message to Congress, he added an appeal for civil rights for African Americans.[2]

It should have been clear to the members of the Republican Congress that if they failed to act on these requests they would be held accountable, accused in the campaign of serving big business and special interests at the expense of the American people. Taft seemed to see what was coming and tried to make adjustments by supporting several bills that brought him a bit closer to the center. The other Republicans, however, either failed to analyze the administration's strategy properly, or, more likely, they thought it would have no impact on the 1948 election, believing instead that their policies and ideas were in favor with the voters, that their time had come, that the 1946 mandate had been clear. But Truman, advised by the young liberals in his administration, was setting the stage for the campaign ahead. He would run against the record of the Eightieth Congress, choosing the ground for the battles to come between the rich man's Congress and the workingman's president.

In the second session, which began in January 1948, the Republicans continued to push against the New Deal and liberalism, still wedded to their mandate of 1946 and still under the impression that the nation's voters had sent them to Washington to eliminate the social programs of Rooseveltism. But with the major exception of labor legislation, the Eightieth Congress had delivered mostly talk when it came to replacing or removing the New Deal. The Congress had followed the administration's lead and passed important legislation in foreign policy, but on domestic issues it had done very little.

One of the most important and visible failures of the Eightieth Congress was its lack of action on housing. Taft had joined a strange-bedfellow alliance in 1945 with Democrat Allen Ellender of Louisiana and "Mr. New Deal," Robert F. Wagner of New York, to produce the Taft-Ellender-Wagner bill (T-E-W), which was designed to provide low- and middle-income housing in the postwar years. The need was apparent because several hundred thousand American soldiers were converging on the nation's urban housing market all at once. The joke "two families in every garage" lost its humor by the beginning of 1946 when home construction fell far behind demand and the housing shortage became acute. The final cost for T-E-W was $90 million, and the bill passed with a voice vote in the Senate in 1948.

It was Taft, however, who took the brunt of the criticism from his own party members for this bill. The head of the National Association of Real Estate Boards called Taft a "fellow traveler held captive by the bureaucracy which is running the government." Kenneth Wherry said Taft had developed a "touch of socialism." Taft argued back, with some degree of prophecy, that "any party that [opposes a housing bill] would have only a short tenure of office and the opposition party would soon enact the legislation anyway, in a much more extreme form."[3] The bill was finally killed by conservative Republicans in the House—smack in the middle of the 1948 presidential campaign. Again, the Republicans failed to act on an issue that affected millions of voters, common people trying to make ends meet in an inflationary economy. The bill's failure also hurt Taft, who was seen by members of the Old Guard as too willing to compromise with the Democratic enemy and by liberal Republicans such as Jacob Javits of New York as not doing enough to pass the bill.

In much the same category was Taft's bill to supply federal aid to education. Taft proposed that $300 million be allocated to assist the nation's poorest states in developing stronger education systems. He used his leadership to push the bill through the more tolerant Senate, but House conservatives killed it. Again Taft, trying to maintain control of the center in his party while portraying himself to voters as a moderate, was criticized by both Republican liberals and Old Guard conservatives.

Both of these bills were major defeats for Taft. The talk among Republican operatives after the passage of Taft-Hartley that Taft would be the 1948 GOP standard-bearer was quickly quieted. Throughout the early months of 1948, when Taft was actively contending for the Republican nomination, he had to fight off constant concerns among his party members that he was not electable, that throughout his career he had come to carry too much baggage, and that he had made too many enemies to defeat nearly any Democratic candidate. But the failure of the housing and education bills made it clear that Taft also had too many enemies in his own party and that his nomination at Philadelphia in June was improbable.[4]

The defeat of these two bills, however, played well into Truman's hands, and he made the most of it during the campaign. He accused the Republicans of succumbing to the demands of the real estate lobby and of being insensitive to the needs of the nation's schoolchildren. It was a strong argument, and people listened.[5]

The passage of the Marshall Plan was the administration's primary foreign policy initiative in the first six months of 1948, and here again the Republicans stumbled and handed the president a powerful campaign issue. The Marshall Plan was a popular program, made even more so by the February communist coup in Czechoslovakia. Even Taft, who had originally opposed the measure, came on board, realizing that he could not afford to oppose such a popular plan. But isolationists and obstructionists in the House wanted the measure cut drastically, and they were willing to sacrifice their party's unity in an election year by dredging up dissensions and party splits in order to the cut the program's funding.

The Senate tried to reduce the administration's request for $6.8 billion to $5.3 billion and then to $4 billion, but the coup in Czechoslovakia in

February eroded conservative support and the $5.3 billion figure was passed. The House followed along. But the House Appropriations Committee, headed by John "Meat Axe" Tabor, threatened to cut the bill to $4 billion, and another struggle ensued between the isolationists and the internationalists in the House. To the American people, however, this Republican infighting seemed only to obstruct a very popular measure. At the same time, the Czech coup dragged the United States into an immediate war scare. For most Americans it was the final proof that the Soviets had intentions of world conquest and that something had to be done. General Marshall called the world situation "very, very serious," and Truman addressed a joint session of Congress on March 17 to call for universal military training and a resumption of the draft.[6] The Marshall Plan finally passed by big margins in both houses, but it was the Democrats who had taken the initiative to contain the forces of international communism, while the Republicans had done little more than squawk about the cost.

The Republicans could claim a few victories in the second session, but in most cases it was Truman who claimed the final victory as the defender of the common man. For instance, the Republicans passed a tax reduction bill over the president's veto, but the bill was clearly designed to reduce taxes only in the highest income brackets, giving virtually no relief to the wage earner. Truman was able to take this issue to the people during the campaign, calling it the "rich man's tax law" and claiming that the tax reduction was the best example of how the Republican Eightieth Congress had done nothing to aid the average American.[7]

The Eightieth Congress also excluded several groups from Social Security benefits—over two presidential vetoes. Truman, in his first term, had made it Democratic party policy to add groups to the rolls of Social Security, and in his State of the Union message in January 1948 he had called on Congress to expand Social Security to include additional workers. In June, just as the campaign was gearing up, Truman vetoed a Republican bill that would have taken some 750,000 people off Social Security. And again, it became fodder for his campaign.[8]

The Republicans also turned down Truman's requests to expand public power. Public power projects had been one of the most successful of the New Deal programs. By 1948 the Rural Electrification Administration (REA) and the Tennessee Valley Authority were on their way to bringing low-cost electricity to the home of nearly every farmer in the nation.[9] The result was higher productivity, modernization, increased sanitation, and convenience. They were popular programs. But these government projects were despised by Republicans as government-supported industries that competed directly with private industries. The Republican stance annoyed farmers who depended on the REA and other public power projects for their electrical power. It also gave Truman another opportunity to accuse the Republicans of being the dupes of big business (which opposed the REA and public power) and special interest groups such as the National Association of Manufacturers.[10] Congress also hurt farmers by cutting funds for soil conservation and crop storage, just as farm prices were beginning to drop in the summer of 1948.

Other liberal proposals by the president met defeat, including a minimum wage bill that died without a hearing and a bill to provide a permanent FEPC that suffered a similar fate.[11] The president's health care proposal was never taken up, and bills designed to deal with education, housing, public power, race issues, and an expansion of Social Security benefits to large groups of workers were also killed. The Taft-Hartley Act passed in the first session weakened the powers of organized labor, and it was clear that the Republicans were moving toward the 1948 election with a great deal of confidence and little fear that large sections of the electorate might find these actions in direct opposition to their needs. Truman, in contrast, pounded these issues home to the American people, placing himself in the role of the candidate who was fighting for the common man against the forces of privilege and wealth. The strategy, of course, worked.[12]

The question has been since 1948, Was the Eightieth Congress truly a do-nothing Congress? In fact, the Eightieth Congress did a great deal. Its work, however, was generally obstructionist and against the fifteen-year-old process of liberal reform. In regard to the election, it is more important that Truman was able to make the do-nothing label stick and use it as an effective campaign issue. The real question concerning the Eightieth Congress is, however, Did the Republicans misinterpret their 1946 mandate and thus move in a direction that the nation did not want to go? And the answer is a resounding yes. The Republicans believed they had been given a mandate to remove the New Deal, to end the era of social legislation in America. The results of the 1948 election show clearly that the Republican-dominated Eightieth Congress had been elected in 1946 for other reasons.

12

The Republicans
Nominate Dewey

The Republicans went to Philadelphia in a mood of exuberance; there seemed little doubt that they would nominate the next president of the United States. *Life* magazine pointed out the nation's general mood: "If ever the Republicans had a mission to choose a candidate capable of carrying a mandate from the people into the White House, it is in 1948."[1] Philadelphia prepared for the big bash. A rubber elephant (only occasionally fully inflated by a vacuum cleaner) adorned the top of the Bellevue-Stratford Hotel, the Republican National Committee headquarters. Flowers decorated the vicinity of the Convention Hall, pretty girls were placed at the city's main intersections to answer questions, and the usual red, white, and blue bunting hung across Philadelphia's main thoroughfares. When the delegates arrived, even the weather seemed to cooperate. The oppressive heat and humidity of the Philadelphia summer was absent, and those delegates who recalled the suffocating 1940 convention held in the same hall breathed a sigh of relief. Not only was that convention a long, hot, and exhausting affair, it was a losing one as well. But now, after fifteen long years exiled in the political wilderness, the Republicans seemed truly on the road to the White House. The atmosphere was upbeat.

The four days of behind-the-scenes haggling, deal-making, and power-broking gave the Republican convention an air of deadlock as the party powerhouses slugged it out for control of convention delegates. But in fact the theme of the convention was the rapid increase of the momentum for Dewey and the sideshow of the anti-Dewey forces who could not come to any accord to stop his blitz to the nomination. When it was over, the *Chicago Tribune* called the convention "one of the greatest party battles ever waged."[2] But it was not. Dewey's momentum was so strong that, as *Newsweek* more accurately reported after the convention, "it was evident that nothing short of the most astute political maneuvering could halt the nomination of the New York governor."[3]

Dewey came to Philadelphia with considerable momentum already under his feet. He had destroyed Stassen in Oregon, and Taft had shown the GOP bigwigs that he was not a strong candidate. Dewey, in contrast, had shown his vote-getting strength. Both men arrived in Philadelphia claiming they were ahead in the delegate count, but Dewey held a substantial lead, carrying just over 300 declared delegates of the 548 needed to win the nomination. In addition, Dewey had at his disposal an undisclosed number of "hidden" delegates that his supporters fed to the press at various points during the convention to keep his momentum moving.[4]

Stassen was forced to accept that he was in third place. On his return from his Oregon primary defeat in May, Stassen stopped off in Topeka, Kansas, to discuss his campaign with Alf Landon, the guru of liberal Republicanism. Landon told Stassen that he did not have enough delegates to win in Philadelphia, thus the best he could do was to influence the outcome of the nomination. It was good advice, but Stassen did not take it. He saw instead a deadlock coming between Taft and Dewey, and he believed he would push through as the compromise candidate. When he arrived in Philadelphia, he made a ridiculous prediction of a Willkie-like deadlocked convention that would come to him on the ninth ballot.[5]

The convention's underdog was Arthur Vandenberg. *Life* said that he was "probably the brightest darkhorse that ever chomped a political oat. . . . It would hardly be surprising if he turns out to be the Philadelphia 'surprise.'"[6] Vandenberg came to the convention with only a few delegates as Michigan's favorite son, but he too seemed ready to march forward when called as the compromise candidate in a Dewey-Taft deadlock. Much to the frustration of Vandenberg supporters (most notably Henry Cabot Lodge Jr. of Massachusetts, Clare Booth Luce, and Vandenberg's son, Arthur Jr.), however, the senator refused to do much to increase his own stock. Talk of his candidacy had begun as early as 1946 and increased after the 1946 election, but Vandenberg seemed to do all he could to remove himself from consideration by insisting that he had no desire to be president.[7] Two days before the convention began, however, and after a great deal of goading from his son, Vandenberg finally agreed to allow Michigan governor Kim Sigler to read a press release stating that he would accept the nomination—but he would not seek it. Vandenberg said later that his only interest was to see that an internationalist plank was included in the Republican party platform for 1948 and to stop the party's isolationists.[8]

Vandenberg's declaration, which was generally unexpected, upset the natural balance that was beginning to coalesce in the days before the convention. A stop-Dewey coalition had just begun to take shape between Taft and Stassen—at best a delicate alliance. To be effective, these two men would have to overcome the antipathy they had developed for each other and then somehow decide which would support the other. That problem was a long way from being solved, but when Vandenberg entered the ring, Stassen decided that the chances for a deadlock were now even greater than before and he broke off all negotiations with Taft. The stop-Dewey movement, at least for the moment, came to an end.[9]

The turning point in the convention came early, when Pennsylvania threw its considerable weight to Dewey. The Pennsylvania forces were divided between the state's governor, James Duff, and Joseph P. Grundy, Pennsylvania's GOP boss, whose conservatism had brought him so far as to call Taft a socialist. A compromise that would have united the Pennsylvania delegation behind House Speaker Joe Martin failed, and then finally both sides agreed to unite behind the state's junior senator, Edward Martin. On Sunday, the day before the convention began, Duff insisted that he controlled forty-five of Pennsylvania's fifty-two votes and that he would throw his support to Taft—or to any stop-Dewey coalition. Whatever happened, it would be the first big shift of the balance in convention delegates, and for Dewey it meant either a substantial gain or a halting of momentum. Dewey's people worked the Pennsylvania delegation for two days. On Tuesday afternoon Edward Martin announced that, as Pennsylvania's favorite son, he was freeing up his delegates and that he would support and in fact nominate Dewey. The delegates on the convention floor apparently believed that Martin's announcement meant that the entire Pennsylvania delegation was going for Dewey, and, as it turned out, it was the beginning of a big blitz by the Dewey forces that finally ended in his nomination. In fact, Martin brought only about forty votes, while Duff remained in control of less than thirty. The numbers were certainly welcomed in the Dewey camp, but the importance was that Dewey won a large bloc of delegates that was supposed to be in the hip pocket of the Old Guard conservatives. It was a devastating blow to Taft's forces, and it got the Dewey bandwagon on the road.[10]

The convention's opening was filled with the usual excitement and accompanying absurdities. Bands roamed the Convention Hall aisles playing theme songs in support of candidates. Banners, confetti, balloons, and cheers carried the day (and night) as television cameras covered the convention for the first time in history—although few Americans had television sets.[11] In her speech before the convention, Clare Booth Luce declared Truman a "gone goose" in one of the 1948 campaign's most memorable moments. She added that Henry Wallace was "Stalin's Mortimer Snerd." The Taft forces showed up on the convention floor and later in the lobby of the Bellevue-

Stratford Hotel with "Eva Tfat" (Taft spelled backward), a four-foot elephant. After some coaxing, the dour and august Taft was persuaded by his supporters to shake the animal's trunk at a press conference. Stassen's support on the convention floor was young and noisy, and to keep his campaign people in proper form, Stassen had eight thousand Stassen-for-President buttons flown to Philadelphia each day of the convention. To add another oddity to the proceedings, a pretty blond in a sailor suit rowed a boat suspended from the top of the Convention Hall above the delegates' heads. The sign along the boat's side read: "Man the Oars and Ride the Crest. Harold Stassen, He's the Best."[12] The parody was clear to the conventioneers: Roosevelt's 1944 theme song had been "Row, Row, Row with Roosevelt."

The sudden shift of Pennsylvania delegates to Dewey forced the other candidates into a flurry of meetings to stop Dewey's surge. On Tuesday afternoon, Stassen, Taft, Earl Warren, Pennsylvania's James Duff (with his twenty-five-plus delegates), and Michigan governor Kim Sigler (representing Vandenberg) met to try to stem the Dewey tide by pooling their delegate support behind one man. Taft, however, refused to support Stassen, and Stassen returned the rebuff by refusing to support Taft. Stassen tried to persuade Taft to support Vandenberg as a compromise, but Taft refused that option as well. The meeting adjourned.[13]

The next morning, the group met again, and it appeared this time that they had come to a compromise. Taft held a press conference to announce that "the Dewey blitz has been stopped" and to claim control of 630 delegates. But it was clear that the stop-Dewey coalition had not gone any further toward agreeing on a candidate, and certainly Taft and Stassen did not control their delegates to the degree that they could swing them all to the other man. Their only real strategy was to stall for time, just as the Dewey people were insisting that balloting begin before the stop-Dewey group could coalesce around a candidate. That afternoon, New Jersey and Missouri shifted to Dewey, then Indiana and Massachusetts. The stop-Dewey coalition met again, and again no candidate was named.[14]

The good weather that had blessed the Republicans on the first three days of their convention deserted them on Thursday. The temperature in the Philadelphia Convention Hall reached a hot and sweaty 102 degrees, and *Time* complained that it was hot enough to grow orchids.[15] On the first ballot, taken on Thursday afternoon, it was clear that the Dewey forces had successfully steamrolled the opposition. Dewey collected 434 delegate votes to Taft's 224. Stassen remained in third with 157, and Vandenberg and Warren collected little more than their own state delegates with 62 and 59.

An hour later, at five o'clock, a second ballot revealed that Dewey was moving quickly to nomination with 515 votes, an increase of 80 votes and only 33 away from the magic number needed to nominate.[16]

The fragile stop-Dewey coalition pushed for a recess to buy time to meet again and bring their forces to bear. But when Dewey's people at the podium did not object to the call for recess it was a signal to many in the Convention Hall that the battle was over. During the second ballot vote, Connecticut, Arizona, and Vandenberg's Michigan had agreed to support Dewey on the third ballot, and their votes would be enough to put Dewey over the top and win the nomination. But in one last act of desperation, Taft called Stassen and asked him to release his delegates to him. Stassen, still blinded by the long-gone hope of a deadlock, said he would consider it after the third ballot. Taft realized that all chances were gone and released his delegates to Dewey; Vandenberg followed, then the reluctant Stassen. That was followed on the floor by the obligatory unanimous ballot for Dewey.[17] Dewey's acceptance speech on Friday, wrote *Life*, was "remarkably earnest and humble." His theme, as it would be throughout the campaign, was unity.[18] The Republicans believed they had nominated the next president.

The only issue remaining was to choose Dewey's running mate. A problem developed when House Majority Leader Charles Halleck of Indiana believed he had been given assurances from Dewey's people that he would be on the ticket with Dewey if he delivered Indiana at the crucial point between the first and second ballots. Halleck did as he was told, delivering the entire Indiana delegation even though fully one-third preferred Taft. *Newsweek* reported: "Halleck's prompt announcement of [Indiana's decision] sent the Dewey stock up another notch." Halleck also had a hand in bringing Missouri over to Dewey—also at that important point in the balloting.[19]

But Halleck must have known that he would not be acceptable to Dewey. Halleck was one of the most powerful isolationists in Congress, and he had pushed hard to slash the Marshall Plan. To the internationalists in the party, particularly Vandenberg and John Foster Dulles, Halleck was anathema. In addition, the isolationist wing of the party was weakening as the Cold War heated up, and it was well beyond having the power to demand that one of its own be placed on the ticket. At the meeting to decide on Dewey's running mate (which was attended by both Vandenberg and Dulles) Halleck was removed from consideration almost immediately. This innerparty bickering would have been of little consequence except that it broke in the press. Halleck appeared spurned and tread on by the ungrateful and insensitive Dewey, while the incident revealed the old party split over foreign policy.[20]

On Friday morning, just before sunup, Dewey and his group decided on Warren. Warren immediately refused, citing the unimportance of the office. He promised, however, to give more thought to the offer. At 11:30 A.M. on Friday, Dewey promised to elevate the vice president's office to cabinet level, and Warren accepted. In the interim, Stassen had been asked to join the ticket if Warren refused, and Halleck had been told the bad news that he was out of consideration.[21]

The ticket received praise in the press. It was young, forward-looking, vigorous. "Barring a political miracle," *Time* reported, "it is the kind of ticket that could not fail to sweep the Republican Party back into power."[22] The newly named chairman of the Republican National Committee, Hugh Scott, called it "a dreamboat ticket."[23] It combined California and New York, which together accounted for one-fourth of the electoral votes needed to win in November.

The Republican party platform generally reflected the Taft-Vandenberg axis in the Senate. Vandenberg, Henry Cabot Lodge Jr. and Dulles made certain that the foreign policy planks reflected their internationalism, while the domestic planks generally contained Taft's fingerprints. At the insistence of Taft's people, the platform included a call for slum clearance and public housing. It also recognized a need for public health, a long-range farm program, old-age security, and conservation of natural resources. Despite objections from the South, planks were added supporting an antilynching law, an end to the poll tax, and desegregation of the armed forces. Not included were support for federal aid to education, despite a push from Taft's people, and an extension of the FEPC in deference to the South. Language was added, however, that called for legislation that would ensure "equal opportunity to work and advance in life [without restrictions because of] race, religion, color, or country of origin."[24] The Republicans also argued in their platform for state control of offshore oil reserves, a major bone of contention between southern states'-rights Democrats and the Truman administration, which wanted federal control over these reserves. It was a clear attempt to drive a wedge between Truman and the disgruntled southern conservatives.[26] All three of the GOP's major players (Dewey, Taft, and Vandenberg) found the platform acceptable. It was a long way from the character of the Eightieth Congress, but it passed easily and quickly.

The convention had presented an air of deadlock, a feeling that the party was stuck between Taft and Dewey and headed for another debacle like

1940. But by the time the convention began, Dewey had won the nomination and Taft had lost it. The primaries in Nebraska, Ohio, and Oregon had made it clear to those who would be voting for the nomination in Philadelphia later in the summer that Dewey was still a strong vote-getter and Taft was not. Electability was the key, and Taft could not convince those who mattered in the party that he could be elected. After the convention it was even clear to him. "Basically," Taft wrote a supporter after the convention to explain his loss, "we were not able to overcome the theory that I would make a weak candidate, an argument that affected politicians more than the average citizen."[26] *Atlantic Monthly*, in contrast, described Tom Dewey as he seemed just after the convention: "He is forward-looking and mature."[27] The Republicans had their man.

13

The Democrats Nominate Truman

While the Republicans resurrected their victorious spirit in the City of Brotherly Love, Truman went on a "nonpolitical" trip to the West. *Life* magazine went to great lengths to show the president in an unflattering light, speaking to empty halls, marching with his "buddies" in parades in Kansas City, spending taxpayers' money, and making mistakes in what was called his "new off-the-cuff style of speaking." *Newsweek* and *Time*, however, noticed that the crowds increased as the president's trip progressed, and in Los Angeles nearly one million people turned out to hear and see Truman. *Newsweek* also noticed a new "human Truman," less stilted in his speech, more natural, more "off the cuff." Even columnists Joseph and Stewart Alsop, who had been critical of Truman since he came to office, wrote of a new, more aggressive Truman who was campaigning like "a county sheriff in the Ozarks."[1] Truman's advisers intended the trip to be a sort of shakedown cruise that would prepare the president for several similar campaign tours to come. It was during this trip that Taft accused Truman of "blackguarding Congress at every whistle stop in the West." The Democratic National Committee responded by sending telegrams to the mayors of every city and town Truman visited: "PLEASE WIRE THE DEMOCRATIC NATIONAL COMMITTEE WHETHER YOU AGREE WITH SENATOR TAFT'S DESCRIPTION OF YOUR TOWN AS A QUOTE WHISTLE STOP END QUOTE."[3] It was another Taft blunder, and it added to Truman's image as a scrappy underdog who represented the common man.

In the months before the July convention the draft-Eisenhower movement had brought a brief flicker of unity to at least two of the several divergent groups in the Democratic party. Rebellious southern Democrats had particularly liked Eisenhower because they thought he could be prevailed upon to support states' rights.[3] The ADA had also thrown its support to Eisenhower, though considering him little more than a vehicle to victory in November, something that most in the party believed Truman could not provide. When Eisenhower refused the nomination, however, these two groups parted ways again, squared off, and prepared for a big convention fight over the volatile issue of civil rights for African Americans.

But the ADA faced a serious problem. When the scheme to unseat Truman and draft Eisenhower abruptly collapsed, it became clear immediately that there was no other Democrat who could possibly take the nomination away from the president. The ADA still believed, however, that Truman could not win in November. To join what appeared to be a losing cause and then to campaign for a candidate whose policies and character the ADA membership generally disliked hardly seemed worth the trouble. In addition, the Truman camp had marked the ADA as a group of traitors and scoundrels—only slightly less so than Wallace himself.

At first, the ADA resolved to work only for state and local candidates, give up on Truman, and then try to jockey for a position of leadership in the reconstruction of the Democratic party after the election. But Loeb and others in the ADA quickly came to see that they still maintained enough power in the party to influence the convention by having an impact on the party platform and even on the party's choice for vice-president. So they set their sights on three convention objectives. First, they would work to lessen the effects of Henry Wallace. The ADA and most liberals had concluded by the summer of 1948 that a split between Wallace and the Democrats was a walk-in for the Republicans, not only in the national election but in state and local elections as well. An attack on Wallace would minimize his impact. Second, they would attempt to have a strong civil rights plank inserted into the party platform at the convention. Not only was this a cause supported by ADA members, it would accomplish their first objective by stealing the civil rights issue from Wallace and the PCA. Civil rights had become one of the biggest *causes célèbre* of the PCA and an important plank in Wallace's platform. If the ADA could force civil rights on Truman and the Democrats, important northern black support would most likely shift to the Democrats. And third, the ADA would work toward drafting Hubert Humphrey, the most dynamic figure among them, as vice-presidential candidate.[4] They would prove successful in two of these three objectives.

The southern Democrats approached the convention with no less diligence in their resolve to keep any strong statement of civil rights out of the Democratic party platform. Like the ADA, they had given up on the possibility of nominating anyone other than Truman, and they intended to make their power felt by influencing the party's campaign platform and possibly by pushing for one of their own for vice-president. Also like the ADA, southern political leaders who had supported Eisenhower were less than popular with the Truman administration, but they believed they still maintained enough power in the party to sway the president away from civil rights at the convention.

All southern state delegates to the convention were free to vote for candidates other than Truman, but only delegates from Mississippi and Alabama were required to bolt the convention if Truman were nominated or if a strong civil rights plank were placed into the party platform. Thus the convention seemed to be on the verge of a fight between the North and the South, between the supporters of civil rights and the supporters of states' rights. The liberals, led by the ADA and Humphrey, had made it clear that a civil rights plank was the primary condition of their support for a Democratic candidate. The South had made it equally clear that it would not support a civil rights plank.

In the middle, of course, was Truman, trying desperately to walk a fine line between these two belligerent groups—but with little success. Truman had made promises (both public and private) to support civil rights, but in a preconvention turnabout he met with Congressman John Rankin of Mississippi and promised that a plank satisfactory to the South would be adopted at the convention. Rankin emerged triumphant from the meeting and told the press that the Democrats would be adopting the 1944 plank, "and I am certain it will be adhered to."[5] Again, Truman's bad balancing act satisfied no one.

Adding to the problems for the Democrats was the strong civil rights platform accepted by Dewey and the Republicans at their convention just three weeks before. Clearly, the Republicans were prepared to scoop up any votes from African Americans or moderate whites that the Democrats might drop as a result of not being able to push through their own civil rights plank. The Republicans had called for an antilynching law, an end to poll taxes, and desegregation of the armed forces. All this, however, had the ring of rhetoric without substance for many African Americans in light of the Eightieth Congress's dismal record on civil rights.[6]

In an attempt to split the Democrats even further, the Republicans had added a platform plank calling for state control of tidelands oil reserves. This question had been a point of contention between the southern states and the federal government since the end of the war. Truman had said that he believed that offshore oil reserves—outside the three-mile limit—should belong to the federal government. Ten southern states that had coastlines were affected, although only Texas and Louisiana had mined significant oil reserves off their coasts. For those two states the money from the reserves was an important addition to their state coffers, but for the rest of the South, the question was states' rights versus federal rights: should the states or the federal government control these reserves? The Republican platform had argued that the reserves belonged to the states. The administration had opted for federal rights. The issue allowed the Republicans to widen the split between the two political philosophies inside the Democratic party.[7]

The Democratic convention began on July 12 in a somber mood of impending defeat. It was a hot and muggy Monday in Philadelphia, with the temperature reaching a dripping 102 degrees in the Convention Hall at midday. There were a few pro-Truman signs: "Keep America Human with Truman." And the delegates were all provided with "Truman Victory Kits" that included a notebook, pencil, lighter fluid, and a whistle—to be used in the Democratic graveyard, *Time* reported.[8] The *New York Times* added that the only optimistic Democrat was a papier-mâché donkey perched above the Convention Hall entrance. It was, of course, supposed to be a combative figure, with its flashing red eyes, smoke belching from its nostrils, and a wagging tail. But even the donkey had trouble. The *Washington Post* reported, "The smoke that he now belches out of his nostrils . . . was at first mistakenly inclined to emerge from the other end of the animal." The red, white, and blue bunting draped over the streets of the city for the Republicans two weeks earlier was by now stained, faded, torn by summer storms, and flapping listlessly in the wind for the Democrats. Philadelphia taxi drivers joked that they should turn in their taxis for hearses, and the delegates themselves compared the convention to a funeral.[9]

One of the few bright spots of the convention was a speech by India Edwards, the feisty head of the Women's Division of the Democratic National Committee. Billed as the "first political speech broadcast on television," Edwards's speech perked up reporters who had quickly become bored with an obviously losing cause. Edwards's job was to get out the female vote, and to that end she spoke about high grocery prices and the rising cost of living, releasing balloons as symbols of inflation. Her speech was touted in the press as the convention's only note of optimism.[10]

A week before, the ADA had issued a press release stating boldly that it intended to be instrumental in writing the party's civil rights plank into the campaign platform. The organization said it would make Truman accountable for his earlier civil rights stance by forcing his own initiatives on the party.[11] "After all," as Humphrey later wrote, "the President did go out on a limb on civil rights long before the convention. The question in the people's minds was 'Did he mean it?' The answer would have been no, if the convention had weasel-worded this declaration."[12] The ADA press release was signed by fifty-one Democrats of various ilks, including many liberals who had briefly transgressed and supported the move to draft Eisenhower earlier in the spring.[13]

Humphrey was the main figure representing the ADA's position on the platform committee, and consequently he has received much of the credit for the civil rights plank that eventually came out of the committee meeting. But accompanying Humphrey were ADA members Esther Murray and Andrew Biemiller. It was the combined efforts of these three that ultimately produced the plank. And all three were determined. "I have always been a very strong civil rights person," Biemiller recalled, "and I made up my mind there was going to be a strong civil rights plank in that platform. . . . I just went there with an idea we were going to have a strong civil rights plank, and I fought for it and got it."[14]

On July 7 the platform committee met to begin the long process of hashing out the party's platform for the campaign. Three days later, Clark Clifford presented to the committee the civil rights plank that Truman would accept. It was virtually the same as the vaguely worded 1944 plank and was clearly designed to maintain control of the disaffected South. Clifford had decided to abandon civil rights at the convention (and abandon the advice from Rowe's memo that the South would not bolt the party) because through the spring political activities in Mississippi and other southern states had indicated that the South might initiate a successful bolt and split the party even further. "As I appraised and analyzed the political situation," Clifford later recalled, "I felt that it was important for us to hold onto the South. . . . I felt that there was no need to mortify the South by pressing for an extreme civil rights plank at the convention." Clifford added, "Most of [Truman's] friends at the time were urging him to go easy with the South."[15]

The ADA responded with its plank, which called for an anti-poll-tax bill, an antilynching bill, an end to discrimination in the armed forces, full and free political participation, equal opportunity in employment, and a permanent FEPC—all policies supported by the president in his February civil rights message and by the PCCR in *To Secure These Rights*. The plank was voted down in a subcommittee meeting and then in the full platform committee—overwhelmed by the strength of Truman's forces. Often the exchange of words in the committee hearing was strained, even heated. Humphrey accused the administration of a "sellout," and at one point Senator Scott Lucas of Illinois, a Truman operative, called Humphrey a "pipsqueak" and accused Biemiller, Humphrey, and the ADA of "attempting to wreck the Democratic party." Finally, Humphrey and Biemiller stormed out of the meeting, promising to take the ADA's minority report to the convention floor for a vote.[16] Southerners on the committee responded with their own rewriting of the platform, insisting that the federal government "shall not encroach upon the reserved powers of the states by the centralization of the government."[17] Sectionalism, the longtime burden of the Democrats, had once again become a divisive factor in the party. *Time* reported that "not since the South rebelled against Stephen Douglas in 1860 has the party seemed so hopelessly torn and divided."[18] Neither side would accept compromise. In the volatile politics of the postwar years there would have to be a winner and a loser.

Finally, after several marathon meetings, the committee (without the ADA) came up with a plank that it passed on to the convention delegates. It called for an end to "all racial, religious and economic discrimination," but it omitted the specifics of civil rights demanded by African Americans and liberals, and, in exchange, it omitted any reference to states' rights.[19]

The ADA delegates, caucusing at a fraternity house near the Convention Hall, chose Biemiller to deliver the ADA-worded minority report to the convention the next day, Wednesday, July 14. On Tuesday night, the ADA was encouraged when a large group of liberal delegates from the northern states opposed the seating of Mississippi's states'-rights delegates. Humphrey saw this as a signal "that many of our civil rights advocates were just as aroused about their beliefs as the state's [sic] rights people were about their own."[20] The ADA delegates then set out on a furious campaign lobbying the northern and western delegations in favor of the ADA minority plank; their main argument was that Truman had no chance to win in November, and that a strong civil rights plank would allow local liberal candidates to win African-American and liberal votes that might otherwise go to Wallace. Truman's people responded with their own late-night lobbying campaign, arguing that even though the ADA proposal contained nothing that Truman had not publicly endorsed himself, the party could not afford to lose the South over this issue.

The ADA minority report would be read to the convention delegates by Biemiller, but it was to be Humphrey who would make the plea to the convention in favor of the ADA-sponsored plank just before the floor vote, and clearly it would be Humphrey's speech that would make or break the plank. But Humphrey began to waffle. He had decided the night before that such a speech might not be politically wise. As a candidate for the Senate, he feared that taking such a strong stand against the White House might place him in direct odds with the administration. It took Biemiller, Joseph Rauh, and others three hours to convince Humphrey that he was the only well-known political figure among them and that a rousing speech from him would be necessary to push the plank through. Finally, at five in the morning, Humphrey agreed to deliver the speech, but only after he was allowed to preface his statements by commending the president for his courageous civil rights stand.[21]

The next day, Wednesday, the South fired the first shot. Former governor of Texas Dan Moody asked the convention to accept a statement affirming states' rights in its platform as it had done in the past: "Traditionally, it has been and it remains a part of the faith of the Democratic party that the Federal Government shall not encroach upon the reserved powers of the states by centralization of [the] government." Two other minority reports were delivered that afternoon, one by an African-American member of the credentials committee who reminded the convention delegates of the racial inequality and cruelty against blacks in the South. He was shouted down by the southern delegations, which brought sympathy for the ADA's upcoming civil rights messages. Biemiller then delivered his report, asking the delegates "to support the president in guaranteeing these basic and fundamental principles: the right to full and equal opportunity of employment, the right to security of persons, and the right of equal treatment in the service and defense of our nation."[22] Then Humphrey spoke: "There will be no hedging," he told the delegates from the podium, "and there will be no watering down, if you please, of the instruments and principles of the civil rights program. . . . We are one hundred and seventy-two years late. . . . I say this," to the states' righters, "that the time has arrived in America for the Democratic party to get out of the shadow of states' rights and to walk forthrightly into the bright sunshine of human rights."[23] The speech catapulted Humphrey from a thirty-seven-year-old mayor of Minneapolis into one of the leaders of American liberalism and into the forefront of the coming civil rights movement. Clifford recalled Humphrey's speech as "high rhetoric—beautifully crafted, eloquent, memorable."[24]

Humphrey's speech carried the day. In the roll-call votes that followed, Moody's resolution was shouted down by a vote of 925 to 309. The Biemiller-Humphrey resolution was adopted 651 1/2 to 582 1/2, with strong support from western and northern delegates. The ADA had scored a rousing success that was about to divide the party.[25]

The southerners had gambled and lost. Generally, the southern and border states had voted to oppose the Biemiller-Humphrey civil rights plank, while the northern and western states had supported it. But it was the support from the northern big city bosses that made the real difference. They desperately needed the African-American urban vote in the upcoming local elections, and they feared that without it their candidates would be swept away in what most expected to be a Republican landslide.[26] Following the vote, Alabama delegate Eugene "Bull" Conner began shouting to chairman Sam Rayburn to announce that the Alabama delegation was going to walk out of the convention. He was not recognized.[27]

That evening, Rayburn asked for nominations from the floor for president. Ellis Handy, representing the Alabama delegation, rose and announced that his state's delegates had been instructed "never to cast their vote for a Republican, never to cast their vote for Harry Truman, and never to cast their vote for any candidate with a civil rights program such as adopted by this convention. We bid you good-bye." In fact, only half the state's delegates had been pledged to walk out, and after trying to wrestle the Alabama standard from a stubborn delegate who refused to leave, an unvanquished thirteen Alabama delegates and the entire Mississippi delegation, led by the 260-pound former governor Hugh White, unfurled a rebel battle flag and strutted out of the convention center into a pouring rain. They had been unsuccessful in bribing the conductor of the convention band to play "Dixie" as they marched.[28]

Most of the southern delegates who remained would not (or could not by prearrangement) vote for Truman. It looked as though Arkansas's Ben Laney would be the recipient of the remaining southern votes, but he made it clear he could not run as the Democratic party's candidate with a strong civil rights plank in the platform. Georgia delegates cast their votes for their senator and favorite son Richard Russell, and most of the South followed. Russell received 263 votes to Truman's 947½. All of Russell's votes were from the South. In the end, North Carolina was the only southern state to vote for Truman's nomination.[29]

For the members of the ADA and most northern liberals the result of the floor fight was an astounding victory. "In the long run," Loeb wrote, "this successful fight may well prove to have a significance as great as the nomination [of Truman]. Finally, after generations of effort, the strangle hold of the reactionary South on the Democratic Party has been broken. . . . It is a momentous occasion," he added. "The result is that the Democratic Party has the most liberal platform ever adopted by a major party in America."[30] To another correspondent, he wrote, it "was the greatest single accomplishment of the ADA or the UDA before it. It will undoubtedly be recorded in the history books."[31] It was indeed the most liberal platform in the nation's history. The South would remain a force in the Democratic party for the future, but the Democrats had come to a crossroads in the summer of 1948 and the party had made a momentous decision. The northern-liberal-urban-black coalition had proved itself more powerful and more important than the votes of the segregationist South and in the future would dominate the political posture of the party. Future Democratic party can-

Truman delivers his acceptance speech at the 1948 Democratic convention. From the Collections of the Library of Congress.

didates would try to straddle the race issue in an attempt to maintain control of both the South and the northern liberals and blacks, but the weight of the issue had begun to tilt toward the North and away from the South in 1948. After the floor vote to accept the ADA-written minority plank, Walter White of the NAACP found a jubilant Biemiller, who recalled, "I never saw a man so happy in my life. He grabbed me as soon as he could get to me . . . and just hugged me all over."[32] White had reason to be happy. The Democrats had chosen the high road. The result was African-American political clout that would manifest itself in long strides toward desegregation in the 1950s and 1960s supported by the strength of the Democratic party. After 1948, the South was forced to follow.

The southerners who rebelled against the party headed off to Birmingham and the road to a second third party and another splintering of the seemingly factious Democrats. The ADA delegates reluctantly supported Truman's nomination; he won easily on the first ballot sometime after midnight on Thursday, July 15. His first choice for vice-president was Supreme Court justice William O. Douglas, but after three days of deliberation with his family in Oregon, Douglas turned the job down on Monday.[33] Truman then turned to an old political hand, Senator Alben Barkley of Kentucky. Barkley had held his state's delegates in line in favor of the president's watered-down civil rights plank and against the Biemiller-Humphrey minority plank.

Truman gave an inspired speech, despite the late hour and despite the broad divisions in the party. In a bold move that changed the attitude of the conventioneers from defeat to hope, the president announced that he would call the Eightieth Congress back into session and force it to make good on the Republican party's platform pledges made just two weeks before. As if awakened from the dead, the convention delegates rose and applauded their candidate. Truman, it seemed, was ready for a fight.

14

The Campaigns

The Democrats had begun their convention under a cloud of doom and gloom; the process seemed little more than a formality to precede their impending November defeat. But on July 18 the *New York Times* reported that the convention adjourned "with fire in its eye, in place of the glazed look of a week ago." The reason for the abrupt change in attitude was a bombshell dropped by Truman in his acceptance speech delivered at 2 A.M. on July 15. He would call Congress back into summer session to make good, as he said, on the Republican campaign platform. "On the twenty-sixth day of July, which out in Missouri we call 'Turnip Day,' I am going to call Congress back." He said he would ask Congress to pass laws to halt rising prices, to meet the growing housing crisis, and to aid education. He would also ask for a national health program, civil rights legislation, "which they say they are for; an increase in the minimum wage, which I doubt very much they are for," and an extension of Social Security coverage and increased benefits, "which they say they are for." And he promised to ask for additional funds for public power projects like the REA that had brought power to most of rural America.

"Now my friends," Truman went on, "if there is any reality behind that Republican platform, we ought to get some action from a short session of the Eightieth Congress. . . . They are going to try to dodge their responsibility . . . but I am here to say that [I am] not going to let them get away with it."[1] Truman and the Eightieth Congress had been conducting an ongoing feud at least since Taft-Hartley was passed, but here Truman made it clear that the record of the Eightieth Congress was going to be a major campaign issue and that he would force Dewey and the Republicans to accept responsibility for its actions—and inactions. Thus the Democrats went home from their convention with a degree of hope that even if the candidate appeared less than promising, there was at least a strategy for victory instead of surrender. Truman, it seemed, had actually had the guts to throw down a gauntlet to the Republicans.

Truman's Turnip Day reference came from an old Missouri adage that said, "On the twenty-fifth of July, sow turnips wet or dry." He later told reporters that "a half pound of seed will sow a couple of acres of turnips," possibly implying that a few seeds sowed in late July would reap great rewards on election day in November.[2] The scheme was hailed by Democrats and the press as innovative, but as a political tactic it was not that new. Although a president had not called back Congress in an election year for nearly one hundred years (and apparently never as a campaign tactic), both Al Smith and Franklin Roosevelt had used the tactic during their terms as governors of New York.[3] Truman's plan for the Turnip Session seemed to have originated in late June, when a memo (most likely compiled by Clifford but emanating from the Wardman Park strategy group) circulated among his campaign staff and advisers.[4] This memo, entitled "Should the President Call Congress Back?," demanded "bold and daring steps." It argued that calling a special session would "focus attention on the rotten record of the 80th Congress . . . force Dewey and Warren to defend the actions of Congress . . . split the Republican party on major issues," and show Truman "leading a crusade for the millions of Americans ignored by the 'rich man's Congress.'"[5] But not all in Truman's circle agreed. George Elsey at first called the idea "unwise" and warned that it might further split the Democratic party. But Clifford and the others prevailed, even winning over Elsey. For Clifford the situation had become desperate; the administration had to move from its defensive posture and inject some spirit into the campaign. Truman "was on his own five-yard line," Clifford recalled later; "there were only three minutes left, and the only thing that could win the game for him was a touchdown. Now, why would he just go ahead and run the plays through the line? He had to try any sort of innovative, surprising, startling kind of tactic that might work because he had everything to gain and nothing to lose."[6]

Truman's call for a special session did push the Republicans into a corner. They had adopted a fairly liberal platform in Philadelphia that included planks regarding issues that the Eightieth Congress had refused even to consider. This, of course, had a great deal to do with Dewey's influence on the convention, and it also exposed the divisions in the Republican party between the liberal Dewey supporters and the Old Guard Taftites. The Republican platform called for federal aid for slum clearance and public housing, an extension of Social Security to cover more Americans, a health plan, the promotion of education, and a fairly significant civil rights plank that included an antilynching law and legislation outlawing the poll tax.[7] This liberal platform was clearly an attempt by Dewey and his supporters to separate themselves from the conservative record of the Eightieth Congress. For Truman and his advisers, however, the division quickly became a campaign issue.

On July 27 the special session began with the president delivering his message to an incensed and even discourteous Republican Congress (many even refused to stand as he entered the chamber). He asked for emergency legislation to stop inflation and solve the housing shortage. He also asked for specific legislation to aid education, increase the minimum wage, and extend Social Security benefits. He asked for action on civil rights, health insurance, a bill to replace the Taft-Hartley Act, and a long-range farm program. Clifford later recalled that this strategy was a gamble. "Our greatest concern," he wrote in his memoirs, was "that they might pass two or three bills during the special session, and try to take the issue of a recalcitrant Congress away from us."[8] But most of this proposed legislation had already been introduced by the administration and rejected by the Republicans. It seemed doubtful that in an eleven-day special session the Republicans would push through major liberal legislation that they had rejected (or refused to consider) during the regular session. Clearly, Truman and his campaign strategists were banking on that probability.

The Republicans were more than accommodating to the Democrats' strategy. Publicly, they said the session was a blatant example of politics, and most promised that nothing would be done. Several congressmen, including Iowa representative Ben Jensen and Ohio senator Frederick Smith, wanted simply to adjourn following Truman's speech.[9] In a radio address, Taft called the entire scheme a "political maneuver," adding that Congress "would be fully justified in adjourning at once until the election is over." He later insisted, with obvious frustration, "I'm not going to give that fellow [Truman] anything."[10] Herbert Brownell, Dewey's campaign manager, made it clear that the Republicans were merely waiting for Dewey to occupy the White House and that they had no intention of doing anything until then: "The Republican platform calls for the enactment of a program by a Republican Congress under the leadership of a Republican President. Obviously this cannot be done in a rump session called at a political convention for political purposes in the heat of a political campaign."[11] And Leslie Arends, chairman of the House Rules Committee, said, "We'll put controls on turnips, but nothing else."[12] House Speaker Joseph Martin admitted that under the circumstances little would be done, but he promised "plenty of action" from the Eighty-first Congress.[13]

From Albany, there was only silence from Dewey. He seemed unaware of the difficulties a special session might cause his campaign. In a letter to his mother he called the session "a nuisance but no more."[14] But as the special session got under way, Dewey apparently began to realize that there would be problems ahead if the Republicans in Congress simply sat on their hands. He sent Brownell to Washington to goad Taft and other congressional leaders into at least passing a semblance of a program. Taft insisted that he would consider only bills that made it out of committee and onto the floor of the Senate on their own initiative, that is, he would not apply pressure to party committee chairmen. Dewey had hoped that Congress would at least pass an amendment to the Displaced Persons Act (which had been passed by the Eightieth Congress and discriminated against Catholics and Jews). Without an amendment, such a bill could hurt his chances in northeastern urban areas.[15] But Congress refused to act.

On August 7 Congress adjourned, despite an eleventh-hour plea from the White House to continue on until the job was completed. The legislators did, however, pass a weak inflation bill that tightened some consumer credit; they rejected the administration-supported housing bill and passed a weaker bill. They voted $5 million to purchase automobiles for disabled veterans and $65 million for the construction of the United Nations building in New York. All other proposals from Truman were either postponed, bottled up in committee, or ignored.[16]

The only action in the Turnip Session that might have been detrimental to Truman's campaign was a filibuster carried on by Democratic senator John Stennis of Mississippi in response to an anti-poll-tax bill called up by Republican Ken Wherry of Nebraska. Clearly, Wherry hoped to turn the tables on the Democrats by calling attention to the divisions in their party and forcing the hand of southern senators over the civil rights issue.[17] This undoubtedly embarrassed Truman, and it may have jeopardized some African-American votes. The NAACP, in what may have been a direct attempt to counter the Republican ploy, issued a press release entitled "What Did the 80th Congress Do on Legislation Supported by the NAACP?" The answer was clear: "nothing on the anti-lynching bill; it refused to act on anti-Jim Crow travel. . . . On the anti-poll tax, it did nothing."[18]

The Eightieth Congress had again done nothing, and Truman was about to let America know it. On August 6 he called it a "do-nothing session."[19] Twelve days later, at a news conference, he called the session the work of "the do-nothing Congress," and he did not let up after that.[20] It was, said Clifford, "an expression that we thought had staying power, and was to become part of the American political language."[21] A memo passed among the Wardman Park group showed that the Democratic strategists were beginning to see the future: "Dewey is in a horrible dilemma. If he speaks, the Congress[ional] Republicans resent it. If he doesn't, the country resents it. . . . The limelight is now on a battle between the President and Congress."[22]

The Turnip Session allowed Truman to distinguish between his own policies and those of the Eightieth Congress instead of going head-to-head against Dewey. Dewey was a liberal Republican. He had a fairly strong civil rights record, and he maintained a strong political association with several organized labor groups in New York. The Republican party platform, engineered by Dewey operatives, was described by none other than FDR aide Samuel Rosenman as fit for any New Dealer to support.[23] Truman was about to begin a campaign against a powerful, experienced candidate whose domestic policies were not much different from his own and whose foreign policy, it was conceded early, would not deviate from the administration's own objectives. The Turnip Session allowed Truman to point to his own agenda that in many ways compared to the New Deal and compare it to the conservative (openly anti–New Deal) record of the Eightieth Congress. Truman was able to cast himself as the candidate of the people against a Republican party that had exhibited little concern for the average American. The Turnip Session also served to split the Republicans even further than they already were, but, more important, that split became apparent to the voters. And it allowed the Democrats to exploit the split by telling voters that Dewey as president, no matter how much he desired to help the average American, would be stymied and stifled by Taft, Joseph Martin, and the Old Guard–run Congress, whose own agenda was directed at destroying the New Deal and promoting the rich on the back of the common man.[24]

Truman and Dewey hit the hustings by train at about the same moment. Truman left Union Station in Washington on the *Ferdinand Magellan,* a train built for Roosevelt, on September 17. Dewey's train, the *Victory Special,* left Albany two days later. Both men had already traveled the nation on campaign excursions: Truman on his "nonpolitical" trip to California in June and Dewey during his various primary fights in the spring. The 1948 election was the last one in which television did not play a significant part, and about the only way to take the election and its issues and symbols to the American people was to speak to them from the back of a train. Radio, of course, was important in carrying campaign messages, and FDR had certainly found success in using it, but a cross-country train trip was still considered the tried-and-true method of campaigning.

The mood of Dewey's campaign was less than vigorous—a kind of going-through-the-motions campaign. All the major polls had shown that the contest was essentially over, that the governor of New York was well on his way to a landslide victory. Consequently, Dewey's campaign strategy did not go far beyond simply avoiding the appearance of taking the voters or the election for granted and helping local and congressional Republican candidates with their campaigns.

In the early going, Dewey received advice from several directions. The Republican party national committee chairman, Hugh Scott, insisted on a vigorous, active campaign to satisfy local party professionals and precinct captains. But for Dewey the campaign message revolved around statesmanship, and he often said he refused to get into the gutter with Truman. He also may have believed that attacking a sitting president might not have boded well for the nation in what was considered a time of crisis. It certainly had not worked in 1944, when Dewey went on the attack against Roosevelt and was promptly trounced. His chief advisers (Russell Sprague, Edwin Jaeckle, and Elliot Bell, his campaign manager Herbert Brownell, and his speechwriter Stanley High) all agreed that the election was already won and that the campaign should proceed along the high road, without major confrontation. Also, Illinois senator Everett Dirksen advised Dewey to be cautious on agricultural issues, relying on the natural loyalty of the nation's farmers to the Republican party.[25] Meanwhile, farm prices were dropping, and Truman was traveling through the farm states attacking the Eightieth Congress for hurting farmers and reminding them that it was the Democrats who had been the party of agricultural rejuvenation in the 1930s.[26]

Dewey's *Victory Special* was more than a campaign train. It was filled out as a portable, yet plush, campaign headquarters. Included were forty-one campaign staffers, along with the candidate's most important advisers. Allen Dulles went along to act as foreign policy liaison between Dewey and Allen's brother John Foster Dulles, who was at the UN conference in Paris. They conferred daily over a teletype machine that accompanied the campaign train. Along for the ride were ninety-two journalists, all of whom were treated well. The food was good, with a variety of choices, but most often roast beef. Reporters and others sent out their laundry and picked it up the next day down the line. The evening fare was usually martinis and bridge. And when the train stopped overnight, reporters were treated to the best hotel facilities in town.[27] On Truman's train, the situation was less comfortable. His entourage may have cavorted late into the night with bourbon and poker, but they washed their clothes in wash basins. Clifford recalled: "We slept in cramped quarters, and . . . how and when to get our laundry done became something of an obsession."[28] Both campaigns had money problems, but it was, surprisingly, the Republicans whose problems seemed to be the worst. Dewey's people had great difficulty raising funds for what was so obviously a sure thing, while the Democrats spent some $700,000 more than Dewey.[29]

The result of the advice Dewey was getting from his advisers and aides was to wage an amazingly listless campaign filled with speeches that seeped with platitudes, triteness, and bromides. When he spoke to workers in industrial districts, he told them that labor must be free: "Unless labor is free," he said often, "none of us are free." In the West he often called for a need to increase the number of fish in the nation's rivers. In late September, in Phoenix, he delivered a speech that has come to symbolize the blandness of his campaign. Here Dewey argued only the obvious: "You know that your future is still ahead of you." Elsewhere he called for such unquestioned objectives as a better future for the nation's children. He said that free enterprise was a good system, that what the nation needed was teamwork, that the nation's industries should be kept strong, that the United States should be cordial to South America, wage peace, tell other lands about America, and stay strong. In Seattle in late September, he said: "We are one people. We are dependent upon one another.... It is imperative that we in America remain strong and grow stronger.... We still have a big job ahead of us and in this I want you to know that your next National Administration will have a warm and urgent interest and an active and constructive part." He also called for "the expansion of existing power facilities wherever possible" and that in "developing our rivers we must also aggressively maintain and perfect the use of fish ladders."[30] Dewey was evasive during press conferences. Often when asked specific questions, he would respond by referring reporters to a past speech in which he covered that issue. Even the always complimentary *Time* magazine began to complain after a while, calling Dewey's speeches "not electrifying" and largely "solemn." *Time* added that the nation's voters must by now be tiring of Dewey's well-worn platitude: "As never before we need a rudder to our ship of state."[31] But it was the *Louisville Courier-Journal* that best summed up the banality of Dewey's speech-making: "No presidential candidate in the future will be so inept that four of his major speeches can be boiled down to these historic four sentences: Agriculture is important. Our rivers are full of fish. You cannot have freedom without liberty. Our future lies ahead."[32]

On at least two occasions Dewey wanted to go on the offensive against Truman, but both times his advisers insisted he moderate his attacks. In Gary, Indiana, Truman seemed to take name-calling about as far as possible by comparing Dewey to Hitler, Mussolini, and Tojo, adding that Republicans "have silently undermined democratic institutions." Dewey wanted to respond, but his advisers insisted he stick to the high road, and his wife reminded him of the problems he had encountered in 1944 when he tried to attack Roosevelt.[33] In a speech in Erie, Pennsylvania, in mid-October, Dewey took the offensive, apparently on his own, and attacked Truman's Taft-Hartley veto. After the speech he was in turn attacked by his advisers and told to avoid all controversy if he wanted to win the election.[34] Dewey relented and continued plodding along, going through the motions.

Such a campaign style can only ignore the issues—and there were issues. Thus every issue that Dewey ignored was, by default, won over by Truman. For instance, Dewey might have forced a further split in the Democratic party by confronting Truman on civil rights, which might have won him large numbers of African-American votes, one of the real prizes of the 1948 election. But Dewey, whose civil rights record needed no apologies, chose instead to ignore the issue, wanting not to alienate African Americans on one side or white southerners on the other. Truman, then, felt no need to defend his own civil rights record during the campaign, and he won that issue (and black votes) by default simply because of the gestures he had made toward civil rights during late 1947 and early 1948.

Dewey also chose to ignore the issue of communism. Wallace became the main conduit for most of the soft-on-communism charges during the campaign, and that left Truman mostly free from criticism on that point. It remained a volatile issue in 1948, but Dewey decided to leave it alone despite advice from Eisenhower that it would be an important issue in the campaign and even after a couple of stumbles by Truman left him vulnerable on the issue.[35] Early in the campaign year Truman said, "I like Old Joe," referring to Stalin. He added that Stalin was a "decent fellow," held hostage by hard-liners in the Politboro.[36] It was hardly a major error, but in one of the most electrically charged eras of the Cold War, when Truman himself had said that Stalin's words could not be trusted, and in the midst of a campaign, such a misstep might have opened wide doors to severe and damaging criticism. The statement brought an uproar from a few Republicans who clearly saw the statement as an opportunity to pin the soft-on-communism badge on Truman. Dewey, however, backed away. In another incident in early August, Truman called the growing Alger Hiss–Whitaker Chambers case a "red herring."[37] This case was beginning to build just as the 1948 campaign was getting under way, and although it did not have any real impact on the election it did seem to back up some Republican arguments that there were, in fact, communists in the State Department.

Whitaker Chambers, a writer and editor for *Time*, had admitted before the House Committee on Un-American Activities that he had been a communist in the 1930s, and among his communist colleagues at that time was Alger Hiss, then a member of the State Department and now, in August 1948, head of the Carnagie Endowment for International Peace.[38] This seemed to offer evidence of what some Republicans had been charging for years: that there were communists among the New Dealers and that communists had influenced American postwar foreign policy—at least partly because Hiss had been an adviser at Yalta. It gave Republicans the ammunition they needed to argue that America was losing the Cold War because communists in the State Department were sabotaging the nation's foreign policy. Truman's remark that it was all a "red herring" might well have given Dewey the opportunity to claim that Truman was being too soft on communism. In fact, most Americans had come to believe that the spy investigations were important to the nation's future—it was a political issue waiting to be picked up.[39] But Dewey had been burned in the 1944 campaign when he had tried to make a connection between FDR and Earl Browder, then the head of the American Communist party. Dewey also found it a degrading issue, beneath his own character, and he was determined to run a clean campaign and stay out of the mud where Truman seemed most at home. When his advisers pushed him to take up the issue, Dewey responded that he would only "fleck it lightly."[40] In late September, in Los Angeles, Dewey made his only strong anticommunist speech, accusing Truman of "giving aid and comfort to the enemies of our system. . . . Millions upon millions of people have been delivered into Soviet slavery while our administration has tried appeasement one day and bluster the next." He concluded with a statement that he had used often, at least since the Oregon primary: "But in this country we'll have no thought police. We will not jail anybody for what he thinks or believes."[41] Again, there was no issue.

Truman opened another door for the Dewey campaign in early October, just as the crisis in Berlin threatened to heat up. Problems there had begun in June when Stalin imposed a blockade of all surface routes through eastern Germany to West Berlin, and Truman reacted with a tremendous airlift of supplies to the stranded people of West Berlin. The situation occasionally sparked through the summer and fall of 1948, and in October it was leaked to the press that Truman was planning to send Chief Justice of the Supreme Court and his good friend, Fred Vinson, to Moscow to try to resolve the problem. But Truman had neglected to inform Secretary of State George Marshall (then in Paris negotiating with the Soviets) of the plan, and Marshall reacted by threatening to resign if Vinson made the trip. Truman backed away immediately, but it appeared in the press that he was trying to circumvent his own secretary of state, the venerable Marshall. It was, recalled Clifford, "the worst mistake of the Truman campaign," and he added, "I was astonished that Dewey did not exploit it."[42] *Time* compared the incident to Truman's mishandling of Wallace's Madison Square Garden speech in September 1946 which embarrassed Truman's then secretary of state James Byrnes and resulted in Wallace's dismissal.[43] Dewey's only response to Truman's blunder was to say of the incident in a speech some ten days later that "the Democrats didn't let their left hand know what their right hand was doing."[44]

With the Republicans quiet on the Vinson issue, Truman was able to turn the slip to his own advantage. In a speech in Miami later in October, Truman defended his plan to send Vinson to Moscow, arguing that he was prepared to do anything for world peace, even if it meant upsetting his secretary of state or jeopardizing his own presidential campaign.[45] Because Dewey did not respond, that is how the incident was generally perceived.

If Dewey seemed reluctant to do battle with Truman on domestic affairs, he was even more unwilling to confront the president over foreign policy. In the 1944 campaign against Roosevelt, Dewey had conceded to a campaign that excluded foreign policy, mostly as a gesture toward a united war effort. Roosevelt's secretary of state Cordell Hull and Dewey's foreign policy adviser John Foster Dulles both agreed that such an abstention was necessary for the good of the country in wartime. Four years later, Dewey took the same route for generally the same reason. Relations between the United States and the Soviets appeared to be growing increasingly worse, and many Americans believed that war was imminent. A united foreign policy was necessary, Dewey and Dulles believed, in the face of the growing Soviet menace. But probably more important, Dewey generally approved of Truman's foreign policy initiatives, as did Dulles and Arthur Vandenberg. Both Dulles and Vandenberg had been involved in most of the major decisions made by the Truman administration on foreign policy issues. This bipartisan foreign policy was heralded by both parties and in the press as presenting a united America, standing in opposition to the forces of world communism. Foreign policy, it seemed, was an issue that must be raised above politics in these times of crisis. But from a political standpoint, the bipartisan plan gave Truman a tremendous advantage. It was extremely popular with the American people, and as president of the United States Truman stood alone at the head of the nation's foreign policy. The rest, including Dewey and the Republicans, appeared simply to follow along behind, approving the president's initiatives. Thus all foreign policy issues were removed from the campaign.

The Republican plan to follow the administration's lead on foreign policy emerged in late July when Vandenberg, Dewey, and Dulles met in

Washington to discuss the party's stance on the Berlin crisis. On July 24 Dewey told reporters that "the present duty of Americans is not to be divided by past lapses but to unite to surmount present danger. We shall not allow domestic partisan irritations to divert us from this indispensable unity." That policy, he concluded, was the Vandenberg policy—which was essentially the administration's policy.[46]

Truman's campaign strategists expected this meeting of the Republican minds to result in Dewey and Vandenberg emerging with an opposition foreign policy stance that they would take into the campaign. For Democratic strategists in the White House, the Republicans seemed to have little choice. The Eightieth Congress was such a liability to Dewey that the natural direction for his campaign was toward foreign policy issues. But the Republicans demurred.[47]

In September, just as discussions over Berlin were going badly in Paris and the administration's foreign policy was vulnerable to attack, Dewey, Vandenberg, and Dulles again sat down to gauge the direction the Republican party's foreign policy should take. And again the policy did not change. To reporters after the meeting, Vandenberg said: "Regardless of political differences at home, we are serving notice on the world that America is united to protect American rights everywhere.... We shall not be in controversy over the basic fact that America is united against aggression and against the foes of freedom." The *New York Times* added that "Senator Vandenberg's statement was construed as a warning that American foreign policy would show no substantial change regardless of who was elected President in November."[48] Again, and seemingly without knowing it, the Republicans conceded the campaign's foreign policy leadership to Truman.

It was Dulles, more than Vandenberg or Dewey, who was the chief architect of this plan. All three men supported Truman's general policy of containment, but Dulles feared that Dewey and Vandenberg would have a falling-out over foreign policy in the middle of the campaign, and he worked hard to keep both men moving in the same direction on foreign policy issues, which meant seeing that Dewey supported Vandenberg's policies. The two meetings between the three men were designed to keep Dewey in line, with Dulles acting more as a mediator between the two Republican leaders than as a conciliator for the administration's policies.[49]

Obviously, Dulles was successful; throughout the campaign, Dewey continued to support the Vandenberg policy that followed the administration's line.[50] Thus the very popular bipartisan foreign policy became Truman's foreign policy, and that freed the president to concentrate on domestic issues, on selling his own domestic program to the people while attacking the record of the Eightieth Congress. Dewey's me-tooism on foreign policy appeared weak in a time of crisis, while Truman appeared in control of the nation's foreign policy decisions.

Dewey's lethargic, issueless campaign drew some criticism, particularly in the press, but no Republican party operatives spoke out against the candidate's campaign style. The strategy in the Republican camp was clear from the beginning—take the high road, say nothing controversial, look like a statesman—and that was the advice Dewey received from his followers and his advisers. In a letter to Dewey just after his nomination, the chairman of the Portland, Oregon, Republican committee advised him as did so many others: "I hope . . . that there be no recriminations against the New Deal or the present administration. . . . I would rather like to see you completely ignore Mr. Truman and his henchmen. . . . I hope that there will be an absolute minimum of discussion on the question of communism. I think it has been discussed entirely too much."[51] Dewey was applauded for his stoic, statesmanlike campaign. When he allowed the Vinson issue to pass without significant comment, *Time* wrote: "It was good judgement and good politics. He would gain both votes and stature by refusing to follow Truman's lead in playing politics with the nation's foreign policy."[52] At about the same time in the campaign, Marquis Childs wrote: "In light of history I believe he will get greater credit for his restraint on the issue of foreign policy than is accorded him today. If peace can somehow be preserved . . . Dewey's contribution will be clear."[53] Obviously, this campaign strategy (or lack of strategy) developed from the Republicans' belief that Dewey's election was a foregone conclusion. American voters had spoken in November 1946; the polls had made it clear that the nation was poised for a change in Washington. The votes had only to be counted in November. The result was a Dewey campaign of going through the motions, a campaign that neutralized most issues, another campaign of Republican me-tooism. Everything played well into Truman's hands.

The most popular aspect of the 1948 campaign was the Truman whistle-stop tour, and it had a significant impact on the outcome of the election. Unfortunately, historians and political scientists often give the tour short shrift because its effects cannot be measured. At the same time, popular writers occasionally make too much of the tour because of its popular appeal. But the significance of the tours (there were several) should not be underestimated. Through the whistle-stop tours, Truman made his face and personality visible to thousands of potential supporters in the last months of 1948, and it clearly made a difference.

The official campaign tour began on September 17. (There had been

trips before, including the so-called nonpolitical trip in June to California.)
The president's entourage included Clifford, special assistant George Elsey,
press secretary Charles Ross, the president's appointment secretary Mathew
Connelly, and a few others, including the president's physician and several
personal aides. Other members of the White House staff joined the group
at various times. Some members of the press, such as Jonathan Daniels of
the *Raleigh News and Observer*, made the entire trip at the president's request, but most pressmen joined the train and traveled with it for only a
short time. Charles Murphy and Oscar Ewing spent most of their time in
Washington feeding information to Clifford and the other speechwriters
on the train.[54]

The plans for the trip seem to have begun sometime in April 1948 after Truman spoke to a radio audience and chose to depart from his prepared
speech and launch into an impromptu discussion of foreign policy. "It was
the best summary of our foreign policy I have ever heard," wrote a *Washington Post* reporter. "If any of his aides were in the hall and failed to make
note of his performance, then they have missed the opportunity of a lifetime. If the President were to go to the people and talk to them as he talked
to us that night, he would be a very hard man to beat in November."[55]
Truman's speaking style, often described as wooden, had caused the nation
to wince at even his most important addresses. Clifford and others had come
to the conclusion that off-the-cuff speaking from an outline or brief notes
was more successful than reading from a prepared text.[56] In June, Clifford
and Oscar Chapman arranged the so-called nonpolitical tour across the
country to California. Officially, Truman was on his way to receive an hon-
orary degree from the University of California, but to Truman and his insiders it was a rehearsal to prepare the president for the campaign swings
that would come in September and October. "We learned a great deal about
how to conduct a campaign," Clifford recalled, "and these lessons were to
serve us well when the final round began in September. Without the June
trip, I doubt the whistle-stops would have succeeded in the fall."[57]

The various (and colorful) terminology associated with the 1948 campaign originated from the whistle-stop tours. The term "whistle stop" came
from Taft, who accused the president of "blackguarding Congress at every
whistle stop station in the West."[58] Of course, Truman made considerable
political hay from the remark by lambasting the Republicans at every little
train station for being insensitive to the needs of small-town America. It
was also on the June trip that Truman first criticized the record of the
Eightieth Congress. In addition, the most enduring symbol of the 1948
campaign, the well-known "Give 'em hell, Harry!" screamed from the audience, originated on that tour. Apparently, on September 17, as the

president's campaign train was about to leave Washington, vice-presidential nominee Alben Barkley called to Truman from the platform: "Mow 'em down, Harry!" According to Clifford, Truman responded, "I'm going to give 'em hell!" The press, covering the president's departure, picked up the line, and it spread across the country. At nearly every stop someone yelled, "Give 'em hell, Harry!" Truman's response was usually: "I'll just tell the truth and they'll think it's hell."[59] "Give 'em hell" has not only become a nationally known symbol of the 1948 campaign and Truman's come-from-behind victory but a symbol for all underdog political candidates, particularly the more feisty ones—a term often used to describe Truman.

The official whistle-stop tour began on September 17 and ended on October 2. Truman covered sixteen states over some eighty-three hundred miles, delivering 126 off-the-cuff speeches before thousands of people. His first stop was Rock Island, Illinois, and from there he went on to the plowing contest in Dexter, Iowa. The *Ferdinand Magellan* then traveled into Missouri, to Denver, Salt Lake City, and west to Los Angeles. Coming back through the Southwest, the train swung through Phoenix and then into Texas, where the president made major speeches at El Paso, San Antonio, Uvalde, and Bonham before heading north to Oklahoma City. From there, the train returned to the Midwest through Missouri, Illinois, Indiana, and then south into Barkley's home state of Kentucky. The campaign continued east into West Virginia and back to Washington on October 2.[60]

Between his first unofficial trip in June until he finally arrived home in Independence on October 31, Truman had traveled some 31,700 miles and delivered well over 350 speeches.[61] Throughout the trips money was in short supply, but generally all other problems were minor. William Bray, who traveled with the president for the entire trip, recalled later that the main problems were too many flowers, politicians who insisted on making long-winded speeches while introducing the president, and high school marching bands that would play only the much-too-slow "Missouri Waltz".[62]

Truman decided that the South (considered safely Democratic by his strategists) would not be visited on the campaign tour, leaving that region mostly to Barkley, who toured by airplane. The president's tour did concentrate hard on Texas, a state that Clifford insisted was crucial to a November win. There, Truman made use of past and future Speaker of the House Sam Rayburn, one of FDR's vice-presidents John Nance Garner, and the young and popular upstart Lyndon Johnson. In perhaps the only public display of criticism on the tour, Truman was booed in Waco for shaking hands with an African-American woman in the crowd.[63]

Part of the whistle-stop strategy was to keep the message simple and

Truman on the campaign trail in Idaho. From the collections of the Harry Truman Library.

brief while giving as many people as possible the once-in-a-lifetime opportunity to view the president of the United States and then to vote for the man in November. In rural areas Truman told farmers that the Republican Eightieth Congress was out to take away the advantages given them by the New Deal. In Dexter, Iowa, he said: "The Republican 80th Congress, under the false mask of economy, cut and threatened to kill the soil conservation program."[64] In Raleigh, North Carolina: "You stand for the Democratic farm program or you stand for the Republican wrecking crew of the 80th Congress." And in Colton, California: "I can prove the Republicans have in mind to sabotage the farm program."[65] In industrial regions he told workers that Taft-Hartley had removed their power to bargain effectively. In Newark, he reminded workers that "the Taft-Hartley Act was passed for one main reason—to weaken the strength of our labor unions so that ultimately wages could be forced down." In Detroit he said: "If the Congressional elements that made the Taft-Hartley Law are allowed to remain in power, and if these elements are further encouraged by the election of a Republican President, you men of labor can expect to be hit by a steady barrage of body blows." Everywhere he attacked the Eightieth Congress. In his Newark speech he added: "In 1946 two-thirds of you stayed at home and didn't vote. We got that awful 80th Congress as a result."[66] In Cleveland he said: "The performance of the do-nothing Congress during the last two sessions . . . has given the country a foretaste of what will happen if the Republicans are successful at the polls." And in Bonham, Texas, he said: "I could go on and on about Republican failures . . . after all, nothing I can say about the Republicans is as bad as their record."[67]

Truman also evoked the Democrats' age-old party line that the Republicans were the instruments of big business, the gluttons of privilege, the harbingers of wealth, and that he was the savior of the common man. In his Dexter, Iowa, speech he said: "The Republican reactionaries want an administration that will assure privilege for big business, regardless of what may happen to the rest of the nation."[68] In Los Angeles he said: "The Republican ideal, as I have seen it in action, is summed up in the phrase, 'big business first.'" And in Indianapolis he told a crowd: "The Republican party . . . favors the interests of a few small powerful business groups at the expense of the rest of the people."[69]

Truman often spoke to as many as fifteen audiences a day, stopping for only a few minutes in a small hamlet to introduce his family, make a few statements about a local incident or issue, and rail at the abysmal record of Congress before moving on. As he traveled, the campaign gained momentum, his simple messages became clearer, his speaking style improved, and more and more people came out to hear him.[70] In Rock Island, Illinois, a crowd of four thousand waited to see Truman at 5:30 A.M. At Dexter, Iowa, at the well-publicized plowing contest, Truman spoke to as many as one hundred thousand people in blazing 110-degree heat. As election results would show, people were listening.

Between October 11 and 16, a second Truman campaign trip hit Ohio, Indiana, and Wisconsin. In the last week of October he took his campaign on another trip, this time to Pennsylvania, than back to Indiana, Ohio, and on to New York, then briefly into New England. On his way to Missouri to wait out the election returns, he again passed through Ohio, Indiana, and Illinois, making more speeches as he went. He arrived in Independence on October 31.[71] On November 1, the day before the election, outside on the front lawn of his house, Truman hit the Republicans one last time: "Tomorrow you will be deciding the principles of the Democratic party—the party of the people—and the principles of the Republican party—the party of privilege."[72]

It is no wonder that Truman's 1948 whistle-stop campaign has become the ultimate example of the underdog winning the day and of how hard work, perseverance, and a big heart can win any victory no matter how illusive. Truman's victory in 1948, won at least in part from the back of a campaign train, has all the makings of a great historical myth. Clearly, the image of a hard fighter up against seemingly impossible odds had an impact on voters in the heartland. At the same time he carried a strong message that won votes.

Dewey, by the character of his campaign, was as responsible for losing the election as Truman was, by the character of his campaign, for winning it. Dewey's overconfidence generated a campaign that either negated the issues (as in domestic policy) or followed the administration's line (as in foreign policy). The overconfidence bred a strategy of making neither promises nor enemies, with the intent of a Republican presidency that would not be burdened by postelection promises to keep or enemies to mollify. At no time was Dewey's campaign directed toward winning the election, confronting Truman, or standing on the issues. The polls made it clear—there simply was no need.

Truman, in contrast, used the powers of his office through 1947 and 1948 to rebuild his coalition. Then he went on the hustings and took his message to the people. He kept his messages simple, appealed to the common man, and attacked the other party for its failings. The character of the campaign forced Truman to make few promises primarily because Dewey raised no issues that would force the president to respond. America listened to Truman because his foreign policy was successful and unchallenged in a time of crisis, and his domestic policy (challenged clearly and directly by the Eightieth Congress) promised some security in a time of economic uncertainty. Dewey could offer neither.

15

The Democratic Party Factions and the Election

By election day, November 3, the Democratic coalition was in place. At best, it was a reluctant coalition; most of its parts finally supported Truman only because there was simply no place else to go.

The southern dissidents (by now tagged the "Dixiecrats" by the press) went to Birmingham after the Democratic convention to form their own party.[1] The Birmingham convention, which convened on July 17, was a wild, raucous affair. Anyone could attend, and some six thousand "delegates" did. The only southern governor there was Mississippi's Fielding Wright, and the only southern senators in attendance were Mississippi's James Eastland and John Stennis. Other southern leaders presumably saw no victories coming from the convention and believed they could only lose political ground by attending. Even Thurmond planned to stay away, but at the last minute several of his supporters prevailed upon him to attend. The leadership of the convention was grabbed by Governor Wright, former Alabama governor Frank Dixon, Mississippi grocery store owner Wallace Wright, Texas judge Merrit Gibson, and Thurmond. With great fanfare under waving Confederate battle flags, Thurmond and Feilding Wright accepted the convention's nominations for president and vice-president.[2]

It was not the Dixiecrats' plan simply to run as another independent party against Truman. They hoped instead to get control of the Democratic party in the South and then have Thurmond and Wright placed on the ballot as the official nominees of the party in each state. If they were not successful, the candidates would be forced to settle for being placed on the ballot as third-party independents.

Throughout the campaign Thurmond tried to focus on states' rights and avoid the volatile race issue. He hoped that the strategy would attract votes and money from southern moderates who were not sensitive to race.[3] But Thurmond and the Dixiecrats were never able to move their campaign very far from the race issue; they were never able to come up with a complete program designed to appeal to a majority of voters even in the South.

Strom Thurmond's Dixiecrat campaign carried him to Florida in October 1948. The state's eight electoral votes went to Truman.

Thurmond addresses the Randolph-Macon student body during his October 1948 stop in Lynchburg Virginia. Both photographs from the archives of the Clemson University Libraries Special Collections Unit.

In addition, loud, boisterous Dixiecrat leaders like Frank Dixon continually raised the question of race throughout the campaign, and the press, looking for controversy and sensation, honed in on race as the primary issue defining the Dixiecrat movement. Consequently, the Dixiecrats never provided much more than a simple plan to pressure the Democratic party to end its civil rights initiative. In the final analysis, the Dixiecrats carried only four states and took only thirty-eight electoral votes. Only South Carolina, Alabama, Mississippi, and Louisiana voted for the Dixiecrat ticket.[4]

Thurmond may have tried to avoid the race issue, but voting patterns in the South showed clearly that support for the Dixiecrat movement came from whites living in the states with the largest African-American populations. Thurmond received 82 percent of the vote in Mississippi, the state with the largest black population, and 72 percent in South Carolina, the state with the second largest African-American population. The next largest black population was in Louisiana, and even though that state's politicians gave little support to the Dixiecrat movement, 50 percent of the voters chose Thurmond.[5] In Alabama, with about the same percentage of African Americans as Louisiana, nearly 80 percent of the votes were cast for Thurmond. In other southern states where the vote for the Dixiecrats was light, Thurmond generally ran the strongest in counties with the largest African-American populations.[6]

The Dixiecrat movement did not represent a new phenomenon. It was, in fact, a call to the past, a last-ditch effort to bring back the southern stranglehold on the Democratic party that prevailed during the first third of the century. And in that endeavor the movement failed. The Democratic party no longer held a special place for the South. The national party no longer sought to protect the South or the southern way of life. Truman and the Democrats had made a pragmatic, bottom-line, political choice to defend civil rights at the expense of southern votes.

The Democratic party after the war was simply not big enough for both southern segregationists and African Americans. Oddly enough, it was not up to either group to make the decision; both would have preferred to remain in the party, but both made it clear that they would leave if the other did not. The Democratic party leadership had to decide between civil rights and states' rights, between northern blacks and southern segregationists. It was a simple decision. The South could deliver fewer electoral votes than the northern urban areas where black voters were now influential and often held the balance of power.

At the same time, the Dixiecrat movement was the beginning of a new age in southern politics. One result of this 1948 decision by the Democrats has been that the white South since then has moved slowly into the Republican party. In 1952 Eisenhower carried Florida, Tennessee, Texas, and Virginia, and he made substantial gains in other southern states. In South Carolina he won 49 percent of the vote, in Louisiana he won 47 percent, in Mississippi he received 40 percent, and in Alabama and Georgia he won between 30 and 35 percent. These votes for Eisenhower came from counties with the largest African-American populations in these states—areas where Thurmond had done well in 1948.[7] In 1956 Eisenhower held Florida, Tennessee, Texas, and Virginia, and he won in Louisiana. In 1964, Republican candidate Barry Goldwater won the states of the Deep South (Mississippi, South Carolina, Georgia, Louisiana, and Alabama). The only other state he won was his home state of Arizona. That same year, in probably the primary symbol of the South's political conversion, Strom Thurmond announced that he would switch from Democratic to Republican affiliation. In 1968, George Wallace, carrying on the Dixiecrat standard, took Georgia, Mississippi, Alabama, Louisiana, and Arkansas, while Republican Richard Nixon took the rest of the South (except Texas), including Thurmond's own South Carolina. In 1972 a full 79 percent of the Mississippi vote went to Nixon, and seven of the eleven old Confederate states gave him over 70 percent of their votes. Clearly, the election of 1948 was a turning point in southern politics and in the politics of the Democratic party.

The Dixiecrat revolt helped to solidify for Truman the northern, urban, African-American coalition that had been targeted by Clifford, Rowe, and the other liberal White House advisers. It allowed Truman to duck the old claim by liberals and African-American leaders that the Democratic party was led by southern racists and still the party of the South and racism. The result was that northern African Americans and white liberals could return to the Democratic party and vote for Truman. The racist right had been purged—or more correctly purged itself. Like Henry Wallace's candidacy on the left, the Dixiecrats on the right gave Truman the appearance of holding the party's center.

Meanwhile, Truman was having a great deal of difficulty shaking his reluctance on the civil rights issue. Through the summer of 1948 he again tried to ride the fence between civil rights and the southern demands. He knew he needed the African-American vote, but he also feared the effects that the bolt of the southern dissidents might have on the election. Probably more important, he also feared the power of southern congressmen who might refuse to support his foreign policy agenda. The civil rights issue, however, was simply too volatile to straddle, with both sides threatening to damage the president's chances in November if the other received concessions.

Truman, however, continued to try. In Virginia, he delivered a speech standing alongside that state's segregationist governor William Tuck. And in Philadelphia in May he spoke at Girard College, a school that openly denied admission to African Americans. But he also remarked to the press that William Hastie, the African-American governor of the Virgin Islands, was his friend, and he entertained members of the African-American press at the White House. For most black leaders, however, these posturings were a long way from fulfilling concrete promises. A. Philip Randolph, for example, warned Truman that if some immediate movement was not made toward desegregating the armed forces African Americans might refuse to fight. They were, Randolph told the president, "in no mood to shoulder a gun for democracy abroad so long as they are denied democracy at home. In particular," he added, "they resent the idea of fighting or being drafted into another Jim Crow army."[8] When most Americans thought war with the Soviets was imminent, such a threat carried considerable weight. To convince African-American leaders and voters that he meant what he said, that he would keep his promises, Truman planned to make some civil rights concessions in July, after the party conventions and after Congress had adjourned.

Truman also avoided the civil rights issue simply because Dewey did not push him on it. The issue was never raised, thus Truman was never forced to defend his civil rights record. For Dewey, civil rights was controversial, and he worked hard to avoid all controversial issues. He may also have believed that he had a chance to win white votes in the South if he kept quiet on civil rights.

Truman's apparent ambivalence on civil rights may have brought misgivings from African-American leaders such as Randolph, but the alternatives for African-American voters were quickly dissipating. The Republicans, one alternative, repeatedly made it clear that all civil rights issues were dead on arrival at Capitol Hill. Republicans in the Eightieth Congress had always been eager to aid conservative southern Democrats in their efforts to kill civil rights legislation in exchange for southern support for key parts of the Republican agenda. This alliance had stifled civil rights legislation in Congress at least since Woodrow Wilson's administration, and in 1948 it was still effective in stalling civil rights bills on the floor of Congress. "What did the 80th Congress do on legislation supported by the NAACP?" asked that organization in the spring. "It did nothing on the anti-lynching bill; it refused to act on anti–Jim Crow travel. . . . On the anti–

poll tax, it did nothing."[9] Walter White conveyed to Robert Taft his disgust with the Republican Congress: "It is inconceivable to us that the Republican party can hope to approach Negroes next fall and ask their votes after these transparent moves on the three minimum civil rights bills."[10] The Republicans, it seemed, were convinced they could win in November, even without support from African-American voters. Also, Wallace, the other possible alternative for African Americans in 1948, was quickly self-destructing under the weight of domestic communist support and a successful campaign by the ADA to portray him as the dupe of the American Communist party and Moscow. By midsummer 1948, Truman was well on his way to winning the support of African Americans. "We believe," wrote the NAACP in support of Truman and the Democratic party's civil rights plank, that "the victory of decency at [the Democratic convention in] Philadelphia marks the greatest turning point for the South and for America which has occurred since the Civil War."[11] In addition, as the Dixiecrat rebellion got under way, the press focused on the Dixiecrat fire-eating white supremacists and their thumping tirades aimed at Truman and the evil Yankee liberals. Among African Americans, Truman's political capital increased proportionately. It quickly became clear to most African Americans that their home was now and for the future with the Democrats and the new liberal coalition. With the civil rights issue his own and Dewey not pushing the point, Truman barely mentioned civil rights through the rest of the campaign. But he refused to repudiate civil rights, claiming over and over that he was bound by the party's platform. Without making considerable concessions, the president easily won the commitment of African-American organizations as the doors to the alternatives closed and the liberal coalition began to come together.

After the convention, on July 26, Truman issued two executive orders that kept his promises and sealed the fate of African-American votes. Executive Order 9980 called for an end to discrimination in the federal government because of race, color, religion, or national origin. Executive Order 9981 was designed to desegregate the armed forces. It stated that "there shall be equality of treatment and opportunity for all persons in the armed sections without regard to race, color, religion, or national origin." It would take several investigations and government commissions, and finally the Korean War, to bring integration to the armed services, but this was the beginning of that process.[12]

On October 25, just a few days before the election, Truman spoke to a crowd of sixty-five thousand African Americans in Harlem, the first American president to do so. The race in New York was running very close, and he hoped that African-American voter strength there would tip the scales in his favor. He told the crowd that he would work for equal rights "with every ounce of strength and determination that I have."[13]

When the votes were counted, it was clear that the overtures, promises, and concessions to African Americans had paid off handsomely for Truman and the Democrats. An NAACP analyst, Henry Lee Moon, had argued in a preelection publication, *Balance of Power: The Negro Vote*, that African-American voters could decide a close election by carrying big cities in states with large electoral votes.[14] So it was that the votes of African Americans were probably the most important aspect of Truman's victory. One of Truman's advisers on civil rights issues, Philleo Nash, estimated that nationwide, Truman received over 80 percent of the African-American vote, much higher than Roosevelt ever got.[15] The big states that went for Truman were California, Illinois, and Ohio. In California, he won by only 18,000 votes. Without the 70,000 African-American votes he received there he would have lost that state's twenty-five electors. In Illinois, another close state, Truman's margin of victory was only 33,000 votes. The African-American vote there was nearly 120,000, and Truman received 85,000 of those votes and took the state's twenty-eight electors. The vote was closest in Ohio, where Truman won by only 7,000 votes. More than 130,000 African Americans voted for Truman in that state, giving the president the state's twenty-five electors. Had any two of those three states gone to the Republicans, Truman would have been left without a majority in the electoral college and the election would have been thrown into the House of Representatives. African-American voters almost gave the big prize of New York to Truman. Truman lost there by a mere 61,000 votes—principally because Wallace took a large enough African American and liberal chunk of the electorate to give the state to Dewey.[16]

Immediately after the election, African Americans announced that they had been the decisive factor in electing Truman.[17] It is too simple to say that African Americans won the election for Truman. A similar set of statistics shows that the votes of organized labor pushed Truman over the top in several important industrial states. It is clear, however, that had African Americans voted for Dewey or Wallace—or even decided to stay home on election day—Truman would have lost the election. But again, the same can be said of labor voters. It is more correct to see the place of the African-American voter in the election of 1948 as part of a strong, new Democratic party coalition of white liberals, organized labor, and African-American voters—all mostly outside the South.

Did Truman support civil rights, or did he latch on to a powerful growing social movement to win votes? Probably both. Clearly, at the president's

Truman and friends celebrate his election on the U.S.S. *Williamsburg*. Pictured, from left to right, are Mon Walgren, Secretary of Agriculture Clinton Anderson, Clark Clifford, President Truman, George Allen, Attorney General Tom Clark, Secretary of the Air Force Stuart Symington, and Oscar Ewing. From the collections of the Harry S. Truman Library, courtesy of the U.S. Navy.

side was a group of political pragmatists whose only job was to win a second term for the president. To push Truman to the left so as to pick up African-American voter strength in the northern urban areas was, for them, little more than a political expediency. At the same time, Truman was genuinely concerned about African Americans. He felt strongly for those African-American men, like Johnny Jones, who had fought in the war and then returned to a hostile South, where their rights were denied by law and their lives were in jeopardy. He also firmly believed that America could not hold the flames of freedom and democracy as an example to the world when freedom and democracy were being denied to a large minority in the United States. These two forces, one personal and one political, motivated civil rights in the Truman administration. Then there was the movement itself: growing, vibrant, with new tactics, strong leadership, a strong financial base for the first time, and newfound political clout. It was moving forward under its own power by 1947, moving faster as a social movement than as a political movement. As the election approached, the two major parties had to decide whether to support the movement and win African-American votes or concede to the rival party. The Democrats embraced the issue. The Republicans would not. And it changed the face of American politics.

By the summer of 1948 most of what Henry Wallace had achieved was gone or was going very quickly. His problem revolved around domestic communist support for his campaign, in addition to his own support for a U.S.-

Soviet accommodation and a belief that Moscow was justified in most of its postwar actions. As Soviet aggressions continued to mount in Eastern Europe, however, Wallace found himself in the uncomfortable position of a Soviet apologist, his views became less and less tenable, and he lost more and more support.

Yet Wallace felt that his political philosophy did not allow him to exclude from his political organization any group that would support him, even communists. After the election he recalled: "We . . . thought that all types of opinion, as long as they believed in our ultimate objective, should be represented in the Progressive party. . . . They were a devoted crowd. I don't know which ones of them were Communists, and it really wasn't my mind to ask that."[18] As the election approached, however, it became clear to Wallace that communist support was killing his campaign, that the communists, despite their enthusiasm, were giving the opposition the ammunition needed to discredit his policies, and he began trying to distance himself from his communist supporters. During a radio address in June in New Hampshire, Wallace allowed himself an unusual display of exasperation over the situation: "I'm never going to say anything in the nature of red-baiting but I must say this: If the Communists would run a ticket of their own this year, we would lose ten thousand votes, but we would gain three million. I know if the Communists really wanted to help us, they would run their own ticket this year and let us get those extra votes."[19] In an interview with Edward R. Murrow at about the same time, he expressed a similar sentiment: "There's no question that support [from the Communists] is a political liability."[20] And in a speech in Seattle he said: "If the Communists want to support me, they must do it on my terms. If the Communists are working for peace with Russia, God bless them. If they are working for the overthrow of the Government by force, they know I'm against them."[21] But by then Wallace had already been branded a communist. A few languid anticommunist statements would not change that impression.

The organization that took the lead in opposing Wallace and his Progressive party bid was the ADA. The ADA had no place for Henry Wallace, and in the months following the Democratic party convention it set out to discredit his campaign. ADA members attacked Wallace on several fronts, but Red-baiting—accusing Wallace of being a communist or at least the dupe of communist interests—was the most effective, and it had an important influence on the outcome of the 1948 election.

The ADA attacked Wallace at every opportunity. The ADA's executive secretary, James Loeb, wrote a friend in reference to the ADA's anti-Wallace campaign: "Every strategy should be used, both the soft strategy and the tough strategy."[22] Even when the ADA agreed with Wallace, it still found room for criticism. On civil rights, for example, the ADA claimed that Wallace was not sincere, that his stand was aimed at exploiting African Americans to further the goals of world communism. Wallace's lack of support for the Truman Doctrine and the Marshall Plan was explained by the ADA as the result of communist influence in the PCA and even a response based on direct orders from Moscow. Wallace's call for peace and a U.S.-Soviet–directed postwar world order was made out to be the worst form of appeasement, and Wallace was described by the ADA (and the ADA-supported press) as a modern-day Neville Chamberlain. The ADA published several anti-Wallace diatribes designed to feed information about Wallace and his supporters to the press. The first, entitled *Henry Wallace: The First Three Months of His Presidential Campaign*, was released to the press in April 1948. The second installment, *Henry Wallace: The Last Seven Months of His Presidential Campaign*, was released in August.[23] These publications accused Wallace of moving "more and more closely to the fluctuations of Soviet policy." They claimed that U.S. Communist party leader William Z. Foster wanted Wallace to run on a third-party ticket in 1948 and that the order for that plan came directly from Jacques Duclos, the French communist leader with direct ties to the Kremlin.[24] The implications were clear: Wallace was running as a Communist party dupe, and his strings were being pulled by Moscow. The ADA sent some eighteen hundred copies of each edition to the most important newspapers in the country, to national politicians and leaders, national labor representatives, Democratic party leaders, and ADA-supported candidates who were being challenged by Progressive party candidates. The information was used effectively to fight Wallace's candidacy. In June, Hubert Humphrey came up with a slogan aimed at the Wallace campaign that was repeated over and over by the anti-Wallaceites: "We are not prepared to see the century of the common man become the century of the Comintern."[25]

On July 22 at the PCA convention in New York the ADA's James Loeb made a dramatic appearance before the PCA platform committee. In what was clearly the hand of peace, the PCA had asked the ADA to send a representative to the committee meeting, but Loeb was determined to represent the ADA himself and turn the event into a media circus that would focus on communist infiltration of the PCA. Days before the meeting, Loeb released to the press the prepared testimony that he planned to deliver to the PCA. It was a harsh, critical, anticommunist harangue that made Wallace out to be little more than a communist dupe. By the time Loeb addressed the committee, they knew exactly what he would be saying. After a seven-and-one-half-hour wait and a final plea from PCA leader

Rexford Tugwell not to speak, Loeb broke what he later called the "super-charged atmosphere": "The Communists and their collaborators guide the major policies and word the major pronouncements of this Party," Loeb claimed. The PCA was "lending itself to the support and extenuation of Soviet totalitarianism and Soviet aggression." It was "a dangerous adventure undertaken by cynical men in whose hands Henry A. Wallace placed his political fortunes." Loeb concluded: "It is our conviction that were the Communists to withdraw from your party today, your organization would soon join that long list of discarded groups which testify eloquently to the inevitable failure of the so-called 'United Front'—which always becomes decreasingly united and increasingly 'front.'" Loeb had to leave the meeting under police guard. He later wrote: "My testimony before the Wallace platform committee got more publicity than almost anything else the ADA has ever done." Tugwell called Loeb's diatribe an "unscrupulous and demagogic denunciation" that was "insincere, hypocritical and immaterial."[26]

The ADA's attacks on Wallace were important to the campaign's final outcome. Since 1946 the Republicans had tried desperately to make the communist name stick to the Democrats, but in the 1948 campaign, the ADA, acting as spokesman for the Democrats at least on this issue, was successful in making American voters believe that Wallace and his supporters were communists. The result, of course, was that the communists supported Wallace and not Truman, thus it was almost impossible to argue that Truman was a communist sympathizer or supported by communists. As a result of the ADA campaign, Wallace and the PCA absorbed the Red-baiting that the Republicans would have thrown at the Truman administration in 1948.

One of the ADA's most effective tactics in this campaign against Wallace was to claim that a vote for Wallace would split the Democrats and elect Dewey. That argument was the most difficult for the Progressives to refute because as Wallace's support grew weaker and weaker any chance to win evaporated and the charge became more and more true. On the last day of September the ADA was able to celebrate its success when the PCA announced the withdrawal of most of its candidates from local elections. Their reason was the same as the ADA had charged: they could not win the elections, and they would only split the liberal vote and facilitate a Republican victory.[27] It was a clear admission that the Wallace third-party move had failed.

Wallace, of course, was not a communist, but by the time the campaign ended and the ADA finished with him, he appeared to the American voter to be a Moscow-driven communist, an apologist for Soviet aggressions, an

Henry Wallace is surrounded by UAW strikers. Much of his organized labor support left him by the end of the election. From the collections of the University of Iowa.

appeaser, and a man who was willing to hand over to the Soviets about anything they wanted—including atomic secrets. Even his old friend organized labor (with the exception of a few communist-dominated unions) deserted Wallace for Truman. And of the old New Dealers, only Rexford Tugwell stood by him.[28] By November, Wallace supporters were nearly nonexistent. Only in New York did Wallace have an impact, and there he only took enough votes away from Truman to give the state to Dewey.

In August, the ADA finally came around to endorsing Truman, but it did little to aid his campaign directly. Instead, it spent most of its time attacking Wallace and assisting the campaigns of liberal congressional candidates around the country. By then the ADA's political agenda was clear. Along with everyone else, the organization expected Truman to lose, and after the postelection dust settled it intended to be the leading liberal organization in the nation. To make that plan succeed, the ADA had to remove all remnants of Henry Wallace. It also hoped to emerge in the leadership role of a new liberal coalition in Congress that would set its sights on the 1952 election. Even though by late summer Wallace was clearly no longer a threat, the ADA continued its inexorable attacks right up to election time. Even on election day Loeb went on national radio to hit Wallace one last time.[29] The ADA not only wanted to destroy Wallace for the 1948 election, it wanted to destroy him for the future.

The Soviets accommodated the anti-Wallace strategy by staging a coup in Czechoslovakia in February. That incident convinced many liberals that compromise with the Soviet Union was impossible and that Wallace's plan for good relations with Moscow was little more than an idealist's fantasy.[30] Then in May, in what was clearly an attempt to show that he could communicate with the Soviets, Wallace wrote an open letter to Stalin calling for talks and disarmament. Stalin, amazingly, replied in what was no less than an open endorsement of Wallace's candidacy for president of the United States.[31] There is hardly a better example of a presidential candidate unable to gauge properly the opinion of the American public, and almost immediately Wallace fell into a campaign abyss. Two months later, in July, as Truman was making a popular stand against the Soviets by flying supplies into Berlin after Stalin closed off that city to western rail traffic, Wallace made another unpopular stand by calling for Truman to give up Berlin "in search of peace."[32] As the Cold War heated up through 1948 and as the nation became more and more offended by the Soviet Union's aggressions, Wallace, it seemed, was prepared to surrender to Moscow at every turn. His objective, as he often said, was peace and understanding— rather than confrontation and war—with the Soviets. But to the American voter, 1948 was a time to stand up to the Soviet Union.[33]

Wallace's defection and eventual third-party bid may have been a factor in pushing Truman toward a more hard-line stance against the Soviet Union to confront and oppose Wallace directly on that issue and to distance himself as much as possible from his "pro-Russian" policies. Certainly, Truman and his secretary of state James Byrnes turned up the fire on the Soviets in the months following Wallace's Madison Square Garden speech, and there is ample evidence that the strategy may have been, at least in part, to discredit Wallace's calls for peace and cooperation with Moscow.[34] But it was also true that the Republican congressional victories in November 1946 jolted Truman into seeing that the America people were looking for something else—a harder line toward Moscow, something that Taft, Vandenberg, and the rest of the Republicans were calling for anyway in response to Soviet aggressions.

In Rowe's memo to the president in late 1947, Wallace was portrayed as a dangerous "fellow traveler" and a "Party liner." Rowe wrote that he believed the Soviets wanted a third party that would split the Democrats and put the Republicans in office because they were "convinced there is no longer any hope that the Truman Administration will submit to the Russian program of world conquest and expansion." Wallace, Rowe believed, also wanted to hand the government over to the Republicans by splitting the Democratic party vote, but his motive was to capture the Democratic party machine and run in 1952. Both presumptions were absurd, but Rowe's strategy for dealing with Wallace was effective: "Every effort must be made *now* . . .—although, of course, by different groups—to dissuade him [from running] and also to identify him and isolate him in the public mind with the Communists."[35] Rowe's "different groups," was, of course, a direct reference to the ADA, the group that would handle the political assassination of Henry Wallace. But the main thrust of Rowe's memo was that Truman should move to the left on domestic issues in an attempt to destroy Wallace's support, which in late 1947 was still considered the administration's greatest threat in the coming election. Through 1948 Truman consumed Wallace's support by making concessions to labor, African Americans, and the cause of liberalism in general. By November, Wallace stood nearly alone.

It was the African-American vote that was the most up for grabs in 1948, and Wallace saw great potential in the northern cities, where polls showed that he was favored by as much as 30 percent of African-American voters. In August, just two months before the election, he headed off on a campaign tour through the South in an attempt to draw the wrath of white southerners and the sympathy (and votes) of northern African Americans. Half of his plan worked.

During his southern campaign swing Wallace openly defied southern Jim Crow laws by refusing to speak to segregated audiences, to stay in segregated hotels, or to eat in segregated restaurants. In town after town through the Carolinas and then into the Deep South in Alabama, Mississippi, and Louisiana, he was booed, egged repeatedly, stoned, and threatened. The most common scream from the belligerents was "Go back to Russia, you nigger-lover!" In Memphis, Wallace's car was attacked by a gang of white thugs. In Durham, a student supporter was stabbed as Wallace spoke. In Birmingham, Wallace was told by Police Commissioner Eugene "Bull" Conner that he could not speak to integrated audiences in the city limits.[36] Wallace's courage at confronting the inequality of southern racism—and making it headline news across the country—won him the respect of many liberals and undoubtedly the support of those northern African Americans whose votes he so coveted as the election approached. But by the summer of 1948 Wallace was no longer a viable alternative for most African-American voters. By then, Wallace's communist connections and the concessions made by Truman and the Democrats had won them over.

Truman kicked off his 1948 campaign with his State of the Union address in January. It was surprisingly liberal in tone, and it was aimed squarely at attacking Wallace's liberal support. The president called for a national health insurance program, a massive housing program, increased federal support for education, increased support for farmers, the conservation of national resources, a rise in the minimum wage, and civil rights.[37] Truman had listened to his advisers and moved to the left on domestic issues with the intention of co-opting Wallace's support among northern African Americans, organized labor, and traditional liberals. As the election approached, Truman and Wallace slowly converged on most domestic issues, and much of Wallace's support began to defect to the Democrats. When it became apparent that Wallace could not win, his followers were faced with either supporting a losing candidate by throwing away their votes or going along with Truman. The first choice was anathema because it might hand the election over to the Republicans. So, presented with the classic American political decision of choosing the lesser of two evils, liberals voted Democratic. By election day Wallace's support was nearly gone.[38] He tallied a pathetic one million votes, less than the Dixiecrats. What had been a possibility for victory, a groundswell, a strong liberal coalition, turned into an embarrassing defeat. When the election was over the *Wall Street Journal* gave the following analysis:

> It is said by political commentators that Mr. Wallace made a bad showing because he got few votes. What they neglect is that Mr. Wallace succeeded in having his ideas adopted, except in the field of foreign affairs. From the time that Mr. Wallace announced he would run for President, Mr. Truman began to suck the wind from the Wallace sails by coming out for more and more of the Wallace domestic program. Now these promises are in Mr. Truman's platform and the men who see eye to eye with Mr. Wallace on domestic, economic and social questions are among those who can rightfully claim a share of the credit for Mr. Truman's victory.[39]

Not surprisingly, the Progressive party leaders, in their postelection remarks, said much the same thing. C.B. Baldwin, the executive secretary of the Progressive party, had this analysis of Wallace's roll in the election:

> It is we who forced the Democrats to don the Roosevelt mantle and promise the people a return to the New Deal. . . . Truman more and more was forced to shape his bid for votes by the standards Henry Wallace set.

> Truman's messages to Congress in January, 1948[,] the civil rights report, and his series of messages to Congress through the spring of 1948 on civil rights, on price controls, on education and housing, on medical care—all registered the pressure of our party and of our campaign.[40]

Both commentators were correct. The administration's shift to the left (as Rowe suggested in his memo) brought in the urban-labor-liberal-black coalition that elected Truman.

Wallace's abortive 1948 presidential campaign followed the predictable pattern of all American third-party activity. That pattern begins with a great deal of enthusiasm and popular support over new ideas, new faces, and new energy. What follows are strong attacks from outside the party and then a move by one of the major parties to take over much of the third party's platform in an attempt to win its followers. In the last step, there is a clear and sharp decline in support for the third party as voters fear throwing their votes away or splitting one of the major parties, which would lead to the election of the opposition. Protest votes seem worthwhile in May but seldom in November. This pattern has been played out several times in American history, and it did in the Wallace campaign of 1948. Unfortunately, Wallace did not see it. He considered himself a student of history, and throughout his campaign, in his speeches and in editorials and articles in *New Republic*, he often referred to the third-party tradition in America, telling his readers and listeners of the great strides made in American politics as a result of the nation's many third-party movements.[41] He was correct that third parties have influenced the American political system, but they do not win elections.

Another reluctant Truman supporter was organized labor. Like the ADA, labor was more interested in the 1948 congressional and state races than in working for the sure-to-be-defeated president. To that end, the CIO-PAC focused on defeating those congressmen who had abandoned organized labor and voted for Taft-Hartley.[42] The other labor power, the AFL, had remained officially outside the political arena in this period, but the passage of Taft-Hartley had forced the AFL to break temporarily from its own dictum of political abstention. In December 1947 the AFL formed Labor's League for Political Action (AFL-LLPA) with much the same purpose as the CIO-PAC: to concentrate on local elections and defeat those in Congress who had supported Taft-Hartley.

In these postwar years organized labor was deeply involved in a colossal internal struggle that would bring the labor vote even closer to Truman and the Democrats as the 1948 election approached. The issue was communism, and the unions had split between those who supported (or were willing to tolerate) communists in the labor movement and those who would not. Communists had always been important in the labor movement, particularly in many of the CIO unions, where they had acted as organizers and foot soldiers. In 1940 and again in 1944 communists had aided in FDR's victories, and most liberals believed they were a legitimate part of the American political system and even of the New Deal coalition. But by 1945 the growing Cold War began to divide the labor movement, and a drive began among several powerful anticommunist labor leaders to purge the communists from the unions. Men such as David Dubinsky of the International Ladies Garment Workers Union, Emil Rieve of the Textile Workers of America, Walter Reuther of the UAW, and CIO executive James Carey were important labor leaders who disliked communism and its influence in organized labor.

The Cold War was the basis of labor's divisive troubles in the postwar years, but labor might not have divided over the issue of communism had it not been for Henry Wallace's third-party bid. CIO president Philip Murray was an ardent anticommunist himself, but he avoided affiliation with both communist and anticommunist organizations to maintain political unity within the CIO.[43] But like most liberals, Murray had come to realize that Wallace's third-party move would draw votes from the Democrats and facilitate the election of the Republicans. Although Murray had lost no love on Truman, it was clear that a Republican would not have vetoed Taft-Hartley. Consequently, like many voters in 1948, Murray realized that he would have to accept Truman. Murray and the anticommunist labor forces also supported Truman's aggressive anticommunist foreign policy, and that caused a further split between labor's communists and anticommunists. To head off a strong third-party move by Wallace that might draw heavily from Truman and other Democrats on the ticket, Murray and the anticommunists in the labor movement began working to isolate Wallace by branding him as a communist sympathizer.[44] By late 1947 Murray's anti-Wallace political strategy had converged with that of the ADA, and in September Murray agreed to support the ADA in its efforts to repeal Taft-Hartley, defeat Wallace, and purge the communists.[45]

With Murray's considerable weight behind the anticommunist factions in the CIO, anticommunism gained momentum among the unions. In August 1947, Murray forced the resignation of the communist editor of *CIO News*, and in November, Walter Reuther announced that all communist officers in the UAW would be fired.[46] This purge had as much to do with the nation's anticommunist mood in the postwar years as with the internal politics of the labor unions, and it had a profound impact on the election of 1948. The purged communists in organized labor were forced into the waiting arms of Henry Wallace, where they all went down to defeat together. The remainder of the union members, by far a large majority of the rank and file, were mostly moderates, liberals, and anticommunists. Like Murray, these men had no love for Truman, but as Truman's presidential campaign developed it became clear that labor (without the influence from communists) had a great deal in common with the president. After Murray's endorsement of the ADA in September 1947, it was only a matter of time before the CIO endorsed Truman, and it did so officially in August 1948. By then the CIO and the remainder of the moderates in the labor movement had come to see that Truman was their only choice and boarded his bandwagon by default. Jack Kroll, the head of the CIO-PAC, announced just after the Democratic convention in July that the nation had found another champion of American labor in Truman.[47] Even A.F. Whitney, who had pledged the entire treasury of the Brotherhood of Railway Trainmen to Truman's political defeat, endorsed the president. William Green and the AFL held to Samuel Gompers's dictum that the big union should not endorse any political candidates. Nevertheless, the AFL-LLPE worked diligently against Wallace, Taft-Hartley, the Eightieth Congress, and the senators and congressmen who had voted for Taft-Hartley.[48] That, for the most part, placed the AFL in the Democratic column, which translated into votes for Truman. Only John L. Lewis remained intransigent, calling the president "Injunction Harry," while the UMW gave all but an official endorsement to Dewey on the grounds that he had never "uttered any statements that reflect upon the integrity or the objectives of the United Mine Workers."[49]

Truman may have been winning the support of labor leaders, but would he win the votes of labor's rank and file? James Rowe wrote in his campaign strategy memo that Truman needed the support of organized labor to win in 1948 and that an unappeased labor might stay home as it had in 1946.[50] In the summer of 1948, the union journal *North American Labor* asked: "Will labor turn out to vote? Or will the workers stay home by [the] millions, as in 1946, and let the election go by default to reaction?"[51] As the election approached, it became increasingly clear that organized labor's rank and file had little choice. Not voting, as the lesson of 1946 had taught, was sure to produce a Republican president and another Republican Congress bent on destroying organized labor and dismantling the New Deal. At the same time, Wallace's association with communism had removed him from consideration, and a protest vote for Wallace would split the Democratic vote and bring in the Republicans. Consequently, Truman received a strong showing from labor in 1948.[52]

The day after the election, Truman strode into the Hotel Muehlbach in Kansas City and announced, "Labor did it."[53] Thirteen years later, his opinion had not changed.[54] In his memoirs, Truman understandably refused to credit the 1948 win to any particular group, although he did write that he won the nation's thirteen largest cities and that California and Ohio had been key states in the election. Labor was certainly important, but it is difficult to attribute the victory to labor votes alone when the president lost such important industrial states as New York, New Jersey, Michigan, Indiana, Connecticut, and Pennsylvania although labor-supported Democrats won congressional victories in those states. One author has pointed out, however, that Truman did well where labor was most active in his favor, although it is clear that even in the strongest labor areas of the country Democratic voter strength fell well below that of the Roosevelt years.[55] Roosevelt's strength among labor voters was immense; Truman's strength was less so, but it was still strong enough to win most labor-heavy parts of the country.

Labor, itself, was successful. A total of 79 incumbents in the House who voted for Taft-Hartley were voted out of office. Of the 84 Democrats who voted for the law, 12 (mostly outside the South) were defeated and replaced by other Democrats. Of the 215 congressmen endorsed by the CIO-PAC, 114 won election. Walter Reuther called it "a batting average which is good in any league."[56] Even the UMW claimed victory, taking credit for defeating 41 congressmen and 6 senators representing coal-producing areas who supported Taft-Hartley.[57] The day after the election, the *New York Times* gave four reasons for Truman's victory. The first three dealt with courage, adherence to the New Deal philosophy, and political tactics. The fourth reason was "the organization of the labor movement, which acquired strength from the middle and the right by shedding the support of the ideological left."[58] In the same article, the *Times* reported that three-fourths of the nation's skilled and semiskilled workers had voted Democratic in the election.[59] In the years after the election, statistical analysts concluded that organized labor played a crucial part in Truman's victory, particularly in the urban industrial districts of Chicago, Los Angeles, Boston, Cleveland, St. Louis, Milwaukee, and San Francisco.[60] In addition, only 11 percent of the union-affiliated workers voted for Dewey, while Truman received 56 percent of their votes.[61]

Truman, however, did not run that well in the industrial states. He lost New York, New Jersey, Pennsylvania, and Michigan, where Wallace received strong support on the left. And he lost Indiana, where the strongly labor, liberal, industrial northwest corridor seldom outvotes the conservative downstate. In several industrial states, particularly Michigan, Indiana, Pennsylvania, New Jersey, and Connecticut, Truman even ran behind a successful Democratic congressional ticket.[62] But his victories in Ohio and Wisconsin (both of which switched from Republican in 1944 to Democrat in 1948) and Illinois and California were due to a strong labor vote and a strong labor get-out-the-vote campaign in the industrial districts of those states. Labor was clearly important as part of that broad, complex coalition of labor, liberals, and urban African-American voters.

Truman's labor stance in 1948 was sincere. He did not decide to support labor in the home stretch just to win its voting power for the election. Although James Rowe's grand strategy set the stage for Truman's victory in 1948, on the labor issue it was Truman's own prolabor legacy that finally emerged and won labor's votes. Truman had been prolabor all his political life, and he would continue to be prolabor in his second term. Consequently, his veto of Taft-Hartley should come as no surprise, and on election day labor responded and supported the president

By election time, Truman had in place a new coalition—albeit a reluctant one. African Americans, organized labor, and the ADA came over to Truman's side in the late summer of 1948 almost by default. The Eightieth Congress had, it seemed, gone to great lengths to make it clear that there was no room in the Republican party for any of these groups, and Henry Wallace, an early alternative for liberals, African Americans, and organized labor, had self-destructed under the weight of the communist issue. The racist harangues of the Dixiecrats had forced the banner of civil rights into Truman's hands, while Wallace's onus of communism kept that burden off Truman's shoulders during the campaign. What had been a disastrously divided party in the face of all the postwar problems of the nation came together, for one brief moment, on November 2, to elect Harry Truman.

16

Postelection Analysis

In the final analysis, Truman received 24,179,259 votes to Dewey's 21,991,291.[1] That translated into a minority victory of 49.6 percent to Dewey's 45.1 percent. In the electoral college, Truman carried twenty-eight states with 303 electoral votes, while Dewey carried only sixteen states and 189 votes. Thurmond took four southern states and 39 electoral votes. Henry Wallace's numbers had little impact, but he took enough votes from Truman in New York to give that state to Dewey; the same may have been true in Michigan and Maryland. Truman won 56 electoral votes from five states that Dewey had won in 1944: Ohio, Wisconsin, Iowa, Colorado, and Wyoming, but he lost nine states and 146 electoral votes to Dewey that Roosevelt had won in 1944: Michigan, Maryland, Delaware, New Hampshire, Oregon, Pennsylvania, New Jersey, New York, and Connecticut.

A Democratic Congress was elected, but it had little to do with Truman's coattails. Truman not only ran behind FDR's 1944 figures in most areas of the country, he often ran behind his own congressional ticket. Nationally, he ran behind his party's congressional ticket by 4 percent while Dewey ran ahead of his party's congressional ticket by over 5 percent. In nineteen states Truman took the state electors but received fewer votes than the Democratic party-endorsed congressional candidates.[2] This is the "reverse coattails" theory devised first by Malcolm Moos in 1952 and then expanded on by R. Alton Lee. This phenomenon most likely occurred because Democrats voted for a congressional candidate but chose to cast their presidential vote for Wallace or Thurmond—or not to cast a vote for president at all. Lee has shown that it was the coattails of labor candidates, along with get-out-the-vote campaigns conducted by organized labor, that in many urban-industrial areas dragged Truman over the top when he might otherwise have lost those areas.[3] It is also true, however, that the coattails of strong liberal candidates in some states pulled Truman along, candidates such as Hubert Humphrey in Minnesota, Guy Gillette in Iowa, Lester Hunt in Wyoming, and Adlai Stevenson and Paul Douglas in Illinois.

Table 1. Election of 1948, Returns by State.

State	Truman	Dewey	Wallace	Thurmond	Total[a]	Electoral
Ala.	—	40,930	1,522	171,443	214,980	11
Ariz.	95,251	77,597	3,310	1	177,065	4
Ark.	149,659	50,959	751	40,068	242,475	9
Calif.	1,913,134	1,895,269	190,381	1,228	4,021,538	25
Colo.	267,288	239,714	6,115	—	515,237	6
Conn.	423,297	437,754	13,713	—	883,518	8
Del.	67,813	69,588	1,050	—	139,073	3
Fla.	281,988	194,280	11,620	89,755	577,643	8
Ga.	254,646	76,691	1,636	85,135	418,844	12
Idaho	107,370	101,514	4,972	—	214,816	4
Ill.	1,994,715	1,961,103	—	—	3,984,046	28
Ind.	807,831	821,079	9,649	—	1,656,212	13
Iowa	522,380	494,018	12,125	—	1,038,264	10
Kans.	351,902	423,039	4,603	—	788,819	8
Ky.	466,756	341,210	1,567	10,411	822,658	11
La.	136,344	72,657	3,035	204,290	416,336	10
Maine	111,916	150,234	1,884	—	264,787	5
Md.	286,521	294,814	9,983	2,489	596,748	8
Mass.	1,151,788	909,370	38,157	—	2,107,146	16
Mich.	1,003,448	1,038,595	46,515	—	2,109,609	19
Minn.	692,966	483,617	27,866	—	1,212,226	11
Miss.	19,384	5,043	255	167,538	192,190	9
Mo.	917,315	655,039	3,998	—	1,578,628	15
Mont.	119,071	96,770	7,313	—	224,278	4
Nebr.	224,165	264,774	—	—	488,940	6
Nev.	31,291	29,357	1,469	—	62,117	3
N.H.	107,995	121,299	1,970	7	231,440	4
N.J.	895,455	981,124	42,683	—	1,949,555	16
N.M.	105,464	80,303	1,037	—	187,063	4
N.Y.	2,780,204	2,841,163	509,559	—	6,177,337	47
N.C.	459,070	258,572	3,915	69,652	791,209	14
N.Dak.	95,812	115,139	8,391	374	220,716	4
Ohio	1,452,791	1,445,684	37,596	—	2,936,071	25
Okla.	452,782	268,817	—	—	721,599	10
Oreg.	243,147	260,904	14,978	—	524,080	6
Pa.	1,752,426	1,902,197	55,161	—	3,735,348	35
R.I.	188,736	135,787	2,619	—	327,702	4
S.C.	34,423	5,386	154	102,607	142,571	8
S.Dak.	117,567	129,651	2,801	—	250,105	4
Tenn.	270,402	202,914	1,864	73,815	550,283	12

Continued on next page

(Table 1, cont.)

State	Truman	Dewey	Wallace	Thurmond	Total[a]	Electoral
Tex.	824,235	303,467	3,918	106,929	1,249,577	23
Utah	149,151	124,402	2,679	—	276,306	4
Vt.	45,557	75,926	1,279	—	123,382	3
Va.	200,786	172,070	2,047	43,393	419,256	11
Wash.	476,165	386,314	31,692	—	905,058	8
W.Va.	429,188	316,251	3,311	—	748,750	8
Wis.	647,310	590,959	25,282	—	1,276,800	12
Wyo.	52,354	47,947	931	—	101,425	3
TOT.	24,179,259	21,991,291	1,157,356	1,169,135	48,793,826[a]	531

Sources: CQ Presidential Elections: 1789-1991 (Washington D.C., 1995), 63, 117; *NYT*, Dec. 11, 1948.

[a]State and national totals include votes cast for minor candidates.

Table 2. Election of 1948.

Candidates	Popular vote	Percent of total	Electoral vote
Truman	24,179,259	49.55	303
Dewey	21,991,291	45.06	189
Thurmond	1,169,135	2.39	39
Wallace	1,157,356	2.37	0

Sources: CQ Presidential Elections: 1789-1991 (Washington, D.C., 1995), 63, 117; *NYT*, Dec. 11, 1948.

Note: Total votes cast, including those for minor candidates: 48,793,826.

Table 3. Election of 1948, Electoral Vote.

Truman (303)		Dewey (189)		Thurmond (39)	
Arizona	4	Connecticut[b]	8	Alabama	11
Arkansas	9	Delaware[b]	3	Louisiana	10
California	25	Indiana	13	Mississippi	9
Colorado[a]	6	Kansas	8	South Carolina	8
Florida	8	Maine	5	Tennessee	1
Georgia	12	Maryland[b]	8		
Idaho	4	Michigan[b]	19		
Illinois	28	Nebraska	6		
Iowa[a]	10	New Hampshire[b]	4		
Kentucky	11	New Jersey[b]	16		
Massachusetts	16	New York[b]	47		
Minnesota	11	North Dakota	4		
Missouri	15	Oregon[b]	6		
Montana	4	Pennsylvania[b]	35		
Nevada	3	South Dakota	4		
New Mexico	4	Vermont	3		
North Carolina	14				
Ohio[a]	25				
Oklahoma	10				
Rhode Island	4				
Tennessee	11				
Texas	23				
Utah	4				
Virginia	11				
Washington	8				
West Virginia	8				
Wisconsin[a]	12				
Wyoming[a]	3				

Sources: CQ Presidential Elections: 1789–1991 (Washington, D.C., 1995), 63, 117; *NYT* Dec. 11, 1948.
[a] States won by Truman in 1948 that had voted for Dewey in 1944
[b] States won by Dewey in 1948 that had voted for Roosevelt in 1944

THE ELECTION OF 1948

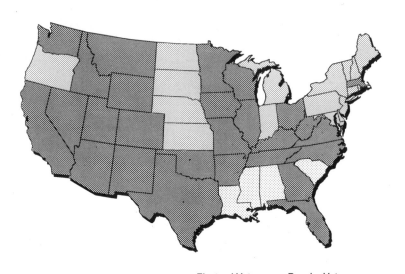

		Electoral Vote (Percent)	Popular Vote (Percent)
	HARRY S. TRUMAN (Democrat)	303 (57%)	24,179,259 (49.55%)
	Thomas E. Dewey (Republican)	189 (36%)	21,991,291 (45.06%)
	Strom Thurmond (States' Rights)	39 (7%)	1,169,135 (2.39%)
	Henry A. Wallace (Progressive)	–	1,157,356 (2.37%)

In Congress, it was a clear mandate for the Democrats—and a disaster for the Republicans not unlike the one they handed the Democrats just two years before. The Democrats now held a majority of 262 to 171 in the House and 54 to 42 in the Senate. Clearly, the Republican-dominated Eightieth Congress had been repudiated by the voters, and just as clearly, Truman had been successful in getting his message across to the people— that the Eightieth Congress had failed.

One important factor in the election statistics is the large stay-at-home vote. If the rate of voter increases in 1940 and 1944 had been the same for 1948, there should have been some fifty-eight million votes cast, ten million more than the actual number. The reason most often given for this apathy is that the outcome of the election was projected in the press and in the polls with such certainty that large numbers of voters saw no need to participate. But if that were true, the stay-at-home vote would have struck both candidates more or less equally, whereas in fact Republicans failed to cast their ballots in much greater numbers than Democrats. Although Dewey ran better than any Republican since Hoover, almost the same number of Republicans (about twenty-two million) voted for Dewey in 1944 as in 1948, whereas in 1952 almost thirty-four million Republicans voted for Eisenhower. Dewey gained no percentage points in 1948 over his showing in 1944, and that was at least in part because he made no inroads at all into Democratic party voter strength. The lack of inspiration for Dewey can only be tied to a bland candidate who conducted a bland campaign. Uninspired voters simply stayed away.

Of course, no one believed Truman would win. The pollsters all called it for Dewey. George Gallup, in his last poll on October 30, gave the election to Dewey by a margin of 49.5 to 44.5 percent.[4] An Archibald Crossley poll published just before the election gave almost the same figures.[5] Elmo Roper wrote on September 9, "My whole inclination is to predict the election for Thomas E. Dewey by a heavy margin and devote my time and efforts to other things." It was his last poll on the election; his prediction of a Dewey margin of victory was a substantial 44.2 to 31.4 percent.[6] *Public Opinion Quarterly*, in its last poll before the election, predicted a Dewey victory of 49 to 44 percent.[7] After the election, a Roper poll showed that only 19 percent of Americans polled had expected Truman to win.[8]

The press was so certain of a Dewey victory that nearly every reporter and news-gathering operation climbed way out on a limb by predicting a big Dewey victory, almost always with embarrassing results. *Newsweek*, on October 11, published a survey of fifty news columnists' opinions on the election. Among those polled were such icons in American journalism as

Marquis Childs, Arthur Krock, and Raymond Moley. All fifty agreed that Dewey would win easily.[9] A poll of the National Press Club gave Dewey the victory by a tally of fifty-to-one. *Time* news correspondents collected their opinions and predicted that Dewey would win in the electoral college by an amazing 350-to-38 margin and that Truman would carry only nine states.[10] Both *Time* and *Life* went so far as to prepare their postelection editions in advance of the election, including articles about the election, photographs of the new Republican president, and even predictions of what the nation would be like under the next four years of Dewey's leadership. Both magazines had to scrap their entire political sections just before press time, and both magazines appeared on newsstands without any mention of the election or its outcome.[11] The *New Republic* conceded defeat in its postelection edition, and *Who's Who* sent its 1949 edition to press with Dewey's address listed as 1600 Pennsylvania Avenue.

According to Clifford, every newspaperman on the president's campaign tour believed that Truman had no chance of winning the election. Even Clifford, the grand strategist, expressed doubt, as did Bess Truman, who made it clear that she did not believe her husband could pull off the upset. The Democratic National Committee, so convinced that its man could not win, had not even bothered to reserve a room for a victory party but the Eightieth Congress, just as certain of victory, voted public funds for a lavish Washington inauguration for its candidate.[12] Henry Wallace, in an election-night broadcast, recognized Dewey as the new president and promised to continue his fight in 1952.[13] And gambling houses could give the president nothing better that a fifteen-to-one long shot at pulling an upset.[14]

Just before the election, Washington began making preparations for an interregnum—one that might be dangerous as tensions grew between the United States and the Soviets over the Berlin crisis. Dewey's foreign policy adviser (and presumably secretary of state after the election) John Foster Dulles met secretly with Truman's secretary of state George Marshall to plan a smooth transition between the Truman and Dewey presidencies.[15] On election day, CIA director Robert Lovett (who would have been Dewey's secretary of defense) suggested to Clifford that the two men work together on the transition.[16] And Dewey, a week before the election, leaked his cabinet choices to the press.

Even Truman may have had his doubts. Only once during the campaign did the candidates' paths cross, at the dedication of New York's Idlewild Airport in late July. During the brief photo opportunity, Truman apparently suggested to Dewey that he might want to have something done about the

Eager to go to press, the *Chicago Daily Tribune* mistakenly pronounced Truman's defeat at the hands of Dewey. From the collections of the St. Louis Mercantile Library Association

plumbing in the White House after the election.[17] It was certainly in Truman's character to make a joke of that nature.

But it was the *Chicago Tribune*, of course, that was forced to eat the most crow. Its own postelection edition, with the headline "Dewey Defeats Truman," was hoisted by the president for photographers to become one of the great icons of American politics. Truman apparently responded, "That's one for the books."[18]

After the election the *New York Times*'s chief political correspondent, Arthur Krock, pronounced the upset "the political whodunnit of the century." For the Republicans, however, the big question revolved around blame. How could they have lost what appeared to be a sure thing? And most important, how did they lose the will of the people, the mandate given them in 1946? Almost immediately, fingers began pointing. The Old Guard blamed

Dewey and the liberals. Not surprisingly, Dewey and his people blamed the Old Guard.

The day after the election, at a press conference at the Roosevelt Hotel in New York, Dewey was clearly dumbfounded. He first blamed the debacle on Wisconsin and Iowa "going contrary to the opinions of everyone." At another press conference three days later in Albany, he was beginning to look at the bigger picture, now blaming the outcome on some three million Republicans who stayed home, he said, out of overconfidence.[19] In a letter to Henry Luce in December, Dewey had another answer: "The farm vote," he said, "switched in the last ten days and you can analyze figures from now to kingdom come and all they will show is that we lost the farm vote which we had in 1944 and that lost the election."[20] But some of Dewey's advisers were beginning to blame the Old Guard, Taft, and the Eightieth Congress. Edwin Jaeckle said that the Republican right had simply been too much "excess baggage" for Dewey to carry with him to victory.[21] And liberals in the party, like Henry Cabot Lodge Jr. concluded that Dewey had not only run a campaign that was too conservative but that Dewey was too conservative to hold the center and win the election.[22] Dewey himself attacked the Old Guard at a Lincoln Day dinner speech in early February: "The Republican party," he said, "is split wide open, with a reactionary group attempting to return it to the philosophy of the Nineteen Twenties." If it succeeded in taking over the party, "you can bury the Republican party as the deadest pigeon in the country." He went on to invite those on the right, those who would destroy the party in order to advance their conservative agenda, to get out of the party.[23]

But Dewey's attack was not playing well among party members. Almost immediately after the election, the vast majority in the party placed the blame for the Republican debacle squarely on Dewey, with the result that the Old Guard again gained strength. And their argument was difficult to refute. Liberals and moderates in the party had controlled the presidential nomination process for the last three elections, and all three candidates had lost. As one party member from the right announced after the election, "These boys [party liberals] have wrecked the party in three different elections. Now it's only fair to give us a chance to wreck it our way."[24] The "me-tooism" of the liberal Republican agenda had clearly failed in the face of the power of the New Deal and the coalition built by Roosevelt. The Old Guard argued that voters were not being given a clear choice between candidates and ideas, that the political system could work (and Republicans could win) only if the candidates were distinctly different.

Clarence Budington Kelland, an outspoken Old Guard operative from

Arizona, used the press to hit hard at Dewey and his supporters. Three weeks after the election, Kelland told *Time*: "Dewey's campaign was smug, arrogant, stupid and supercilious. . . . It was a contemptuous campaign, contemptuous alike to our antagonists and to our friends. The Albany group proved themselves to be geniuses in the art of stirring up an avalanche of lethargy. No issue was stated or faced." Then, in an article in *American Mercury* in February, Kelland appeared to be laying down the agenda for the party's future. He again blamed Dewey for the loss, claiming that he failed to draw a line between the policies of the two parties. The campaign, Kelland added, amounted to a "spineless dodging of issues" that was laden with "opportunism and appeasement and indefinite, shallow generalities. . . . We must cast aside forever the me-too appeasement of which we have been guilty," he wrote. "Me-too is not a policy. The Republican Party never has adopted it. Only certain leaders, lacking in courage and moral integrity, have enunciated it as belonging to us."[25] By mid-July Kelland and others on the Republican right succeeded in forcing Republican National Committee chairman (and Dewey supporter) Hugh Scott out of office and replacing him with Guy Gabrielson, a conservative supported by Taft's people. The surge in the Old Guard's power was also felt in the now Democratic-dominated Eighty-first Congress. Republican party liberals attempted to oust the venerable Taft as Policy Committee chairman and replace him with Lodge. Other liberal Young Turks, as they were called, tried to push conservatives from key Republican positions in favor of more liberal Republicans, but all lost—and it became clear whose strength was building in the party.[26]

The reverberations from the 1948 defeat continued to empower conservative Republicans in the months after the election. In July, Kelland led a move that set up the National Republican Round-up, a meeting of conservative minds for the purpose of promoting the policies of the party's right as a statement of principles and objectives for the national party. Then in December the Republican National Committee met in Chicago to repudiate the "me-tooism" of Willkie, Dewey, and the party's left. They promised that the 1950 campaign would be run in direct opposition to Truman and his policies, which they called socialist. The result was the *Statement of Republican Principles and Objectives* published in February 1950.[27]

The Republican debacle in 1948 and the resulting repercussions within the party brought the party's right to power and repudiated its liberal wing for about a four-year period, from the election of 1948 to the nomination of Eisenhower in the summer of 1952. It was during those four years that McCarthyism, the Republican party–inspired Red Scare, had its beginnings and reached its peak. McCarthyism had its origins in many events and issues and even in the depths of the national character that had developed an irrational fear of domestic communism. But McCarthyism was certainly fueled by the power of the Republican right in Congress, power that it had attained as a result of the 1948 election and postelection maneuverings.

Truman's victory has been well analyzed through the decades. Samuel Lubell, in his *Future of American Politics*, proposed several theories to describe Truman's upset. He was the first to present the Ohio thesis: that it was Ohio that finally tilted the election in Truman's favor in the early hours of November 3, that Ohio had gone for Dewey in 1944, and that Truman had worked harder for votes in Ohio than probably any other state except possibly New York. Lubell then looked deeper to find a key to this thesis in Ohio's German-American farmers. This group, Lubell argued, had voted against the Roosevelt administration during the war, but in 1948 they returned to the Democratic party and pulled Ohio over at the last minute.[28] Clearly, Ohio was important, and even Truman agreed that Ohio and California were keys to his victory.[29] Pinning the entire election down to a few German-American voters in Ohio, however, seems ludicrous in the analysis of a nationwide presidential election that can carry so many factors and variables. In fact, Truman received fewer votes in Ohio in 1948 than Roosevelt received in 1944 when Roosevelt lost the state to Dewey.[30] Jules Abels, in his *Out of the Jaws of Victory*, concluded that the urban labor vote, and not German-American farmers, was the deciding factor in Ohio.[31] More than anything else, the importance of Ohio seems to be that the numbers were close there and that the returns were reported late the morning after the election.

It was Lubell, also, who first explained that the Wallace and Thurmond third parties did more to help Truman than hurt him in 1948, and here is a viable and important explanation for Truman's victory.[32] Wallace's campaign pulled votes from the left away from Truman, but it also insulated Truman from Republican claims that the Democratic party was soft on communism and infiltrated with communists and communist sympathizers. Red-baiting had played well for the Republicans in 1946, and they certainly would have used it as an issue again in 1948, but that thunder was stolen when Wallace took the communists and their allies out of the Democratic party. That made the Democrats appear less leftist and more centrist at a time when the nation was generally moving away from the policies and ideologies of the left. This new stance allowed moderates who might otherwise have been alienated by the party's left-wing leanings that had supposedly prevailed during the Roosevelt years to support Truman. Much the same occurred on the right. The Dixiecrat campaign removed from the Democratic party the southern racist element that was so noxious to northern liberals and African Americans. Both of these groups might well have supported Wallace, but they returned to the Democrats in big numbers when the southerners left the party and took the race issue with them. The result was big votes for Truman from the northern–urban–liberal–black coalition that his strategists had targeted. Of course, James Rowe had been substantially correct in his campaign strategy memo to the president in the fall of 1947: the South remained in the party and voted for Truman—with the exception of the thirty-nine electoral votes that went to Thurmond. California and Illinois together gave Truman fifty-three electoral votes.[33] In both of those states the popular vote was close, and both states had large numbers of urban African Americans, labor voters, and liberals, many of whom voted for Truman. The trade-off for Truman in those two states alone easily negated the Dixiecrat "revolution." So it was, as Lubell pointed out in the early 1950s, that the Wallace and Thurmond campaigns actually helped rather than hurt Truman.

Lubell has also shown that Truman won in the nation's cities, although his margin of victory there was well below Roosevelt's.[34] According to Lubell, urban America had become the political bastion of the Democratic party beginning in 1928, when for the first time more urban dwellers voted Democratic than Republican. Roosevelt added to those majorities through the 1930s and early 1940s. The figures for the Democrats dropped off considerably in 1948, however, and analysts at the time assumed that the decline was owing to a siphoning off of liberal votes to Wallace in the northeastern urban areas. In a revised third edition of his original work, however, Lubell showed that the decline in Democratic party strength in the cities in 1948 was the beginning of a general decline that continued until 1960, when John Kennedy again pulled up urban voting strength for the Democrats.[35] Of course, Truman won a plurality in New York City, Philadelphia, Pittsburgh, Detroit, and Baltimore, but he lost New York State, Pennsylvania, Michigan, and Maryland. Nevertheless, Lubell's figures show that Truman had drawn on a nationwide urban constituency. The urban issues that helped Truman were housing, his prolabor stance, inflation control, and civil rights.

Other analysts saw the key to Truman's victory not in the cities but on the farm. That thesis did not escape Lubell, but it has been Allen Matusow, in his important work, *Farm Policies and Politics in the Truman Years*, who has best developed this thesis. Matusow showed that an obscure provision in the Commodity Credit Corporation charter passed by the Eightieth Congress at the end of the first session made it impossible for the federal government to build grain storage bins near farms. The fall of 1948 brought a harvest of record-breaking overproduction and drastic price declines in the grain-producing states. With no bins available, farmers could not deposit their grain and collect support payments. As commercial storage space began to disappear and surpluses piled up, farmers were forced to dump their grain early, and that caused prices to fall even further. Truman was able to use this issue in the last two months of the campaign when the situation in the farm belt was at its worst. The president and his secretary of agriculture, Charles Brannan, hit the hustings in the Midwest and the plains states with the message to farmers that the Republicans and the Eightieth Congress had denied them storage rights in a time of overproduction. A Republican victory, Truman told farmers, would bring more of the same. He added that the Republicans would probably move to cut other government programs that farmers had come to depend on such as price supports and funding for rural electrification. Truman won the agricultural states of Illinois and Missouri, but Matusow showed that his victories there came because of big urban votes in Cook County, Illinois, and Kansas City and St. Louis, Missouri, not from the farm vote. Matusow did, however, attribute Truman's victories in Ohio, Wisconsin, and Iowa to the farm vote. If the forty-seven electoral votes in those three states had gone to Dewey (as they had in 1944), the election would have gone to the House of Representatives.[36] Matusow added that farmers in 1948 remembered the help they had received from the New Deal. Now, after over fifteen years of support from the Democratic party, farmers saw the Republicans as risky. Farmers, Matusow concluded, were simply acting with customary conservatism by voting Democratic.[37] Irwin Ross, in *The Loneliest Campaign*, stated that the farm vote in Wisconsin and Iowa was crucial to Truman's victory, but he concluded that it was the urban vote in Ohio and Illinois, and not the farm vote, that gave those states to Truman.[38]

It is a truism of the American two-party political system that voters are often forced to vote for candidates because they have nowhere else to turn. It might also be true, in the most cynical of minds, that candidates win by default rather than by their ability to appeal to the hearts and minds of the majority of the electorate. In 1948 several groups found themselves with nowhere else to go on November 2; Truman was their only choice. For many who were disenchanted with Truman the reality had become clear that a vote for either Wallace or Thurmond meant a split in the Democratic vote and an advantage for the Republicans. Much of organized labor, for instance, had not been convinced by election time that Truman was working in their best interest. But for them, Wallace had become an unacceptable alternative, and the Republicans in the Eightieth Congress had shown that there was no place for organized labor on the right. Most southern whites who saw no advantage in dividing the Democratic party also had no place to go but to Truman. Anticommunist liberals, like those who filled the ranks of the ADA, were also among the politically homeless of 1948. The ADA and its allies searched and connived in an attempt to upset Truman for just about anyone from Dwight Eisenhower to William O. Douglas. They too were forced to settle for Truman. Big city bosses such as Frank Hague, Jake Arvey, and William O'Dwyer were Democrats with important power bases but with no place to defect. Polls showed that farmers came to Truman only in the eleventh hour of the campaign. And even African Americans who had been infatuated with Wallace in 1946 and 1947 had come to realize that a vote for Wallace would give an advantage to the Republicans, who had made no efforts to alleviate their plight. Truman, of course, made many of the right moves to bring these groups around to the Democratic party, but generally they came over reluctantly and very late, at least in part because there was no place else to go. It is not too much of an exaggeration to say that Truman won in 1948 by default.

It also might be said that the Republicans did as much to lose the election in 1948 as the Democrats did to win it. Probably the greatest Republican blunder was to accept at face value that the landslide in the 1946 congressional elections was not only a Republican mandate but a conservative mandate, when it clearly was not. The 1946 victories gave the Republicans a dose of overconfidence that produced a conservative leadership in the Eightieth Congress and a very hard line on domestic issues. The Republican leaders never seemed to consider the possibility that they might lose the presidential election (and even control of Congress) in 1948 if they failed to do a better job of legislating than the Democrats had done since Roosevelt died. As conservative domestic legislation came to dominate the agenda of the Eightieth Congress—with seemingly little regard for the political consequences—Republican political capital slipped in the minds of an American public that was not yet ready to give up on the policies of FDR and the New Deal. Truman, of course, made the best of these failings. At the same time, the Republicans allowed the president to do as he pleased in building domestic coalitions, in taking the lead of the popular bipartisan foreign policy, in making points with various political groups, and generally increasing his own political capital at their expense.

Meanwhile, public opinion polls continued to show that Dewey had little to fear from Truman in November. Consequently, Dewey's only campaign strategy seemed to be to avoid making promises that he would have to keep after the election. The result was a remarkably bland, uninspired campaign that confronted no issues and answered no questions.

In 1948, communism was a significant issue for the first time in a presidential election. But instead of the Republicans attacking the Democrats on the issue, Truman and the ADA successfully used Red-baiting to isolate Wallace and undercut his support. The Red-baiting of Wallace, however, would come back to haunt the Democrats later. As Allen Yarnell has written, "The 'respectable' liberal community led by the president had legitimized red-baiting."[39] According to Yarnell and others, the Red-baiting of Wallace in 1948 showed how effective that strategy could be in the early Cold War hysteria of the late 1940s and early 1950s. By 1952 the Republicans had resurrected the issue and were using it effectively against the Democrats, even against the ADA Democrats who had used it so effectively against Wallace in 1948.

It was more important to American voters, however, that Truman had successfully contained international communism. In a poll conducted in late 1946 a full 62 percent said they distrusted the Russians. In the summer of 1948, 56 percent said the United States should intervene militarily rather than lose control of Western Europe, and 61 percent wanted to do more for Western Europe than simply send aid.[40] It was President Truman who had stopped the advances of communism in Greece, Turkey, Iran, and West Berlin. The Truman Doctrine and the Marshall Plan had both been successful in stopping the spread of communism in Western Europe, and most Americans saw these foreign policy initiatives as appropriate responses to Soviet power. Truman had been with Churchill at Westminster College in Fulton, Missouri; he had appointed hard-line anticommunists such as Byrnes, Forrestal, and Marshall and dealt with Stalin with a firm hand. Truman took this anticommunist record into the 1948 election and won. And for the first time in U.S. history a presidential candidate had shown that the anticommunist issue could win votes, that there was a large sector of the American public who believed strongly in stopping communism and would vote for the candidate who did the most (or claimed he would do the most) to curtail the communist threat. It was a lesson that future presidential candidates would learn. It was Truman's successful anticommunist campaign of 1948, against the Soviets on one hand and against Wallace on the other, that set the stage for future campaigns in which the most anticommunist candidate drew the most votes.

At the same time, the foreign policy that Truman took into the election of 1948 was bipartisan and popular. It was also vehemently anticommunist, based on the policy of containment, and directed mostly at Wallace. All this undoubtedly hardened public attitudes in America toward communism (both domestic and foreign), severely damaged U.S. relations with the Soviet Union, and may well have brought on a witch-hunt mentality at home. The 1948 election also brought American communists out into the open. Generally a quiet, almost clandestine movement before 1948, American communism came up from underground to work openly for Wallace's campaign. And almost immediately after the election, they became the targets of federal and state investigations.

Truman won in 1948 because of a broad urban-liberal-black-labor coalition that he and his advisers had consciously forged through 1947 and 1948. Strategy for building that coalition began immediately after the Democratic debacle in November 1946 and continued unabated for two years. Again, Clifford was the point man at the head of the liberal Wardman Park group. James Rowe's memo was the strategy's constitution and by-laws. High points were the veto of Taft-Hartley in 1947, the appointment of the President's Committee on Civil Rights, and the decision to fight the record of the Eightieth Congress instead of Dewey. Wallace in the end did not remove the liberals from the Democratic party; he removed only the far left and the communists, a small and insignificant group by 1948. The liberals remained the powerful core of the party in the form of anticommunist ADA types, labor, and northern urban African Americans. There were other factors. One cannot deny the significance of the whistle-stop campaign, particularly in bringing the farmers over to the Democratic side in the last weeks before the campaign. Truman himself deserves a great deal of credit for evoking a fighting spirit that was clearly appealing to the American commoner, both urban and rural. Just as Truman deserves credit for his character in the victory, Dewey deserves credit for his lack of it in defeat. His dour, boring campaign of platitudes and overconfidence may well have done as much for Truman as any Clifford stratagem.

The Democratic party has always been made up of groups, and in this period they might best be described as voting blocs. Rowe recognized this in his memo written in September 1947, and that was its genius. He recognized that these groups were essentially liberal and that a few gestures (sincere or otherwise) in their various directions would bring them back into the party and win the election for the Democrats. He realized that several of these groups might have become alienated from Truman, but they had not been alienated from the party, and, certainly, they had not become Republicans. Truman, Clifford, and others in the White House were willing to give up the communists and left-wing Democrats to Wallace and the conservative southerners to Thurmond. What Truman held on to was the middle of the Democratic party, which in 1948 was essentially a liberal majority of the American electorate. If there were conservative elements among the president's electorate they came from farmers in the Midwest and West and from southern poor to middle-class whites who gave Truman their votes probably because they could not face voting Republican or splitting the Democratic vote by voting for Thurmond.

The election of 1948 was the greatest upset in American political history. It was the first presidential election since 1932 that did not include FDR and the first presidential election since the end of the war. It was bound to be significant. There were new issues to be confronted for the first time such as communism (at home and abroad), an inflation economy (instead of a depression economy), the newfound political power of northern urban African Americans and labor. Seeing the volatility of the postwar political world, groups in the Democratic party struggled for power, and they all seemed to move toward 1948 with a "succeed or destroy" attitude toward the party. One important theme of the 1948 election is always the deep splits in the Democratic party, but it was in the Republican party that the split was the most disastrous. The Democrats healed their wounds for one brief moment, just long enough to vote Truman into office, but the Republican left-right split produced for Truman the issue of the Eightieth Congress, and that issue carried the president right into his November victory.

The election of 1948 shaped postwar politics in both parties. For the Democrats, at least through Jimmy Carter's election in 1976, the goal would be to maintain the coalition—pacify the various groups—by holding on to the party's political center as Truman did. For the Republicans, the answer would be to heal the wounds between the left and the right—as Eisenhower would do through the 1950s—and to expand the party's voter base, particularly into the South.

The election reaffirmed the strength of the American party system, the strength of both parties, and the strength of the American electorate. The impact was great.

Notes

Abbreviations

EP   *Papers of Dwight D. Eisenhower*
GMMA   George Meany Memorial Archives
HSTL   Harry S. Truman Library
LC   Library of Congress
MDAH   Mississippi Department of Archives and History
NYT   *New York Times*
PCCR   President's Committee on Civil Rights
PP   Public Papers of the Presidents
WPRL   Walter P. Reuther Library
WSHS   Wisconsin State Historical Society

1. "Had Enough?" The Elections of 1946

1. See Gallup Poll tracking from July 1945 to October 1946 in *Washington Post*, July 11, 1947. In a June 1946 *Fortune* magazine survey, 33 percent said that Truman was not capable of handling the job of president.

2. William E. Leuchtenburg, *In the Shadow of FDR: From Harry Truman to Ronald Reagan* (Ithaca, N.Y., 1989), 23; *Newsweek*, Sept. 13, 1946. Alonzo Hamby has concluded that Truman chose to stay out of the campaign. See Hamby, *Beyond the New Deal: Harry S. Truman and American Liberalism* (New York, 1973), 136-37. On this same point, see also Harold F. Gosnell, *Truman's Crises: A Political Biography of Harry S. Truman* (Westport, Conn., 1980), 315.

3. *Newsweek*, Nov. 4, 1946; Leuchtenburg, *Shadow of FDR*, 23. *U.S. News*, Sept. 13, 1946, reported that "Mr. Hannegan is now trying to convince the voters that President Truman is a follower of Mr. Roosevelt in spirit and in action as well as in title and prerogatives."

4. *U.S. News*, Nov. 15, 1946. Similar comments continued in the press until the 1948 election. See, for example, *U.S. News and World Report*, Feb. 20, 1948.

5. David E. Lilienthal, *The Journals of David E. Lilienthal, vol. 2, The Atomic Energy Years, 1945-1950* (New York, 1964), 434.

6. Ickes resigned in February 1946, Wallace on September 20. Truman also did not get along with FDR's advisers who were tied to labor, such as Democratic National Committee chairman Hannegan. See *U.S. News*, Sept. 13, 1946.

7. Truman's appointees also brought a great deal of political inexperience to the White House. Only Secretary of State James Byrnes, Wallace, and Hannegan had worked in a national election campaign. See *U.S. News*, Sept. 13, 1946; and Truman to Jonathan Daniels, Feb. 26, 1950, in Robert H. Ferrell, ed., *Off the Record: The Private Papers of Harry S. Truman*

(New York, 1980), 174. Ferrell sees Truman's appointments as "first rate," particularly in the Departments of State and Defense. See Ferrell, *Harry S. Truman: A Life* (Columbia, Mo., 1994), 185-87.

8. In a postelection analysis, *Fortune* (March 1947) estimated that 23 percent of FDR's supporters turned Republican in 1946. The defection of Democrats to the GOP over the anticommunist issue was anticipated early; see *Fortune*, March 1946. See also Robert Griffith, *The Politics of Fear: Joseph R. McCarthy and the Senate* (Amherst, Mass., 1970), 38.

9. Quoted in Joseph C. Goulden, *The Best Years: 1945-1950* (New York, 1976), 226.

10. *U.S. News*, July 21, Sept. 13, 1946.

11. Quote in Goulden, *Best Years*, 226. The communist issue sent large numbers of Catholics back into the Republican party in this election. Many Catholics had become Democrats in 1928 as a result of Al Smith's campaign for president. Communism was a factor in the election of Henry Cabot Lodge Jr. in Massachusetts and in local and congressional elections in Pennsylvania, Michigan, and Illinois. See *U S News*, Nov. 15, 1946. For a discussion of one campaign in which communism was a major factor, see Jerry Voorhis, *Confessions of a Congressman* (Garden City, N.Y., 1947), 335-42; and Stephen E. Ambrose, *Nixon: The Education of a Politician* (New York, 1987), 138-40.

Joseph Stalin asked American voters to support candidates backed by the CIO-Political Action Committee. Republicans used this effectively against CIO-PAC candidates. See *Life*, Nov. 4, 1946.

12. For a preelection discussion of Truman's problems with minorities, see *U.S. News*, Nov. 1, 1946. On the FEPC and how it related to the election of 1946, see William C. Berman, *The Politics of Civil Rights in the Truman Administration* (Columbus, 1970), 6-7, 24-28, 32-33.

13. *U.S. News*, Nov. 15, 1946.

14. *U.S. News*, Nov. 1, 15, 1946.

15. *Fortune*, March 1947.

16. Quoted in Gary Reichard, *Politics as Usual: The Age of Truman and Eisenhower* (Arlington Heights, Ill., 1988), 31.

17. These quotes can be found in several places. See James R. Green, *The World of the Worker: Labor in the Twentieth Century* (New York, 1980), 194-95; David McCullough, *Truman* (New York, 1992), 506; Goulden, *Best Years*, 122. See also *U.S. News*, Oct. 18, 1946.

18. *Newsweek*, Nov. 4, 1946. Truman believed that Lewis's threatened strike of late 1946 helped defeat the Democrats in 1946. See Harry S. Truman, *Memoirs*, 2 vols. (New York, 1956), 1:556.

19. *U S News*, Nov. 15, 1946; *New Republic*, Nov. 18, 1946; and *NYT*, Nov. 11, 1946.

20. *Fortune*, May 1946.

21. Ibid.

22. *U.S. News*, July 12, 1946.

23. *Fortune*, May 1946.

24. Ferrell, ed., *Off the Record*, 100.

25. *Newsweek*, Nov. 11, 1946.

26. *U.S. News*, Oct. 25, 1946.

27. *Time*, Nov. 18, 1946.

28. For Truman's analysis of all this see Truman, *Memoirs*, 2:41.

29. *Life*, Nov. 4, 1946. The Gallup Poll is reported here. See also, *U S News*, Nov. 1, 1946.

30. *Cong. Rec.*, 80th Cong., 1st sess., 244-51. See also *NYT*, Nov. 11, 1946.

31. *New Republic*, Nov. 18, 1946; *NYT*, Nov. 11, 1946.

32. *Newsweek*, Nov. 18, 1946; *Time*, Nov. 18, 1946.

33. Hamby, *Beyond the New Deal*, 78-81; Ferrell, *Truman*, 220.

34. *U.S. News*, Nov. 15, 1946. There is an additional postelection discussion of the Republican "mandate" in *U.S. News*, Nov. 11, 1946.

35. *Newsweek*, Nov. 18, 1946.

36. William S. White, *The Taft Story* (New York, 1954), 57.

37. This hard line as a result of the election was anticipated by the press; see particularly *Newsweek*, Nov. 18, 1946; *U.S. News*, Nov. 15, 1946.

38. Arthur Schlesinger Jr., "How We Will Vote," *Atlantic Monthly*, Oct. 1946, 37.

39. *U.S. News*, Nov. 15, 1946. Harold Ickes thought it was a good idea. See Leuchtenburg, *In the Shadow of FDR*, 23. Truman began referring to Fulbright as "Senator Halfbright." See Clark Clifford, *Counsel to the President: A Memoir* (New York, 1991), 83. After the election the *Chicago Sun Times* called for Truman's resignation. See *NYT*, Nov. 7, 1946. See also Herbert S. Parmet, *The Democrats: The Years After FDR* (New York, 1976), 61.

40. *U.S. News*, Nov. 15, 1946.

2. Clark Clifford and Democratic Party Campaign Strategy

1. *Newsweek*, Nov. 18, 1946. Several Truman advisers in the White House agreed, particularly Secretary of the Treasury John Snyder, Secretary of Agriculture Clinton Anderson, and John Steelman, who had an important role as assistant to the president.

2. Leon H. Keyserling, "Leon H. Keyserling," in *The Truman White House: The Administration of the Presidency, 1945-1953*, ed. Francis H. Heller (Lawrence, Kan., 1980), 191. The group was meeting by December 27, 1946. See Dave Morse to Clark Clifford, Dec. 27, 1946 in Subject Files, Clark Clifford Papers, HSTL. For a more complete discussion of the Wardman Park group, see Gary A. Donaldson, "The Wardman Park Group and Campaign Strategy in the Truman Administration, 1946-1948," *Missouri Historical Review*, 86, no. 3 (April 1992): 282-94.

3. Other attendees included Assistant Secretary (later Secretary) of Agriculture Charles F. Brannan, and George M. Elsey, David Bell, J. Donald Kingsley, and John Thurston, all assistants to Clifford and Ewing. Democratic National Committee chairman J. Howard McGrath also attended occasionally. See interview with William Batt Jr., HSTL; and Keyserling, "Keyserling," 191.

4. Interviews with Oscar R. Ewing and Girard C. Davidson, HSTL.

5. Interview with Clark Clifford, HSTL. See also Clifford, *Counsel*, 85. Keyserling agreed. "I deserve eighty-five percent of the credit for pressing the issues with the Ewing group, but . . . Clifford deserved eighty-five percent of the credit for persuading the President" (interview with Leon H. Keyserling, HSTL).

6. Interviews with Clifford and with Davidson.

7. Clifford made an additional comment on this point in his interview, Truman Library: "It was an unceasing struggle during those two years, and it got to the point where no quarter was asked and none was given." For the other side of the argument, see interview with John Snyder, HSTL. See also Clifford, *Counsel*, 79-80.

8. Interview (combined) with Charles Murphy, Richard Neustadt, David Stowe, and James Webb, HSTL.

9. The changing nature of postwar American liberalism is discussed in Alan Brinkley,

The End of Reform: New Deal Liberalism in Recession and War (New York, 1995), 265-71; and Allen J. Matusow, *The Unraveling of America: A History of Liberalism in the 1960s* (New York, 1984), 3-29.

10. Clifford, *Counsel*, 84.

11. Interview with Clifford. Keyserling referred to it as "watering the tree at the bottom" ("Keyserling," 191-92).

12. Clifford, *Counsel*, 85.

13. Interviews with Clifford and with Keyserling.

14. Interviews with Ewing and with Clifford.

15. Interviews with Davidson and with Ewing.

16. See particularly Alonzo Hamby, *Man of the People: A Life of Harry S. Truman* (New York, 1995), 340; and Hamby, *Beyond the New Deal*, 182-83.

17. Interview with Clifford.

18. Keyserling, "Keyserling," 215-16; interviews with Davidson and with Clifford.

19. For a more in-depth discussion of the memo, its significance, and its origins, see Gary A. Donaldson, "Who Wrote the Clifford Memo? The Origins of Campaign Strategy in the Truman Administration," *Presidential Studies Quarterly* 23, no.4 (Fall 1993), 747-54.

20. James Rowe, memo to Clifford, "'Cooperation'—or Conflict?—The President's Relationship with an Opposition Congress," Dec. 1946, Subject Files, Clifford Papers.

21. Clifford, *Counsel*, 191.

22. Clifford referred to his part in changing the memo as "revise and update" (ibid.). In *New Yorker*, in 1991, Clifford gave Rowe credit for the original draft but referred to his own as "an extensive revision." See Clifford, "Annals of Government: Serving the President, The Truman Years," *New Yorker*, April 1, 1991, 60. In a *Washington Post* article in May 1991, Clifford was willing to give Rowe more credit. He was quoted as saying that his own "changes in the memorandum were not great." See E.J. Dionne Jr., "Clark Clifford and the Mystery of the Memo," *Washington Post*, May 22, 1991, 81, 89.

23. James Rowe to James Webb, "The Politics of 1948," Sept. 18, 1947, copy in interview with Rowe, 129-61.

24. All the following quotes come from Rowe's confidential memo to Budget Director James Webb entitled "The Politics of 1948," Sept. 18, 1947. A copy of the memo is in the appendix of the interview with Rowe, pp. 129-61. The memo from Clifford to Truman is entitled "Memorandum for the President" (Nov. 19, 1947), and is substantially the same as the Rowe memo. All quotes included here are in both memos. A copy of the Clifford memo is in the Clifford Papers.

25. Rowe to Webb, "The Politics of 1948," Sept. 18, 1947, copy in interview with Rowe, 128.

3. The Eightieth Congress and the Question of Mandate

1. Quoted in Jules Abels, *Out of the Jaws of Victory* (New York, 1959), 139.

2. Michael P. Poder, "The Senatorial Career of William E. Jenner" (Ph.D. dissertation, University of Notre Dame, 1976), 106.

3. On the debate over aid to England, see press release, Feb. 25, 1948, Political Files, Robert A. Taft Papers, LC. On the debate over the International Monetary Fund, see James T. Patterson, *Mr. Republican: A Biography of Robert A. Taft* (Boston, 1972), 291-295; and David Baldwin, *Economic Development and American Foreign Policy, 1943-1962* (Chicago,

1966). A good source for the foreign policy split in the Republican party is Walter Sloan Poole, "The Quest for a Republican Foreign Policy, 1941-1951" (Ph.D. dissertation, University of Pennsylvania, 1968).

On the unilateralists in the Republican party, see John Lewis Gaddis, *Strategies of Containment: A Critical Appraisal of Postwar American National Security Policy* (New York, 1982), 120; and Poole, "Quest for a Republican Foreign Policy," 117.

4. Quote in Eric F. Goldman, *The Crucial Decade—and After* (New York, 1960), 55. Taft fully intended to lead the way in abolishing several New Deal programs. See Taft to Gabriel Kaye, Nov. 4, 1946, Letters Sent Files, Taft Papers; and Taft speech in New York, Jan. 9, 1947, copy in Special Files, ibid.

5. On Taft's stand on education, see Robert A. Taft, *Education and Federal Aid* (n.p., n.d.), copy in Political Files, Taft Papers. On education, see also Taft's speech in Atlantic City, Mar. 6, 1947, copy in Special Files, ibid. On Taft's general philosophy, see "Taft's Political Credo," in Political Files, ibid. Taft, however, hated Truman's health care plan and worked to kill it. See pamphlet *What Should Congress Do About Health Insurance*, Special Files, ibid.

6. The Byrnes-Vandenberg relationship is explained well in Poole, "Quest for a Republican Foreign Policy," particularly 112-14. See also *NYT*, March 1, 1946; and James Byrnes, *All in One Lifetime* (New York, 1958), 355. For Vandenberg's opinion of his place in foreign policy and the Truman administration, see Arthur H. Vandenberg Jr., ed., *The Private Papers of Senator Vandenberg* (Boston, 1952), 378-79, 446. For Vandenberg's opinion of Byrnes, see pages, 225 and 243.

7. For Truman's glowing opinion of Vandenberg, see Truman, *Memoirs*, 2:281.

8. Patterson, *Mr. Republican*, 340; White, *Taft Story*, 146. For Taft's statements on foreign affairs and his opposition to the administration's foreign policy, see particularly press release to CBS News, March 3, 1948; and press release on the European Recovery Program, Feb. 25, 1948, both in Political Files, Taft Papers. See also Taft to Charles R. Hook, Dec. 31, 1947, Letters Sent Files, ibid.

9. Quoted in Patterson, *Mr. Republican*, 340.

10. *U.S. News*, Nov. 18, Dec. 22, 1946; *Newsweek*, Nov. 11, 1946. *Newsweek* claimed that the "Democrats have overstayed their time."

11. Joseph Martin, *My First Fifty Years in Politics* (New York, 1960), 179.

12. *NYT*, Jan. 3, 1947.

13. *Cong. Rec.*, 80th Cong., 1st sess., 36. This quote is from a radio address by Taft read into the *Congressional Record*. See also White, *Taft Story*, 56-57.

14. See *Time*, Nov. 18, 1946. Henry Z. Scheele, *Charlie Halleck: A Political Biography* (New York, 1966), 111-12.

15. The chairmen were Harold Knutson, Ways and Means; John Tabor, Appropriations; Jesse Wolcott, Banking and Currency; J. Parnell Thomas, Un-American Activities; Charles Eaton, Foreign Affairs. Eaton was an internationalist.

16. White, *Taft Story*, 58, 60.

17. Even his most sympathetic biographer agreed. See Patterson, *Mr. Republican*, 341-42.

18. Taft to Landon, May 17, 1948, Special Files, Taft Papers. Taft may have taken the position because liberal Republican George Aiken of Vermont was in line for the chairmanship of the committee. See Patterson, *Mr. Republican*, 338. A news release, Dec. 23, 1946, stating which chairmanships Taft would take is in Special Files, Taft Papers.

19. Quoted in Patteson, *Mr. Republican*, 339.

20. By senority rights, Taft should have chaired the Finance Committee. He chose to remain a member of that committee.

21. It was recorded in the *Columbus* (Ohio) *Dispatch* on December 24, 1946, that Bricker would not run in 1948. See also unidentified Bricker aide to Taft, Dec. 24, 1946, in Special Files, Taft Papers.

22. See Eleanor Bontecou, *The Federal Loyalty-Security Program* (Ithaca, N.Y., 1953), 237-255; Susan Hartmann, *Truman and the 80th Congress* (Columbia, Mo., 1971), 20, 28. The Loyalty Review Board was created by Executive Order 9835. It is often argued that Truman set up the Loyalty Review Board to head off the extremes of House Committee on Un-American Activities, then about to come under control of J. Parnell Thomas. See McCullough, *Truman*, 551. In an interview with Carl Bernstein, Clifford insisted that the loyalty program was only a "political problem" designed to take the issue from the Republicans and win the 1948 election for Truman. See Carl Bernstein, *Loyalties: A Son's Memoir* (New York, 1989), 195-98.

23. *PP: Truman, 1947*, 1-12.

24. Ibid., 13-39, 40-97. Truman's press conference on the budget given on January 8, 1947, is on pages 40-55. Knutson was chairman of the House Ways and Means Committee. Tabor chaired the House Appropriations Committee.

25. Hartmann, *Truman and the 80th Congress*, 27-46.

26. *NYT*, Jan. 23, 1947; Hartmann, *Truman and the 80th Congress*, 41-43. Clifford, Secretary of Labor Lewis Schwellenback, and Leon Keyserling of the Council of Economic Advisors opposed the bill. They believed it violated the Fair Labor Standards Act, the hallmark of labor legislation during the New Deal years. Attorney General Tom Clark, Secretary of Commerce Averell Harriman, and Secretary of the Navy James Forrestal supported it. See *PP: Truman*, 1947, 243-44.

27. Truman regarded Marshall highly. See Truman, *Memoirs*, 2:136.

28. *U.S. News*, March 21, 1947; *NYT*, March 18, 1947. For more on the public's appreciation of this supposedly amicable period, see *NYT*, Dec. 31, 1946, and Feb. 27, 1947. See also Susan Hartmann, *Truman and the 80th Congress*, 27-46.

29. *NYT*, Feb. 6, 10, 11, 15, 1947.

30. Lilienthal agreed to have his name withdrawn at any time during the confirmation process if he became an embarrassment to the administration. See Clifford, *Counsel*, 179; Lilienthal, *Journals*, vol. 2, 143-44.

31. *NYT*, Mar. 11, April 2, 3, 4, 10, 1947; *PP: Truman, 1947*, 131; Vandenberg, ed., *Papers of Senator Vandenberg*, 355; Hartmann, *Truman and the 80th Congress*, 32-35; Lilienthal, *Journals*, 2:143-44. For Truman's response to the vote and Vandenberg's comments to Lilienthal after the vote, see Lilienthal, *Journals*, 2:166. See also Patterson, *Mr. Republican*, 344.

32. Quoted in Hartmann, *Truman and the 80th Congress*, 38.

33. *PP: Truman, 1946*, 262-66; ibid., *1947*, 268-72.

34. *NYT*, Nov. 12, 1946. Taft's early plans for a labor bill are evident in a speech delivered in New York, Jan. 9, 1947, copy in Special Files, Taft Papers.

35. Copy of Hartley press release, April 10, 1947, in American Federation of Labor Papers, Department of Legislation, GMMA.

36. *CIO News*, March 10, 1947.

37. *NYT*, April 18, 1947.

38. White, *Taft Story*, 68.

39. *Cong. Rec.*, 80th Cong., 1st sess., 4965-86, 6392-93, 6441-45, 6536, 7488-89, 7535.

See also R. Alton Lee, *Truman and Taft-Hartley: A Question of Mandate* (Lexington, Ky., 1966), 49-79; Melvyn Dubofsky, *The State and Labor in Modern America* (Chapel Hill, 1994), 202-7; *NYT*, April 18, 1947. For Taft's role in the Senate, see Patterson, *Mr. Republican*, 352-66. Patterson concluded that Taft staved off more extreme antilabor intentions in the House (366).

40. The best source on Taft-Hartley is Lee, *Truman and Taft-Hartley*. See also Dubofsky, *The State and Labor*, 202-7; and Hartmann, *Truman and the 80th Congress*, 82-90. On Clifford's input on the veto decision, see Donaldson, "Wardman Park Group," 291. Truman's veto of Taft-Hartley is in *PP: Truman, 1947*, 288-97. See also "Radio Address to the American People on the Veto of the Taft-Hartley Bill," ibid., 298-301. Here Truman calls the bill a "shocking piece of legislation. "

41. *PP: Truman, 1947*, 428.

42. *NYT*, Sept. 17, 27, 1947. As early as late July, Taft was making speeches entitled "Why Things in Congress Have Been so Slow" and "The Republican Record." See speeches under these titles dated July 31, 1947, in Political Files, Taft Papers.

43. *PP: Truman, 1947*, 279-81, 342-44. The Senate failed to override the veto by five votes.

44. *PP: Truman, 1947*, 497-98.

45. *NYT*, Oct. 29, 1947.

46. *PP: Truman, 1947*, 432. See also *NYT*, (Sept. 12, 14, 1947).

47. Dean Acheson, *Present at the Creation: My Years in the State Department* (New York, 1969), 219; James Forrestal, *The Forrestal Diaries*, ed. Walter Millis, (New York, 1951), 248-49. Clifford also pushed Truman for a forceful address. See Clifford, *Counsel*, 132. For the strategy of the speech being devised among Truman's aides, see particularly Clifford to George Elsey, March 8, 1947, George Elsey Papers, HSTL; and Joseph Jones, "Chronology, Drafting of the President's Message of March 12, 1947" (n.d.), Joseph Jones Papers, HSTL.

48. *PP: Truman, 1947*, 176-80.

49. The Senate passed the aid package for Greece and Turkey by a vote of 67 to 23. The House went along 287 to 107, and Truman signed the bill on May 22. On the Truman Doctrine, see Melvyn P. Leffler, *A Preponderance of Power: National Security, the Truman Administration and the Cold War* (Stanford, 1992), 142-47.

50. Taft to Charles R. Hook, Dec. 31, 1947, Letters Sent Files, Taft Papers; David W. Reinhard, *The Republican Right Since 1945*, (Lexington, Ky., 1983), 33. See also Leffler, *Preponderance of Power*, 157-65; and Frank Kofsky, *Harry S. Truman and the War Scare of 1948: A Successful Campaign to Deceive the Nation* (New York, 1993), 124-41.

4. Henry Wallace and the Split of the Democratic Left

1. Manuscript in Henry Wallace Papers, University of Iowa, Iowa City, Iowa. Also in *Vital Speeches of the Day*, 14 (Aug. 1, 1948): 620-23.

2. John Morton Blum, ed., *The Price of Vision: The Diary of Henry A. Wallace, 1942-1946* (Boston, 1973), 263.

3. Quoted in Curtis Macdougall, *Gideon's Army*, 3 vols. (New York, 1965), 1: 91-92. For a slightly different opinion on which speech made Wallace an important political figure, see Hamby, *Beyond the New Deal*, 25.

4. *Washington Post*, July 18, 1944; *NYT*, July 18, 1944.

5. Truman, *Memoirs*, 1:558. Truman told his secretary of state James F. Byrnes in the

fall of 1945 that he needed Wallace "because of his influence with labor." See Byrnes, *All in One Lifetime*, 373.

6. Blum, ed., *Price of Visions*, 432, 631.

7. Ibid., 631.

8. *Life*, Dec. 16, 1946.

9. A transcript of Wallace's Madison Square Garden speech dated September 12, 1946, is in Wallace Papers, and a copy is in Subject Files, Clifford Papers. See also, Wallace to Truman, July 23, 1946, Progressive Party Papers, University of Iowa, which contains most of the material and statements that Wallace used in his Madison Square Garden speech. Beyond these often-quoted statements, Wallace had very little criticism of America's foreign policy toward the Soviets in this speech. Several times he was hissed and booed when he spoke of the need for Moscow to understand America's own postwar aims. Several days after the speech, the leaders of the American Communist party felt a need to calm their rank and file concerning several anti-Soviet remarks that Wallace had made. Eugene Dennis, the Communist party national secretary, wrote that the Communist Party was "disoriented by the unjust and harmful remarks by Wallace on the Soviet Union. . . . Because of this, the comrades failed to grasp the fact that Wallace, in his own way and within the limitations of his position, was challenging the main line of the Byrnes-Vandenberg policy. Cited in Irving Howe and Lewis Coser, *The American Communist Party, 1919-1957* [New York, 1962], 470. See also Eugene Dennis, *The Third Party and the 1948 Elections* (New York, 1948); and Blum, ed., *Price of Vision*, 612-28, 661-69. See particularly Blum's comments on page 669.

10. Byrnes had just delivered his "Stuttgart speech" on September 6 in which he stated the nation's new hard line against the Soviets. Many regarded Wallace's Madison Square Garden speech on September 11 to be in direct response to Byrnes's speech. The Stuttgart speech is in *Vital Speeches of the Day*, 12 (Sept. 15, 1946); 706-9.

11. See telegrams and copy of State Department communique in President's Secretary's Files, Harry S. Truman Papers, HSTL.

12. James F. Byrnes, *Speaking Frankly* (New York, 1947), 239-43.

13. A transcript of Truman's September 12, 1946, press conference is in Subject Files, Clifford Papers. See also Blum, ed., *Price of Vision*, 612; Byrnes, *All in One Lifetime*, 71; *NYT*, Sept. 13, 1946.

14. A transcript of Truman's September 13, 1946, press conference is in Subject Files, Clifford Papers; and in Political Files, Truman Papers. See also Byrnes, *All in One Lifetime*, 372. In another speech in Madison Square Garden a year later (as a commemoration to his 1946 speech) Wallace said: We read [the original Madison Square Garden speech] over page by page in the White House a year ago yesterday" (manuscript copy, Sept. 11, 1947 in Wallace Papers).

15. Truman, *Memoirs*, 1:557. See also George Curry, "James F. Byrnes," in Robert H. Ferrell and Samuel Flagg Bemis, eds., *The American Secretaries of State and Their Diplomacy* (New York, 1965), 14:254, 258.

16. Byrnes, *Speaking Frankly*, 240; Byrnes, *All in One Lifetime*, 372; *Time*, Sept. 30, 1946. See also Truman, *Memoirs*, 1:559.

17. Byrnes, *Speaking Frankly*, 241.

18. Clifford, *Counsel*, 121, 109. Clifford and others in the administration shared this fear. See particularly Gael Sullivan to Clifford, June 2, 1947, Subject Files, Clifford Papers.

19. See Gael Sullivan to Clark Clifford, June 2, 1947, Subject Files, Clifford Papers. It

reads in part: "Wallace is a major consideration in 1948. Something should be done about [him] before he gets himself too far committed to a Third Party. "

20. Harvey Klehr and John Earl Haynes, *The American Communist Movement: Storming Heaven Itself* (New York, 1992), 114; Joseph Starobin, *American Communism in Crisis, 1943-1947* (Cambridge, Mass., 1972), 169-72.

21. Macdougall, *Gideon's Army*, 1:19; *NYT*, July 31, 1944.

22. Steven M. Gillon, *Politics and Vision: The ADA and American Liberalism, 1947-1985* (New York, 1987), 6-7, 16. "Statement of Policy," June 28, 1947, in Progressive Party Papers, said that this policy of government ownership was in no way to be construed as socialism. See also Macdougall, *Gideon's Army*, 1:114-20.

23. *New Republic*, March 24, 1947. Wallace made the same statement in a speech on NBC radio, March 13, 1947, manuscript copy in Wallace Papers. The speech was also printed in the *Washington Post*, March 20, 1947.

24. Macdougall, *Gideon's Army*, 1:170.

25. *NYT*, June 23, 1947. *New Republic*, July 14, June 30, Oct. 4, 6, 1947, Jan. 5, 1948; and *Vital Speeches*, 4:174. See also manuscript of Wallace speech, March 31, 1947, Wallace Papers. A copy of the speech appeared in *PM*, April 1, 1947.

26. *New Republic*, June 2, Sept. 1, 1947; manuscript copy of speech; May 19, 1947, in Wallace Papers.

27. Manuscript, Sept. 11, 1947, in Wallace Papers; *NYT*, Sept 11, 1947.

28. *Nation*, Dec. 20, 1947, 668. This article pushed Wallace to make a decision. See Wallace interview, Columbia Oral History Collection.

29. Manuscript copy of speech in Wallace Papers. See also Wallace, "I Shall Run in 1948," *Vital Speeches of the Day* 14 (Jan. 1, 1946): 172-74. Wallace said he made the decision to run on December 29. See Wallace interview; and Starobin, *American Communism in Crisis*, 165-66, 290.

30. *PM*, Dec. 30, 1947.

31. Upton Sinclair to Henry Wallace, July 15, 1948, President's Secretary's Files, Truman Papers. Sinclair sent Truman a copy of the letter.

32. *Life*, March 1, 1948.

33. *Nation*, March 13, 1948.

34. For these deals, see Starobin, *American Communism in Crisis*, 188-89; and Macdougall, *Gideon's Army*, 3:866, 2:545.

35. Eleanor Roosevelt's column was syndicated. See undated clippings in Subject Files, Clifford Papers. The article was reprinted in *ADA World*, Jan. 8, 1948.

5. Truman Versus Organized Labor

1. *NYT*, Sept. 9, 1945.

2. See particularly Truman to John J. Dempsey, Jan. 26, 1946, Official Files, Truman Papers.

3. Truman to Bess Truman, Jan. 23, 1946, in Margaret Truman, *Harry S. Truman* (New York, 1972), 304-5.

4. *CIO News*, March 12, 1945. See also Lee, *Truman and Taft-Hartley*, 30; Eight states were considering right-to-work laws in 1945.

5. For labor's fears of federal antilabor legislation, see *CIO News*, Nov. 12, 1945. For a general discussion of these bills and what they entailed, see Harry A. Millis and Emily Clark

Brown, *From the Wagner Act to Taft-Hartley: A Study of National Labor Policy and Labor Relations* (Chicago, 1950), 356-62.

6. Gallup Poll, "Public Opinion on Case Bill," June 1946, copy in Official Files, Truman Papers. In a public opinion poll taken in 1946, 74 percent agreed that the government should take over the mines being struck by the UMW. See Hadley Cantril, *Public Opinion, 1935-1946* (Princeton, 1951), 824.

7. Quoted in William Leuchtenburg, *Franklin Roosevelt and the New Deal* (New York, 1963), 243.

8. Joel Seidman, *American Labor from Defense to Reconversion* (Chicago, 1953), 135.

9. Quoted in Saul Alinsky, *John L. Lewis: An Unauthorized Biography* (New York, 1949), 302.

10. *Wall Street Journal*, Aug. 22, 1944.

11. For the influence of communism in American labor unions after the war, see Robert H. Zieger, *The CIO, 1935-1955* (Chapel Hill, 1995), 253-93.

12. *NYT*, June 22, 1946. The Hobbs bill (HR 653) that was approved by the House (78th Cong., 1st sess.) was later included in the vetoed Case bill, then separately passed and signed as the Hobbs Act in July 1946. The bill removed the exemption of labor unions from the Federal Anti-Racketeering Act. Truman signed the bill despite protests from labor. See Millis and Brown, *From the Wagner Act to Taft-Hartley*, 332-33.

13. *Life*, Jan. 21, 1946.

14. For the growth and development of the CIO-PAC, see Zieger, *CIO*, 444-46; and James C. Foster, *The Union Politic: The CIO Political Action Committee* (Columbia, Mo., 1975).

15. Cantril, *Public Opinion*, 824.

16. Gallup Poll, "Public Opinion on Case Bill."

17. See particularly *Life*, Jan. 28, Feb. 4, 1946.

18. *NYT*, May 27, 1946.

19. *Life*, May 13, 1948.

20. *Life*, May 20, 1948.

21. "Report to the President's Council of Economic Advisors Submitted by Philip Murray, President of CIO," Dec. 12, 1946, CIO Secretary-Treasurer's Office Files, CIO Papers, WPRL. See also Council of Economic Advisors, "The Impact of Foreign Aid Upon the Domestic Economy," Oct. 1947, James E. Webb Papers, HSTL.

22. Seidman, *American Labor from Defense to Reconversion*, 221.

23. Ibid., 240-41. In the last half of 1946 consumer prices increased by 15 percent; food prices increased by nearly 30 percent. Those increases are reflected in the real wage statistics cited here. See also Lee, *Truman and Taft-Hartley*, 17. For a similar breakdown of United Auto Workers' average weekly wages before and after the war, see Walter Reuther, Press Release, Feb. 21, 1947, UAW President's Office Files: Walter Reuther, Walter P. Reuther Papers, WPRL. According to Reuther, the average auto worker made $35.76 per week in 1940 but a real wage of only $33.50 in 1946.

24. W. Reuther to Truman, Oct. 26, 1946 UAW President's Office Files: Walter Reuther, Walter Reuther Papers.

25. George F. Addes (CIO secretary-treasurer), press release, Oct. 6, 1946, ibid.

26. Seidman, *American Labor from Defense to Reconversion*, 241.

27. *CIO News*, Sept. 3, 1945. For a breakdown in the automobile industry as reported by the CIO, see Walter Reuther, press release, Feb. 21, 1947, UAW President's Office Files: Walter Reuther, Walter Reuther Papers. According to Reuther, the auto industry would earn

as much as $2 billion in before-tax profits in 1947 as opposed to its 1936-1941 average earnings of $460,000 per year.

28. *CIO News* was understandably obsessed with such questions; see particularly Aug. 20, Sept. 3, 1945. Truman's economic advisers also feared the possibility of a postwar depression. See Council of Economic Advisors, "The Impact of Foreign Aid Upon the Domestic Economy," Oct. 1947, Webb Papers.

29. Executive Order 9599; *NYT*, Aug. 17, 1945. This was also included in Truman's September message to Congress. See *PP: Truman, 1945*, 283, and *NYT*, Sept. 7, 1945.

30. *NYT*, Sept. 18, Nov. 27, 1945.

31. *NYT*, Nov. 2, 17, Dec. 1, 3, 13, 1945,; *Life*, Nov. 22, 1945, Dec. 9, 1946.

32. *CIO News*, Mar. 18, 1946; and Seidman, *American Labor from Defense to Reconversion*, 226-27. A year later Reuther claimed that 1946 industry profit reports confirmed his claims that the auto industry was, in fact, capable of paying higher wages in 1946 (UAW-CIO Press Release, April 20, 1947, UAW President's Office Files: Walter Reuther, Walter Reuther Papers).

33. *NYT*, Dec. 3, 4, 1945.

34. *CIO News*, Dec. 10, 1945.

35. *NYT*, Dec. 13, 1945.

36. *Life*, June 3, 1946.

37. Clifford, *Counsel*, 88.

38. Ibid., 89.

39. *PP: Truman, 1946*, 277-80; *NYT*, May 25, 1946.

40. Clifford, *Counsel*, 91. See also *Cong. Rec.*, 79th Cong., 2d sess., 5801; Truman, *Memoirs*, 1:501. See also Seidman, *American Labor from Defense to Reconversion*, 236; and Lee, *Truman and Taft-Hartley*, 36.

41. *NYT*, May 27, 1947; *Life*, June 10, 1946; *CIO News*, June 3, 1946.

42. *Newsweek*, June 10, 1946; *NYT*, May 27, 1946. Taft told Congress that the bill violated "every principle of American jurisprudence." But he also stated that had the railroad strike not been settled, he would have supported the bill (*Cong. Quart.* 2 [1946]: 300).

43. Rankin to Truman, n.d., Official Files, Truman Papers.

44. See *CIO News*, Feb. 4, 11, 1946.

45. *PP: Truman 1946*, 289-97.

46. Ewing to Truman, n.d. (Dec. 1946), Political Files, Oscar Ewing Papers, HSTL.

47. Lewis and Krug were bitter personal enemies. See Melvyn Dubofsky and Warren Van Tine, *John L. Lewis: A Biography* (New York, 1977), 470.

48. Clifford, *Counsel*, 93; *NYT*, Nov. 18, 1946.

49. Clifford, *Counsel*, 93.

50. Ibid., 92.

51. Truman's approval rating climbed to 62 percent. See *Public Opinion Quarterly* (Winter 1946-47): 428.

52. Clifford, *Counsel*, 92.

53. *PP: Truman, 1947*, 3-5.

54. Tally, June 12, 1947, in Subject Files, Clifford Papers. According to Alton Lee, these figures represent only a selection of over 750,000 telegrams, postcards, and letters that came to the White House, with the vast majority urging veto of the bill. Lee cites the *New York Herald*. See Lee, *Truman and Taft-Hartley*, 81.

55. Green to Clifford, May 20, 1947, Subject Files, Clifford Papers.

56. Bowles to Truman, May 23, 1947, ibid.

57. Wyatt to Truman, June 10, 1947, ibid.; *ADA World*, May 5, 1947. Many in the ADA did not expect Truman to veto Taft-Hartley. See *ADA World*, April 26, 1947.

58. *Washington Post*, June 23, 1947. A Gallup Poll on Taft-Hartley is in *Washington Post*, May 23, 1947.

59. *PP: Truman, 1947*, 279-81; *NYT*, June 21, 1947. See Robert Taft's reply to the veto in *NYT*, June 21, 1947; and Fred Hartley's reply the next day, *NYT*, June 22, 1947.

60. *Cong. Rec.*, 80th Cong. 1st sess., 7489, 7538.

6. The ADA and the Splintering of Postwar Liberalism

1. *ADA World*, March 2, 1948.

2. See various requests for funds, open descriptions of the organization's financial plight, and summaries of various financial reports in ADA Administrative Files, Americans for Democratic Action Papers, WSHS. At one point in 1948 the ADA could claim only five thousand paying members, four thousand of whom were located in New York and Chicago. See "Confidential Memo," Feb. 20, 1948, UAW President's Office Files: Walter Reuther, Walter Reuther Papers.

3. James Rowe to James Webb, "The Politics of 1948," Sept. 18, 1947; copy in interview with Rowe, 129-61.

4. James Loeb, untitled manuscript, Jan. 16, 1947, ADA Administrative Files, ADA Papers.

5. Gillon, *Politics and Vision*, 10.

6. *UDA Bulletin*, June, 1941.

7. Loeb to Wallace, Dec. 1944, UDA Administrative Files, ADA Papers.

8. Loeb to Wallace, Sept. 21, 1946, ibid.

9. On this point, see *ADA World*, June 16, 1947.

10. Loeb, untitled manuscript, Jan. 16, 1947. See also "Minutes" of ADA conference held January 4, 1947, both in ADA Administrative Files, ADA Papers. In another writing, Loeb added, "Progressivism has been cruelly crippled legislatively." See Loeb, untitled manuscript, Nov. 14, 1946, UDA Administrative Files, ADA Papers.

11. From "List of Founders of Americans for Democratic Action," Jan. 9, 1947, ADA Administrative Files, ADA Papers.

12. *NYT*, Jan. 4, 1947.

13. ADA press release, Jan. 4, 1947, UDA Administrative Files, ADA Papers. Schlesinger wrote a more strongly worded statement. See Schlesinger draft, Dec. 13, 1946, ibid.

14. "ADA Constitution," n.d., ADA Administrative Files, ADA Papers; ADA press release, Jan. 4, 1947, UDA Administrative Files, ADA Papers.

15. Loeb to Patrick Gordon-Walker, Aug. 31, 1947; and Wyatt to Loeb, July 18, 1947, ADA Administrative Files, ADA Papers. Murray may also have hoped that by withholding support he could force the two groups to merge. See Gillon, *Politics and Vision*, 22-23.

16. In the *New Republic* issue immediately following Truman's election in November, Straight published an article by Arthur Schlesinger in what appeared to be the spirit of forgive and forget. See *New Republic*, Nov. 8, 1948.

17. *New Republic*, Jan. 17, 1947.

18. Reprinted in *Cong. Rec.*, 80th Cong., 1st sess., A1329; and in *Washington Post*, March 20, 1947.

19. *New Republic*, March 24, 1947.

20. *NYT*, March 30, 1947.

21. See David D. Lloyd to "All Chapters," March 10, 1948. ADA Administrative Files, ADA Papers. This statement urged support for the ERP bill.

22. See *ADA World*, April 12, 1947.

23. *ADA World*, April 26, May 30, 1947. On the ADA's push for a veto of Taft-Hartley, see Wilson Wyatt to Truman, June 10, 1947, Subject Files, Clifford Papers.

24. See particularly Gael Sullivan to Clifford, June 2, 1947, Subject Files, Clifford Papers.

25. ADA, "Statement on Political Policy," April 11, 1948, copy ibid.

26. *ADA World*, June 5, 1948.

27. Quoted in Irwin Ross, *The Loneliest Campaign: The Truman Victory of 1948* (New York, 1968), 73; and Clifton Brock, *The Americans for Democratic Action: Its Role in National Politics* (Washington, D.C., 1962), 88.

28. *PP: Truman, 1948*, 1-10.

7. The Loosening of Old Chains

1. Steven F. Lawson, *Running for Freedom: Civil Rights and Black Politics in America Since 1941* (New York, 1991), 14.

2. Raymond Wolters, *Negroes and the Great Depression: The Problem of Economic Recovery* (Westport, Conn., 1970), 124-25, 148-55; John A. Salmond, "The Civilian Conservation Corps and the Negro," *Journal of American History* 52, no. 1 (June 1965): 75-88.

3. For more on this group, see Henry Lee Moon, *Balance of Power: The Negro Vote* (Garden City, N.Y., 1948), 28-30. For Ickes's feelings and opinions on civil rights, see Harold L. Ickes, *The Secret Diary of Harold L. Ickes*, 3 vols. (New York, 1954), 2:115; and Ickes, "To Have Jobs or to Have Not," *Negro Digest*, Jan. 1946.

4. Several important African-American leaders felt that the New Deal was not going far enough to help poor blacks. Among this group were Ralph Bunche and A. Philip Randolph. See Bunche, "A Critical Analysis of the Tactics and Programs of Minority Groups," *Journal of Negro Education* 4 (July 1935): 308-20; and Bunche, "The Programs of Organizations Devoted to the Improvement of the Status of the American Negro," *Journal of Negro Education* 88 (July 1939): 539-47. On Randolph, see Paula F. Pfeffer, *A. Philip Randolph: Pioneer of the Civil Rights Movement* (Baton Rouge, 1990), 33-35.

5. For an analysis of African-American political activity in selected northern cities in the 1940s, see Moon, *Balance of Power*, 146-73. The proportion of African Americans living in the South in the postwar period declined from 75 to 63 percent. See U.S. Housing and Home Finance Agency, *Housing of the Nonwhite Population, 1940-1947* (Washington, D.C., 1948), 4. Consequently, the number of African Americans moving to northern cities after the war increased dramatically. See *US News and World Report*, Feb. 20, 1948.

6. Walter White, *A Man Called White* (New York, 1948), 186-88. Nancy J. Weiss, *Farewell to the Party of Lincoln: Black Politics in the Age of FDR* (Princeton, 1983), 278-79.

7. Weiss, *Farewell to the Party of Lincoln*, 276-77.

8. Richard M. Dalfiume, *Desegregation of the U. S. Armed Forces: Fighting on Two Fronts, 1939-1953* (Columbia, Mo., 1969), 40-41.

9. Weiss, *Farewell to the Party of Lincoln*, 287.

10. Pfeffer, *Randolph*, 47-49.

11. Press release, June 12, 1941, Philleo Nash Papers, HSTL.

12. Quoted in *Ebony*, Nov. 1958.

13. Of some eight thousand complaints submitted to the FEPC, over two-thirds were dismissed. Both unions and employers frequently disregarded FEPC orders with no penalty. See Pfeffer, *Randolph*, 50-51. See also Richard M. Dalfiume, "The 'Forgotten Years' of the Negro Revolution," *Journal of American History* 55, no. 1 (June 1968): 90-106.

14. Lawson, *Running for Freedom*, 6.

15. White, *A Man Called White*, 35.

16. *Colliers*, Nov. 22, 1947.

17. See various clippings from the African-American press in Nash Papers. See also Truman's pathetic apology to Adam Clayton Powell: "I am sure that you will realize, however, the impossibility of my interference . . . in the management or policy of a private enterprise such as the one in question." The African-American press printed the letter and made it clear that the DAR, having been chartered by Congress in 1890, was not a private organization. The letter is in Nash Papers.

18. Donald R. McCoy and Richard T. Reutten, *Quest and Response: Minority Rights and the Truman Administration* (Lawrence, Kan., 1973), 71.

19. *New York Daily News*, Oct. 28, 1948.

20. James Rowe to James Webb, "The Politics of 1948," Sept. 18, 1947, copy in interview with Rowe, 129-61. Most of the nation's African-American newspapers supported Dewey in 1948.

21. William Batt to Gael Sullivan (the memo was forwarded to Clifford), April 20, 1948, Subject Files, Clifford Papers.

22. *NYT*, June 22, 1948.

23. Anonymous memo to Oscar Ewing, April 5, 1948, Political Files, Ewing Papers.

24. Anonymous (Ewing?), undated (spring 1948?) memo to Clifford, ibid.

25. William Batt to Gael Sullivan, April 20, 1948, Subject Files, Clifford Papers.

26. Rowe, "The Politics of 1948."

27. Anonymous, undated memo to Clifford, Political Files, Ewing Papers.

28. That the Truman administration was concerned about these factors can be seen in "Files of the Facts," undated manuscript compiled by the Democratic National Committee in Nash Papers.

29. President's Committee on Civil Rights, *To Secure These Rights: The Report of the President's Committee on Civil Rights* (Washington, D.C., 1947), 100.

30. *PP: Truman, 1947*, 311-12.

31. *PP: Truman, 1948*, 122.

32. Robert K. Burns, "The Comparative Economic Position of Manual and White-Collar Employees," *Journal of Business* 54 (Oct. 1954): 260; *Statistical Abstracts of the United States* (1962), 312.

33. Philip S. Foner, *Organized Labor and the Black Worker, 1619-1973* (New York, 1974), 270.

34. Ibid., 270-74.

35. Lawson, *Running for Freedom*, 9.

36. Gunnar Myrdal, *An American Dilemma* (New York, 1944), 1002-4, 1009. See also Harvard Sitkoff, *A New Deal for Blacks: The Emergence of Civil Rights as a National Issue, The Depression Decade* (New York, 1978), chap. 8.

37. Quoted in Steven Lawson, *Black Ballots: Voting Rights in the South, 1944-1969* (New York, 1976), 100.

38. Manning Marable, *Race, Reform, and Rebellion: The Second Reconstruction in Black America, 1945-1990* (Oxford, Miss., 1991), 26.

39. *Life*, Dec. 16, 1946.

40. *Cong Rec.*, 80th Cong., 1st sess., 7-8; *Life*, (Dec. 16, 1946, Jan. 13, 1947; *Newsweek*, Sept. 1, 1947. The best source on Bilbo is A. Wigfall Green, *The Man Bilbo* (Baton Rouge, 1963). For a look at southern racism at mid-century, see Theodore G. Bilbo, *Take Your Choice: Separation or Mongrelization* (Poplarville, Miss., 1947).

41. White, *A Man Called White*, 324. See also Daniel F. Byrd (president of the Louisiana chapter of the NAACP) to White, Aug. 26, 1946, NAACP Papers, LC.

42. Clyde R. Miller to Arthur Hays Sulzberger, Aug. 22, 1946; and NAACP press release, Aug. 28, 1946, both in NAACP Papers. For the press accounts of the murder, see *New York Post*, Aug. 20, 1946; and *PM*, Aug 21, 1946.

43. White, *A Man Called White*, 325; *Shreveport Times*, March 2, 1947.

44. NAACP Press release, March 3, 1947, NAACP Papers.

45. NAACP press release, Sept. 20, 1946, NAACP Papers; White, *A Man Called White*, 322-28; Robert A. Garson, *The Democratic Party and the Politics of Sectionalism, 1941-1948* (Baton Rouge, 1974), 194-98.

46. White to William Hastie, Sept. 26, 1946; and White to Truman, Aug. 16, 1948, both in NAACP Papers.

47. White, *A Man Called White*, 330.

48. Ibid., 330-31.

49. Philleo Nash later revealed to historian Barton Bernstein that the president was well aware of the violence in the South and that a plan to set up a civil rights committee was already in the works. See Barton J. Bernstein, "The Ambiguous Legacy: The Truman Administration and Civil Rights," in *Politics and Policies of the Truman Administration*, ed. Bernstein (Chicago, 1970), 276, 307. See also Garson, *Democratic Party and the Politics of Sectionalism*, 199-200. For Truman's recollections, see Truman, *Memoirs*, 2:210. Nash advised Truman on civil rights issues.

50. White, *A Man Called White*, 331-32; White to William Hastie, Sept. 26, 1946, NAACP Papers. The President's Committee on Civil Rights did not report its findings until October 1947.

51. Executive Order 9809, Dec. 5, 1946, copy in Nash Papers; Executive Order 9809, 11 *Federal Register* 14153.

52. Also named to the committee were Rev. Francis J. Haas, the bishop of Grand Rapids, Michigan, and former head of the now defunct FEPC; Francis Matthews, the former head of the Knights of Columbus and a Chamber of Commerce executive; New York rabbi Rolland B. Gittelson; president of the University of North Carolina Frank Graham; and president of Dartmouth College John S. Dickey. Other members included Henry K. Sherrill, a prominent Episcopal bishop; Morris Ernst from the American Civil Liberties Union; Philadelphia city solicitor Sadie Alexander; and M.E. Tilly, a prominent southern liberal.

53. White to Marshall, Dec. 6, 1946, NAACP Papers.

54. Carr to White, March 27, 1947; Carr to Roy Wilkins, Feb. 27, 1947; and White to Marshall, Dec. 6, 1946, NAACP Papers. White and Marshall both appeared before the committee.

55. Niles to Mathew J. Connelly (Truman's appointment secretary), June 16, 1947, Subject Files, Clifford Papers.

56. *PP: Truman, 1947*, 311-13; *NYT*, June 30, 1947.

57. Quoted in William E. Pemberton, *Harry S. Truman: Fair Dealer and Cold Warrior* (Boston, 1989), 115.

58. White, *A Man Called White*, 348-49.

59. President's Committee on Civil Rights, *To Secure These Rights*, 151-73. See also V.O. Key, "Use of Federal Grants-In-Aid as a Device for Preventing Discrimination in the Providing of Public Services," unpublished manuscript, n.d., Papers of the President's Committee on Civil Rights, HSTL.

60. White to Truman, Oct. 28, 1947, NAACP Papers.

61. Bethune to Truman, Oct. 31, 1947, Official Files, Truman Papers.

62. David K. Niles, "Public Interest in the President's Civil Rights Program," Feb. 16, 1948, memo in Nash Papers. Large numbers of copies were sent out by the Americans for Democratic Action. See ADA press release, March 11, 1948, ADA Administrative Files, ADA Papers. The ADA began immediately to push Truman to enact the provisions of *To Secure These Rights*. See Henderson to Truman, July 22, 1948, ibid.

63. *PP: Truman, 1948*, 121-26.

64. *Washington Post*, Feb. 3, 1948.

65. *U.S. News and World Report*, May 21, 1948.

66. *Newsweek*, March 1, 1948. The Democratic candidate had also received the support of the Democratic party boss in the Bronx, Ed Flynn and New York City mayor William O'Dwyer, another powerful figure in the Democratic party. On Truman's reaction to the Isacson victory, see Robert H. Ferrell, ed., *Truman in the White House: The Diary of Eben A. Ayers* (Columbia, Mo., 1991), 246, 266.

67. *NYT*, Feb. 18, 1948. See also various poll reports collected in Political Files and Subject Files, Clifford Papers, and in Nash Papers.

68. *U.S. News and World Report*, May 21, 1948. See also, Moon, *Balance of Power*, 10-11.

8. The End of Southern Dominance in the Democratic Party

1. Truman was also perceived as a midwestern New Dealer, which added to his appeal as a vice-presidential candidate. Just after his nomination, Truman called himself "a progressive Southerner" who believed in states' rights and was "not interested one whit in the question of 'white supremacy'" (*NYT*, July 19, 1948).

2. Copy of Thurmond speech in President's Personal Files, Truman Papers. In Louisville in October 1947 Thurmond said: "We who believe in a liberal political philosophy, in the importance of human rights as well as property rights, in the preservation and strengthening of the economic and social gains brought about by the efforts of the Democratic Party will vote for the election of Harry Truman and . . . I believe we will win." See Nadine Cohodas, *Strom Thurmond and the Politics of Southern Change* (New York, 1993), 123.

3. On the significance of the two-thirds rule, see Harold Bass, "Presidential Party Leadership and Party Reform: Franklin D. Roosevelt and the Abrogation of the Two-Thirds Rule," *Presidential Studies Quarterly* (Spring 1988): 303-17.

4. In the Seventy-ninth Congress, 43 of the 102 southern Democrats in the House cast less than 50 percent of their votes with the majority of their party. See Garson, *The Democratic Party and the Politics of Sectionalism*, 168.

5. In the House, a Republican-southern coalition of 149 Republicans and 87 southerners passed the bill.

6. James Rowe to James Webb, "The Politics of 1948," Sept. 18, 1947, copy in interview with Rowe, 129-61.

7. George Elsey to Clifford, n.d., Elsey Papers.

8. *PP: Truman, 1948*, 121-26.

9. *NYT*, Feb. 4, 1948. A crowd of two hundred burned a cross at the county courthouse in Swainsboro.

10. *Time*, Feb. 16, 1948.

11. *Cong. Rec.*, 80th Cong., 2d sess., A1512.

12. Quoted in Charles P. Roland, *The Improbable Era: The South Since World War II* (Lexington, Ky., 1976), 60; and in Francis Butler Simpkins and Charles P. Roland, *A History of the South* (New York, 1972), 500. See similar comments in the *Norfolk Journal and Guide*, Feb. 7, 1948; *Arkansas Gazette*, Feb. 2, 1948; *Montgomery Advertiser*, Feb. 3, 1948; and *Atlanta Journal*, Feb. 3, 1948. The *Norfolk Journal and Guide*, Feb. 7, 1948, insisted that the president's speech was "politically motivated" and that "only the blindly prejudiced will deny that what he has done is more of a political *liability* than it is a political *asset*." All clippings are in "States' Rights Scrapbook," Mississippi Department of Archives and History, Jackson, Miss.

13. *PP: Truman, 1948*, 127.

14. *NYT*, Feb. 6, 7, 8, 1948; Jackson *Clarion Ledger*, Feb. 6, 1948. Governor Fielding Wright of Mississippi had warned in his inaugural address in January 1948 that Democratic party support for civil rights would cause the South to bolt the party (*Jackson Daily News*, Jan. 20, 1948).

15. *NYT*, Feb. 24, 1948. *Jackson Clarion-Ledger*, June 10, 1948; and *Jackson Daily News*, Feb. 24, 1948. Those attending the meeting included Thurmond, Texas governor Beauford Jester, Arkansas governor Ben Laney, and North Carolina governor R. Gregg Cherry. A transcript of the February 23, 1948, meeting between McGrath and the southern governors can be found in Senatorial Records, J. Howard McGrath Papers, HSTL. Another copy is in the John Redding Papers, HSTL. Redding was the publicity director for the DNC. See also John M. Redding, *Inside the Democratic Party* (Indianapolis, 1958), 136-40. The *New York Times*, Feb. 24, 1948, reported that McGrath "would not yield on a single point as they fired question after question at him." See other comments in V.O. Key, *Southern Politics in State and Nation* (New York, 1949), 329; and Bernstein, "Ambiguous Legacy," 285.

16. Garson, *The Democratic Party and the Politics of Sectionalism*, 239; Redding, *Inside the Democratic Party*, 136-40; *NYT*, Feb. 24, 1948. See also Records of the Democratic National Committee, HSTL. Quote from Cohodas, *Thurmond*, 136.

17. Thurmond's denunciation of Smith and the other racists was harsh: "We do not invite, we do not need, the support of Gerald L.K. Smith or any other rabble rousers who use race prejudice and class hatred to enflame the emotions of our people" (*New York Daily News*, July 20, 1948).

18. *NYT*, March 13, 14, 1948; *States Righter*, April 1948, copy in "States' Rights Scrapbook."

19. *Jackson Clarion-Ledger*, May 11, 1948. Cohodas, *Thurmond*, 144-46.

20. Garson, *The Democratic Party and the Politics of Sectionalism*, 262; *NYT*, May 11, 1948.

21. Gallup Poll, April 9, 1948, unidentified newspaper clipping in Records of the Democratic National Committee. Democratic party operatives feared that if the South left the party, there would be a severe decline in party funds. See *Washington Post*, Feb. 13, 1948.

22. *PP: Truman, 1948*, 254. Truman finally issued two executive orders on July 26 (following the convention and the bolt by the South). Executive Order 9980 established a Fair Employment Board in the Civil Service Commission to deal with discrimination among federal employees. Executive Order 9981 began the long process of desegregating the armed forces. See *Federal Register*, 4311, 4314.

23. Garson, *The Democratic Party and the Politics of Sectionalism*, 265, 268; William Batt to Clifford, June 11, 1948, Subject Files, Clifford Papers.

9. The Eisenhower Phenomenon

1. See Gallup in *Newsweek*, Oct. 6, 1947; Gallup in *Life*, Oct. 13, 1947; Roper in *Fortune*, Feb. 1948; *Public Opinion Quarterly* (Summer 1948): 360; *Public Opinion Quarterly* (Winter 1947-48), 667; Gallup in *ADA World*, June 5, 1948.

2. An account of an early attempt to interest Eisenhower in the presidency is in Harry C. Butcher, *My Years with Eisenhower: The Personal Diary of Captain Harry C. Butcher, USNR* (New York, 1946), 434. See also *Washington Post*, Jan. 13, 1947. The quote is from John Gunther, *Eisenhower: The Man and the Symbol* (New York, 1952), 133.

3. *Time*, Dec. 2, 1946; *Life*, Dec. 2, 30, 1946.

4. Gallup Poll cited in *Reader's Digest*, Dec. 1947; *Time*, Dec. 2, 1946.

5. Louis Galambos and Alfred D. Chandler Jr., eds., *The Papers of Dwight D. Eisenhower*, 9 (Baltimore, 1983) #1700 (Aug. 21, 1947), 1890.

6. Gunther, *Eisenhower*, 133.

7. *EP*, #1742 (Sept. 18, 1947), 1933.

8. *EP*, #1837 (Oct. 31, 1947), 2027.

9. *EP*, #1720 (Dec. 18, 1947), 1909. See also Galambos notes, *EP*, 1909. The editorial was by Roy Roberts, a leader of the draft-Eisenhower movement. See *Life*, Aug. 25, 1947.

10. *EP*, #1800 (Oct. 16, 1947), 1987. Eisenhower made a similar statement to Cornelius Vanderbilt. See *EP*, #1828 (Oct. 29, 1947), 2017.

11. *EP*, #1800 (Oct. 16, 1947), 1986-87.

12. Galambos notes in *EP*, 2193-94.

13. *NYT*, Jan. 13, 1948. For the difficulty Eisenhower had in composing the letter, see Forrestal, *Forrestal Diaries*, 365-66; and note to Lynn Townsend White, *EP*, #2016 (Jan. 29, 1948), 2211. See also Peter Lyon, *Eisenhower: Portrait of a Hero* (Boston, 1974), 379-80.

14. *EP*, #1998 (Jan. 22, 1948), 2191-93; *NYT*, Jan. 24, 1948.

15. Quoted in Gunther, *Eisenhower*, 137. Eisenhower told Walter Bedell Smith, "I have experienced a great sense of personal freedom that I was rapidly losing" (*EP*, #2009 [Jan. 28, 1948], 2205).

16. *NYT*, Dec. 18, 1946.

17. Paul Walter to Taft, July 30, 1947, two letters, Political Files, Taft Papers.

18. See *The Taft Story*, n.d., campaign pamphlet, and Bill McAdams to Clarence Brown, "Confidential Memo," titled "Outline of Public Relations and Publicity Program," n.d. (fall 1947?), Political Files, Taft Papers. See also Patterson, *Mr. Republican*, 396-99.

19. B.E. Tate to Taft, Dec. 24, 1947, Political Files; Taft to Solbert, June 30, 1948, Letters Sent Files. See also Taft to Richard B. Scandrett, Dec. 31, 1947, Letters Sent Files, all in Taft Papers. Even Taft's sympathetic biographer James T. Patterson has had to admit that it is impossible to make a silk purse out of a sow's ear. See Patterson, *Mr. Republican*, 399.

20. A Gallup Poll that month showed that only Stassen among the three Republican candidates had any chance of defeating Truman. Dewey, the poll showed, would lose to Truman by 46-41 percent, Taft would lose 51-31 percent, and Stassen would win 44-42 percent. Truman's strong showing here can be attributed to foreign policy successes. See collected polling data, dated January 2, 1948, in Political Files, Taft Papers.

21. The often-quoted remark is from the wife of Kenneth Simpson, GOP leader in New York County. See Goulden, *Best Years*, 23.

22. From Reinhard, *Republican Right*, 40.

23. Quoted in Goulden, *Best Years*, 373.

24. *NYT*, Sept. 12-14, 1947; *Newsweek*, Sept. 29, 1947. See also Patterson, *Mr. Republican*, 378-82.

25. *NYT*, July 6, 1947.

26. Forrestal, *Forrestal Diaries*, 325.

27. *Newsweek*, Nov. 24, 1947, March 15, 1948. See also William Manchester, *American Caesar: Douglas MacArthur, 1880-1964* (Boston, 1978), 521.

28. Joseph McCarthy, "Dear Folks" letter to the people of Wisconsin, March 31, 1948, copy in Special Files, Taft Papers. MacArthur's campaign in Wisconsin was supported by the Hearst-owned *Milwaukee Sentinel*. McCarthy headed the Stassen-for-President club in Wisconsin. See Michael O'Brien, *McCarthy and McCarthyism in Wisconsin* (Columbia, Mo., 1980), 82-83. In April, the *New York Times* predicted a MacArthur victory in Wisconsin (*NYT*, April 1, 3, 4, 1948). For the Wisconsin campaign, see Carolyn J. Mattern, "The Man on the Dark Horse: The Presidential Campaigns of Douglas MacArthur, 1944 and 1948" (Ph. D. dissertation, University of Wisconsin, 1976), 180-241. Mattern has little to say about McCarthy's influence.

29. See, for example, Dewey's speech in Milwaukee, April 1, 1948, in *Public Papers of Thomas E. Dewey*, 12 vols. (New York, 1948?), 6:575-78.

30. Patterson, *Mr. Republican*, 400-405; Richard Norton Smith, *Thomas E. Dewey and His Times* (New York, 1982), 488; Reinhard, *Republican Right*, 42-43.

31. Following the June convention Taft wrote to thank some of his supporters. In several notes he wrote: "After the Nebraska primary, I realized that it was an up-hill fight," and "I was never very optimistic after the Nebraska primary." See particularly Taft to Oscar Solbert, June 30, 1948, and Taft to Abba Hillil Silver, June 29, 1948, both in Letters Sent Files, Taft Papers; and Taft to B. Carroll Reese, June 30, 1948, Political Files, Taft Papers.

32. *NYT*, Jan. 26, 1948.

33. P.W. Walter to Taft, July 17, 1947, Political Files, Taft Papers.

34. Taft to Stassen, Jan. 28, 1948, ibid.

35. *NYT*, Jan. 26, 1948. The letter from Taft to Stassen dated January 28, 1948, is an apology by Taft for this public statement.

36. Smith, *Dewey*, 488.

37. *Public Papers of Thomas E. Dewey*, 6:470, 598-602, 606, 613-17, 633.

38. Ibid., 351; Smith, *Dewey*, 488.

39. *Newsweek*, May 31, 1948.

10. The Democrats and the Eisenhower Diversion

1. Bowles to Loeb, and Loeb to Wyatt, March 5, 1948, ADA Administrative Files, ADA Papers. See also *Washington Post*, May 17, 1948.

2. Gallup Poll in *Newsweek*, Oct. 6, 1947; *Public Opinion Quarterly* (Summer 1948): 360; Roper poll in *Fortune*, June 1948.

3. *Nation*, March 13, 1948. See ADA statement of policy adopted at the convention in UAW President's Office Files: Walter Reuther, Walter Reuther Papers.

4. Loeb to ADA national offices, March 10, 1948, ADA Administrative Files, ADA

Papers. See also Loeb to W. Reuther, March 4, 1948, UAW President's Office Files: Walter Reuther, Walter Reuther Papers.

5. *NYT*, April 13, 1948; "Statement on Political Policy," April 11, 1948, ADA Administrative Files, ADA Papers. Loeb had decided as early as March 8, 1948, that Eisenhower would be the savior of the Democrats. See Loeb to Carl Auerbach, March 8, 1948, and Loeb to National Offices, March 10, 1948, ADA Administrative Files, ADA Papers.

6. Niebhur to Loeb, June 23, 1948, ADA Administrative Files, ADA Papers; *NYT*, June 13, 1948.

7. *Time*, March 15, 1948. *Time* said it was an "extraordinary idea." See also *NYT*, March 25, April 13, 1948). There was some significant dissension among the liberal ranks. Walter White of the NAACP opposed the movement. See *New York Herald Tribune*, April 4, 1948; and press release, April 8, 1948, NAACP Papers. Bill Green of the AFL also opposed it. See Green to A.J. Sabath, May 18, 1948; and Green to J. Roosevelt, July 2, 1948, AFL Department of Legislation Files, AFL Papers.

8. James Roosevelt, *My Parents: A Differing View* (Chicago, 1978), 327.

9. *PM*, March 29, 1948.

10. *NYT*, March 25, 27, April 2, 1948.

11. *EP*, #34 (April 12, 1948), 10:25.

12. Quoted in Stephen E. Ambrose, *Eisenhower: Soldier and President* (New York, 1990), 477-78.

13. *Time*, April 19, 1948, 25.

14. Truman, *Memoirs*, 2:185.

15. Lyon, *Eisenhower*, 386. For additional analysis, see Arthur Krock, *Memoirs: Sixty Years on the Firing Line* (New York, 1968), 243. Cabell Phillips, *The Truman Presidency: The History of a Triumphant Succession* (New York, 1966), 196-97.

16. Phillips, *Truman Presidency*, 197; Truman, *Memoirs*, 2:218; Merle Miller, *Plain Speaking: An Oral Biography of Harry S. Truman* (New York, 1974), 339. Arthur Krock, in his *Memoirs*, 242-44, has a similar story.

17. Dwight D. Eisenhower, *Crusade in Europe* (Garden City, N.Y., 1948), 444. See also Eisenhower, *Mandate for Change* (Garden City, N.Y., 1963), 5. Truman later denied it. See Miller, *Plain Speaking*, 339.

18. Robert Ferrell, ed., *Dear Bess: The Letters from Harry to Bess Truman, 1910-1959* (New York, 1983), 516.

19. Truman, *Memoirs*, 2:186.

20. Interview with Clifford.

21. *NYT*, July 4-5, 1948.

22. *EP*, #106 (July 5, 1948), 10:124.

23. *NYT*, July 6, 1948.

24. *NYT*, July 7-9, 1948.

25. *Newsweek*, July 7, 1948.

26. *EP*, #110 (July 8, 1948), 10:129; *NYT*, July 3, 6, 1948. See also *Time*, July 12, 1948, 12. According to Arthur Krock, Secretary of the Army Kenneth Royall helped Eisenhower draft the statement. See Krock, *Memoirs*, 243.

27. *NYT*, June 20, 1948.

28. *NYT*, July 10, 1948.

29. *EP*, Galambos notes, 10:130.

30. *NYT,* June 23, 1948; *Newsweek,* July 19, 1948. Walter Reuther also came out for Douglas in this period. See *NYT,* July 8, 1948.

31. *New Republic,* June 14, 1948.

32. *NYT,* July 10, 1948. See also *New York Herald-Tribune,* July 12, 1948. *Time* (July 19, 1949) quoted Douglas with more irreverence: "I never was a-runnin,' I ain't a-runnin,' and I ain't goin' tuh."

33. *New York Post,* July 12, 1948; *NYT,* July 12, 1948. *Time* (July 19, 1948) described Pepper as "the last drummer in the Eisenhower parade." The CIO-PAC may have pushed Pepper to run as a favorite son representing labor. See Foster, *Union Politic,* 115.

34. Henderson to Leo Rosten, Oct. 4, 1948, ADA Administrative Files, ADA Papers.

35. Bowles to T.E. Dudley, June 18, 1948, ibid.

36. Loeb to Niebuhr, June 24, 1948; and Loeb to Wyatt, June 24, 1948, ibid.

37. Truman called James Roosevelt, Jacob Arvey, the ADA, and Frank Hague all double-crossers and double-dealers. See Ferrell, ed., *Off the Record,* 141.

11. The Do-Nothing Eightieth Congress's Second Session

1. Quoted in Ross, *Loneliest Campaign,* 55-56.

2. *PP: Truman, 1948,* 1-10.

3. Quoted in Patterson, *Mr. Republican,* 391; and Smith, *Dewey,* 476. The Wherry quote is from Marvin Stromer, *The Making of a Political Leader: Kenneth S. Wherry and the United States Senate* (Lincoln, 1969), 164.

4. On Taft's supposed unelectability, see Taft to Sinclair Weeks, July 1, 1948, Letters Sent Files, Taft Papers. On the point that Taft was too liberal for the far right in his party, see Taft to John J. Williams (conservative senator from Delaware), June 30, 1948, ibid. In that letter Taft apologizes to Williams for being "too liberal with government money."

5. Truman told voters in Louisville: "For three years, the real estate lobby, operating through the Republican party, has blocked [housing] legislation" (*NYT,* Oct. 1, 1948). The next day he said the Eightieth Congress "delivered a body blow at millions of our veterans by refusing to provide a descent housing program" (*NYT,* Oct. 2, 1948). See also *PP: Truman, 1948,* 305-6. A week later, in Buffalo, he said: "Republican policies are depriving millions of American families of the housing they need" (*New York Herald Tribune,* Oct. 9, 1948). And on education: "I made a recommendation to the Congress that the Federal government make a contribution to the support of the schools of the nation. No action—no action" (*NYT,* June 15, 1948). "I asked for aid to education for the benefit of the children of this country. No action by the Republican Congress" (*New York Herald Tribune,* Sept. 24, 1948).

6. See *PP: Truman, 1948,* 182-86.

7. Some good examples of Truman's arguments are in *NYT,* June 15, Oct. 30, 1948. The tax cut reduced taxes in the under $2,400 bracket by 3 percent, in the $10,000 bracket by 8 percent, for those who made $20,000 by 15 percent, and for those whose income exceeded $100,000 by up to 65 percent. See Goldman, *Crucial Decade,* 56.

8. Truman told an audience in June: "Now do you know how Congress has broadened the base of Social Security? They've just taken 750,000 people off Social Security and sent me a bill to that effect" (*NYT,* June 15, 1948). Then in late September he said: "Have the Republicans extended social security? They have not" (*NYT,* Oct. 1, 1948). Groups to be excluded by the Republican bills included newspaper and magazine vendors, door-to-

door salesmen, home workers, taxi drivers, and truck drivers. See *PP: Truman, 1948*, 205-6, 354-55.

9. Since 1935 the REA had loaned nearly $3 billion to REA co-ops. Of those subscribers, 67 percent were farmers. By 1953 over 2.5 million farms in the United States would be connected to REA lines and American agriculture would be electrified. See D. Clayton Brown, *Electricity for Rural America: The Fight for the REA* (Westport, Conn., 1980), 113.

10. In Bonham, Texas, Truman told an audience of voters, most of whom received their power from the REA, that "the Republican 80th Congress wasn't willing to bring low cost electric power to consumers when that would stand in the way of the profits of private power monopolies" (*New York Herald Tribune*, Sept. 28, 1948. See also *PP: Truman, 1948*, 278, 389-91.

11. On the minimum wage issue the Democrats wanted a sixty-five-cent minimum, but when the Republicans went along with the proposal, Truman increased his request to seventy-five cents. See Hartmann, *Truman and the 80th Congress*, 148-49.

12. *New York Herald Tribune*, Sept. 24, 1948.

12. The Republicans Nominate Dewey

1. *Life*, June 21, 1948.

2. *Chicago Tribune*, June 25, 1948.

3. *Newsweek*, July 5, 1948.

4. *Newsweek*, June 28, 1948.

5. Ibid.

6. *Life*, June 21, 1948; *Atlantic Monthly* (June 1948) predicted a Stassen-Vandenberg ticket.

7. See various quotes of "noncandidacy" in Vandenberg, ed., *Private Papers of Senator Vandenberg*, 421-22; and *Life*, March, 11 1946. Clare Booth Luce pleaded with Vandenberg to take on Dewey, "this little chap who looks like the bridegroom on a wedding cake" (Smith, *Dewey*, 496). This quote is variously credited to Ethel Barrymore and Alice Roosevelt Longworth. See McCullough, *Truman*, 672.

8. Vandenberg, ed., *Private Papers of Senator Vandenberg*, 426-27; *Newsweek*, June 28, July 5, 1948. Vandenberg also said later that he believed he was too old to be president at age sixty-five, that his wife was too frail to be first lady, that he had attracted too many bitter enemies, and that American voters do not elect presidents from Congress (Vandenberg, ed., *Private Papers of Senator Vandenberg*, 434-37. Vandenberg was also satisfied with Dewey.

9. The best discussion of this is in *Newsweek*, July 5, 1948.

10. In exchange, Dewey chose Pennsylvania congressman Hugh Scott to be Republican National Committee chairman. See Smith, *Dewey*, 495-96. The best press report of this issue is in *Newsweek*, July 5, 1948. See also *NYT*, June 24, 1948; *Time*, July 5, 1948; and *Life*, July 5, 1948. See also Reinhard, *Republican Right*, 46.

11. *Life*, July 5, 1948. *Life* referred to "several million watchers." Dewey conducted the first telecast news conference in history. See *Time*, July 5, 1948; *Life*, July 5, 1948.

12. *Time*, June 28, 1948; *Newsweek*, June 28, July 5, 1948; *Life*, July 5, 1948.

13. *Newsweek*, July 15, 1948; *Time*, July 5, 1948; *NYT*, June 23, 1948. The idea of a Taft-Stassen ticket was promoted most often by Robert McCormick, publisher of the *Chicago Tribune*. See Patterson, *Mr. Republican*, 412. See also Taft to Robert McCormick, Letters Sent File, June 29, 1948, Taft Papers.

14. *Newsweek*, July 15, 1948.

15. *Life*, July 5, 1948; *Time*, July 5, 1948.

16. *Newsweek*, July 5, 1948.

17. *NYT*, June 25, 1948; *Newsweek*, July 5, 1948. Stassen tried to get in touch with Eisenhower at Columbia to persuade him to come to Philadelphia and accept the nomination. Eisenhower did not reply. See Smith, *Dewey*, 498-99.

18. *Life*, July 5, 1948. Dewey's acceptance speech is in *Time*, July 5, 1948.

19. *Newsweek*, July 5, 1948.

20. The best source on this is *Newsweek*, July 5, 1948. See also Reinhard, *Republican Right*, 47-48; and Goulden, *Best Years*, 380. Goulden characterizes this event as a "double-cross." See also *NYT* editorial, "Surely Not Mr. Halleck," June 23, 1948. Scheele, *Halleck*, 120-21. Taft had no part in choosing Dewey's running mate. Taft had wanted Dwight Green, governor of Illinois. He was never considered. See Taft to Green, June 29, 1948, Letters Sent Files, Taft Papers.

21. *Newsweek*, July 5, 1948; Smith, *Dewey*, 500.

22. *Time*, July 5, 1948.

23. Quoted in Smith, *Dewey*, 501.

24. Kirk Porter and Donald B. Johnson, *National Party Platforms, 1840-1964* (Urbana, 1966), 452-53.

25. Ernest R. Bartley, "The Tidelands Oil Controversy," *Western Political Science Quarterly* (March 1949): 135-53.

26. Taft to Abba Hillel Silver, June 29, 1948. See also Taft to Sinclair Weeks, July 1, 1948, both in Letters Sent Files, Taft Papers.

27. *Atlantic Monthly*, July 1948.

13. The Democrats Nominate Truman

1. *Life*, June 21, July 26, 1948; *Newsweek*, June 21, 1948; *Time*, June 21, 1948.

2. See numerous telegram receipt copies, various dates through June and July, 1948, Records of the Democratic National Committee. Among the "whistle stops" were San Francisco, Chicago, and Los Angeles.

3. Eisenhower was supported in the South by Senators McClellan, Hill, Sparkman, Johnston, and Eastland and by Governors Tuck of Virginia, Laney of Arkansas, Jester of Texas, and Thurmond of South Carolina. Governor Wright of Mississippi would not support him. Thurmond went to New York on July 8 to meet with Eisenhower in an attempt to persuade him to run as a Democrat. He refused. See Cohodas, *Thurmond*, 155.

4. The ADA announced that Humphrey would attempt to write a civil rights program into the Democratic party platform in a press release dated July 5, 1948, Political File, ADA Papers. The release was signed by the biggest names in the ADA, including James Roosevelt and Franklin Roosevelt Jr., Robert F. Wagner Jr., Will Rogers Jr., Paul Douglas, Henry Morgenthau, and Chester Bowles. Humphrey agreed to have his name placed in nomination for vice-president at the convention. See Minutes of ADA Executive Meeting, June 28, 1948, ADA Administrative Files, ADA Papers.

5. *NYT*, June 23, 1948.

6. Porter and Johnson, *National Party Platforms*, 452-53. See also Berman, *Politics of Civil Rights in the Truman Administration*, 104. The *Chicago Defender* was the only major African-American newspaper to endorse Truman. Most others supported Dewey because

he had a fairly good record on civil rights as governor of New York. See Cecelia Van Auken, "The Negro Press in the 1948 Presidential Election," *Journalism Quarterly* 26, no. 4 (Dec. 1949), 431-35.

7. Bartley, "Tidelands Oil Controversy," 135-153. See also *St. Louis Post-Dispatch*, Aug. 20, 1948.

8. *Time*, July 18, 1948.

9. *NYT*, July 12, 1948; *Life*, July 26, 1948; Goulden, *Best Years*, 383. It rained two days later, and the donkey had to be removed.

10. India Edwards, *Pulling No Punches: Memoirs of a Woman in Politics* (New York, 1977), 120,

11. ADA press release, July 5, 1948, Political Files, ADA Papers.

12. Humphrey to John Kenneth O'Brien, Aug. 20, 1948, letter quoted in *North American Labor*, Sept. 1948.

13. ADA press release, July 5, 1948, Political Files, ADA Papers.

14. Interview with Andrew J. Biemiller, Truman Library. Biemiller had refused to support the draft-Eisenhower movement and by convention time had broken with the ADA over the issue.

15. Interview with Clifford. Years later in his memoirs Clifford wrote: "In my view, this was the wrong time, the wrong place, and the wrong way to further the civil rights cause." (*Counsel*, 218). For Truman's side, see Truman, *Memoirs*, 2:213; Forrestal, *Forrestal Diaries*, 458; and Ferrell, ed., *Off the Record*, 141-43. See also *NYT*, July 12, 1993.

16. Clifford, *Counsel*, 219; *ADA World*, Aug. 7, 1948; *North American Labor*, Sept. 1948; Brock, *Americans for Democratic Action*, 97.

17. Quoted in Gillon, *Politics and Vision*, 48.

18. *Time*, July 19, 1948.

19. In past Democratic party platforms the South had allowed vague civil rights references as long as states' rights was included. See *Time*, July 19, 1948; and Democratic National Committee, *Official Proceedings of the Democratic National Convention* (1948), 109-16. One meeting lasted thirty-six hours (*North American Labor*), Sept. 1948. See Humphrey's analysis of the events in ibid.

20. *North American Labor*, Sept. 1948.

21. Interview with Biemiller. See also Gillon, *Politics and Vision*, 49.

22. DNC, *Official Proceedings of the Democratic National Convention*, 109-16, 181; *NYT*, July 19, 1948. *ADA World*, Aug. 7, 1948. Joseph Rauh wrote the minority report delivered by Biemiller. See also, interview with Biemiller; *Life*, July 22, 1948.

23. *NYT*, July 15, 1948; DNC, *Official Proceedings of the Democratic National Convention*, 192.

24. Clifford, *Counsel*, 219.

25. *NYT*, July 15, 1948; *ADA World*, Aug. 7, 1948.

26. DNC, *Official Proceedings of the Democratic National Convention*, 202-10; *NYT*, July 15, 1948; *ADA World*, Aug. 7, 1948.

27. Cohodas, *Thurmond*, 167.

28. *NYT*, July 19, 1948; Richard D. Chesteen, "'Mississippi Is Gone Home!': A Study of the 1948 Mississippi States' Rights Bolt," *Journal of Mississippi History* 32, no. 1 (Feb. 1970): 43-59; Key, *Southern Politics in State and Nation*, 332; Cohodas, *Thurmond*, 167. See also Memphis *Commercial Appeal*, July 15, 1948. The attempted bribe was $50. See *Jackson Daily News*, July 15, 1948. See Clifford's recollections in Clifford, *Counsel*, 220.

29. *NYT*, July 15, 1948. The Mississippi delegation did not vote. Russell did not ac-

cept the votes from the southern delegations with enthusiasm. He was a powerful senator, next in line for the chairmanship of the Senate's Armed Services Committee. To lead a rebellion against his own party might have ended his career. See Cohodas, *Thurmond*, 168-69.

30. Loeb to J.G. Schultte, July 27, 1948; Loeb to Robert H. Richter, July 27, 1948, ADA Administrative Files, ADA Papers.

31. Loeb to David C. Williams, Aug. 2, 1948. See similar statements in Loeb to Humphrey, July 28, 1948; and Loeb to Eleanor Michnun, July 27, 1948, all ibid.

32. Interview with Biemiller.

33. Truman, *Memoirs*, 2:222. Truman wanted Douglas badly and was less than satisfied with Barkley. See Ferrell, ed., *Truman in the White House*, 265.

14. The Campaigns

1. *PP: Truman, 1948*, 408; Truman, *Memoirs*, 2:241-42.

2. *NYT*, July 16, 1948. See also R. Alton Lee, "The Turnip Session of the Do-Nothing Congress; Presidential Campaign Strategy," *Southwestern Social Science Quarterly* 44 (Dec. 1963): 261. Turnip Day was July 25, a Sunday in 1948. The special session convened the next day, Monday, July 26.

3. William Batt (director of the Democratic party's research division) made this point to Clifford in a memo dated July 19, 1948, arguing that a special session would be effective (Speech Files, Clifford Papers). See also Ferrell, ed., *Truman in the White House*, 265-66.

4. This memo is in Clifford's awkward writing style. Others have disagreed. Ross, *Loneliest Campaign*, 134-36, argued that William Batt was the author. Hartmann, *Truman and the 80th Congress*, 193, argues convincingly that Batt was the author. Truman, thirteen years later, insisted that the idea was his own. See Truman interview with Alton Lee cited in "Turnip Session of the Do-Nothing Congress," 121.

5. Unsigned memo, "Should the President Call Congress Back?," June 29, 1948, in Samuel I. Rosenman Papers, HSTL. A second copy is in the appendix of the interview with Leon Keyserling. A third copy can be found in the Speech Files, Clifford Papers.

6. Elsey to Clifford, undated memo, Political Files, Clifford Papers; interview with Clifford. Clifford made a similar statement to the press on "Turnip Day." See *Newsweek*, July 26, 1948. A similar quote appears in Clifford, *Counsel*, 222.

7. *Cong. Rec.*, 80th Cong., 2d sess., A4661-62.

8. *PP: Truman, 1948*, 416-21; Clifford, *Counsel*, 223.

9. *Cong. Rec.*, 80th Cong., 2d sess., 9376; *Time*, July 26, Aug. 2, 1948.

10. "Address of Senator Taft over the National Broadcasting Company and the Mutual Broadcasting Company," July 28, 1948, manuscript copy in Speech Files, Taft Papers; Taft quoted in Robert J. Donovan, *Conflict and Crisis: The Presidency of Harry S. Truman, 1945-1948* (New York, 1977), 411; Reinhard, *Republican Right*, 51. This remark further alienated Dewey's wing of the party from the Taftites. See Patterson, *Mr. Republican*, 422.

11. *NYT*, July 21, Aug. 2, 1948.

12. Smith, *Dewey*, 513.

13. *Time*, July 26, 1948.

14. Dewey to Annie Dewey, July 12, 1948, Thomas E. Dewey Papers, Rush Rhees Library, University of Rochester, Rochester, New York.

15. *Time*, Aug. 16, 1948.

16. Hartmann, *Truman and the 80th Congress*, 197. Hamby, *Man of the People*, 452-53. The housing bill was introduced by Wisconsin senator Joseph McCarthy.

17. *Time*, Aug. 9, 1948; *Newsweek*, Aug. 16, 1948.

18. "What Did the 80th Congress Do on Legislation Supported by the NAACP?," undated press release, NAACP Papers. Walter White of the NAACP had actually expected civil rights action in the special session because of the Republican party's strong civil rights statement in its convention platform. See White, "Memo to Branches," July 26, 1948, ibid.

19. *NYT*, Aug. 7, 1948.

20. *NYT*, Aug. 13, 1948. *Time* wrote (Aug. 16, 1948) that the record of the special session "made it easy for Truman to plant the do-nothing label on Congress."

21. Clifford, *Counsel*, 223-24.

22. Anonymous memo, July 27, 1948, Political Files, Ewing Papers.

23. Smith, *Dewey*, 504.

24. See particularly, *PP: Truman, 1948*, 504-5.

25. Smith, *Dewey*, 515.

26. For a few examples, see *New York Herald Tribune*, Sept. 25, 28, Oct. 20, 1948; *NYT*, Sept. 19, Oct. 7, 1948, and *PP: Truman, 1948*, 399-400. The price of corn had fallen from $2.29 per bushel in June to $.96 in October.

27. *NYT*, Sept. 20, 1948; Smith, *Dewey*, 526.

28. Clifford, *Counsel*, 227.

29. Smith, *Dewey*, 531.

30. *Public Papers of Thomas E. Dewey*, 6:505, 519, 661, 649, 670-73, 657-58, 651-55, 662.

31. *Time*, Oct. 25, 1948. *New York Times* also hit Dewey hard in October for his listless campaign. See *NYT*, Oct. 12, 1948.

32. *Louisville Courier Journal*, Nov. 18, 1948.

33. Dewey's advisers who opposed his attacking Truman were James Hagerty, Paul Lockwood, and Edwin Jaeckle. See Smith, *Dewey*, 536.

34. *NYT*, Oct. 12, 1948; Smith, *Dewey*, 531; Reinhard, *Republican Right*, 51; Donovan, *Conflict and Crisis*, 426.

35. Eisenhower to Dewey, Sept. 10, 1948, Dewey Papers.

36. Quoted in Clifford, *Counsel*, 200-201.

37. *NYT*, Aug. 6, 1948.

38. There are several good sources on this case. See Allen Weinstein, *Perjury: The Hiss-Chambers Case* (New York, 1978), 4-8. On August 5 Hiss testified before the committee that the charges were false.

39. See Gallup Poll in *Washington Post*, Sept. 5, 1948.

40. Smith, *Dewey*, 506-8. Dewey may also have been reticent on the Hiss-Chambers issue because his chief foreign policy adviser, John Foster Dulles, had hired Hiss at the Carnegie Endowment in late 1946. See Ronald W. Pruessen, *John Foster Dulles: The Road to Power* (New York, 1982), 369-70.

41. *NYT*, Sept. 25, 1948.

42. Clifford, *Counsel*, 233. On the decision to send Vinson to Moscow, see Ferrell, ed., *Truman in the White House*, 276-78.

43. *Time*, Oct. 18, 1948.

44. *NYT*, Oct. 12, 1948.

45. *NYT*, Oct. 19, 1948.

46. *NYT*, July 25, 1948.

47. Anonymous memo, July 27, 1948, Political Files, Ewing Papers.

48. *NYT,* Sept. 11, 1948.

49. Pruessen, *Dulles,* 373; Michael A. Guhin, *John Foster Dulles: A Statesman and His Times* (New York, 1972), 160. Other foreign policy advisers pushing Dewey to follow the Vandenberg policy were Elliot Bell and McGeorge Bundy.

50. For an example of Dewey's support for the bipartisan foreign policy, see *NYT,* Oct. 13, 1948.

51. Donald R. Van Boskirk to Dewey, July 1, 1948, Dewey Papers. Dewey responded that he intended to follow the advice. See Dewey to Boskirk, July 6, 1948, ibid.

52. *Time,* Oct. 18, 1948.

53. Quoted in Smith, *Dewey,* 530.

54. Charter Heslep, "Campaign Train," n.d., manuscript, Charter Heslep Papers, HSTL; William Bray, "Recollections of the 1948 Campaign," n.d., manuscript in Political Files, Clifford Papers. Two accounts by participants in the tours are Ferrell, ed., *Truman in the White House,* 238-86; and Edwards, *Pulling No Punches,* 220-22. Good secondary sources on the whistle-stop campaign include McCullough, *Truman,* 654-69; Gosnell, *Truman's Crises,* 400-21; and Goulden, *Best Years,* 392-408.

55. *Washington Post,* April 18, 1948. Truman's own account is in Truman, *Memoirs,* 2:209-10. See also Clifford, *Counsel,* 199. Another account is in Donovan, *Conflict and Crisis,* 394.

56. Truman's speaking style was of great concern to the White House strategists. See anonymous, undated memo, "Footnotes on the Opportunities of the White House in the Political Battles of 1948: Criticism of Presidential Speeches over the Last Months," President's Secretary's Files, Truman Papers. The author insisted that the message be simple: "The American people do not care about a professor's approach. . . . The listener wants to hear about one thing at a time. Since the basic issues are *great* issues, they can be told in monosyllable language. "

57. Clifford, *Counsel,* 199-200. See *Life's* sarcastic article on Truman's "so-called nonpolitical" trip west, June 21, 1948.

58. Quoted in Goulden, *Best Years,* 370.

59. Clifford, *Counsel,* 226. See the same account in Goulden, *Best Years,* 393.

60. Bray, "Recollections"; and Hamby, *Man of the People,* 457.

61. The figures are from Truman's own account in *Memoirs,* 2:254. Other accounts give different numbers. See, for instance, McCullough, *Truman,* 654.

62. The flowers were sent to veterans' hospitals, politicians were encouraged to say only, "I am proud to present the President of the United States," and marching bands were asked to play the local high school fight song (Bray, "Recollections"). The campaign could not afford to buy a single radio broadcast. For the trip's money problems, see *NYT,* Sept. 26, 1948; Lee, *Truman and Taft-Hartley,* 140; and Donovan, *Conflict and Crisis,* 418.

63. Interview with Alben Barkley, Truman Library; Clifford, *Counsel,* 229.

64. *NYT,* Sept. 19, 1948.

65. *New York Herald Tribune,* Oct. 20, Sept. 25, 1948.

66. *NYT,* Oct. 8, Sept. 7, 1948.

67. *New York Herald Tribune,* Oct. 27, Sept. 28, 1948.

68. *NYT,* Sept. 19, 1948.

69. *New York Herald Tribune,* Sept 24, Oct. 16, 1948.

70. On the growing size of the crowds to meet Truman, see Ferrell, ed., *Truman in the White House,* 279.

71. Bray, "Recollections. "
72. *NYT*, Nov. 2, 1948.

15. The Democratic Party Factions and the Election

1. The credit for the name "Dixiecrat" is usually given to William Weisner, editor of the *Charlotte News*, who could not squeeze "States' Rights Democrats" into a headline. It was not uncommon for Dixiecrats to refer to themselves as "the Jeffersonian wing of the Democratic Party." See *Jackson Clarion-Ledger*, July 19, 1948.

2. The official convention of the States' Rights Democrats was held in Houston on August 11. Thurmond and Wright accepted their party's formal nomination there. *Newsweek* (Oct. 10, 1948) called Wallace Wright "the principal financial backer and guiding spirit of the Dixiecrats." See also Memphis *Commercial Appeal*, July 18, 1948, for a description and size of the Birmingham convention.

3. *NYT*, July 20, 1948.

4. A Truman elector from Tennessee bolted and raised the final total to 39 electoral votes. Some leaders in the movement had hoped that as many as 142 electoral votes would go to Thurmond. See *Jackson Clarion-Ledger*, Oct. 3, 1948.

5. Key, *Southern Politics in State and Nation*, 341-44.

6. See Garson, *The Democratic Party and the Politics of Sectionalism*, 312; Cohodas, *Thurmond*, 189-90; and Alexander A. Heard, *A Two-Party South?* (Chapel Hill, 1952), 251-55, 20-33.

7. Garson, *The Democratic Party and the Politics of Sectionalism*, 319-21.

8. David K. Niles to Mathew Connelly, Jan. 20, 1948, Office Files, Truman Papers. See also a series of letters from important African-American leaders to J. Howard McGrath making many of the same threats: Randolph to McGrath, Feb. 2, 1948, Robert M. Moore to McGrath, Feb. 5, 1948, and Grant Reynolds to McGrath, Aug. 1, 1948, all in McGrath Papers. See also *Pittsburgh Courier*, April 10, July 3, 1948.

9. NAACP press release, n.d., NAACP Papers.

10. White to Taft, May 20, 1948, ibid.

11. NAACP press release, July 15, 1948, ibid.

12. Executive Orders 9980 and 9981 in *Federal Register* 4311 and 4314. See Richard Dalfiume, *Desegregation of the U. S. Armed Forces: Fighting on Two Fronts, 1939-1953* (Columbia, Mo., 1969), 157. Truman may have issued the orders to avoid a confrontation with A. Philip Randolph, who had announced that unless the administration began desegregating the armed forces immediately he would initiate an antidraft campaign (civil disobedience and nonregistration) among African Americans. See Berman, *Politics of Civil Rights in the Truman Administration*, 117.

13. *PP: Truman, 1948*, 923-29. In the final days of the campaign the president made several speeches calling for "basic rights" and "respect for the dignity of men and women without regard to race, creed or color." See ibid., 854, 868, 923-29. See also *NYT*, Oct. 30, 1948.

14. Moon, *Balance of Power*.

15. Nash to Truman, Dec. 6, 1948, President's Secretary's Files, Truman Papers.

16. *Pittsburgh Courier*, Dec. 13, 1948; *Chicago Defender*, Nov. 13, 1948. Wallace voters most likely prevented Truman from taking Michigan and Maryland. An NAACP postelection survey showed that 69 percent of all African Americans in the nation's major

cities had voted for Truman (Henry Lee Moon, "What Chance for Civil Rights," *Crisis*, Feb. 1949, 42-45). See comprehensive election results in *NYT,* Dec. 11, 1948.

17. *Chicago Defender,* Nov. 13, 1948; *Pittsburgh Courier,* Dec. 13, 1948. *Chicago Defender* (Nov. 13, 1948) also claimed that black votes kept Florida, Georgia, and Texas from going to the Dixiecrats.

18. Wallace interview.

19. Manuscript of radio address, n.d. (June 1948), in Political Files, ADA Papers. Quote also in *Baltimore Sun,* June 28, 1948.

20. Murrow interview in Macdougall, *Gideon's Army,* 2:423.

21. Seattle speech on May 22, quoted in ADA pamphlet, *Henry A. Wallace: The Last Seven Months of His Presidential Campaign* (N.p., n.d.), copy in Political Files, ADA Papers. In 1950 Wallace admitted that the communists had taken over his party and that it was a major mistake to allow it to happen (Address by Wallace at the Second National Convention of the Progressive Party, Chicago, Feb. 24, 1950, Progressive Party Papers).

22. Loeb to Harry Girvetz, Sept. 18, 1948, ADA Administrative Files, ADA Papers.

23. Copies of both in Political Files, ADA Papers, and in Oscar L. Chapman Papers, HSTL.

24. ADA publication, written by William Dufty and Elizabeth Donahue, *Henry A. Wallace: The First Three Months of His Campaign,* n.d. (April 1948), Political Files, ADA Papers.

25. *ADA World,* June 5, 1948.

26. Tugwell to ADA, July 16, 1948; Loeb to Robert H. Ellis, Aug. 4, 1948; "Testimony of James Loeb Before the Platform Committee of the Progressive Party," July 22, 1948; Loeb to David C. Williams, Aug. 2, 1948; Loeb to Eleanor Mishnun, July 27, 1948; Loeb to Ronald Reagan, Aug. 8, 1948; and Loeb to Bowles, Aug. 6, 1948, all in ADA Administrative Files, ADA Papers. See *Los Angeles Herald Express,* July 22, 1948, clipping ibid; Tugwell quote in Richard J. Walton, *Henry Wallace, Harry Truman, and the Cold War* (New York, 1976), 317-18.

27. C.B. Baldwin, executive secretary of the Progressive party, insisted that he had planned to withdraw the candidates all along. Thirteen Progressive party candidates were withdrawn. See Progressive Party Papers. See also *NYT,* Oct. 1, 1948, and "Report to the National Committee of the Progressive Party," Progressive Party Papers, LC.

28. By August even Tugwell was voicing misgivings about communist influence in Wallace's campaign. See *New York Post,* Aug. 20, 1948. See his postelection explanation: Tugwell, "Progressives and the Presidency," *Progressive,* April 1949.

29. Radio speech by Loeb, Nov. 2, 1948, manuscript copy in ADA Administrative Files, ADA Papers. The ADA's official endorsement of Truman came on August 29, 1948. Copy of endorsement in UAW President's Office Files: Walter Reuther, Walter Reuther Papers.

30. In a speech on February 27, 1948, Wallace argued that "the Czech crisis is evidence that a 'get-tough' policy provokes a 'get-tougher' policy" (manuscript in Progressive Party Papers). Wallace later said that his public position on the Czech crisis was "my greatest mistake." See Edward L. Schapsmeir and Frederick H. Schapsmeir, *Profits in Politics: Henry A. Wallace and the War Years, 1940-1965* (Ames, Iowa, 1970), 186; David A. Shannon, *The Decline of Communism: A History of the Communist Party in the United States since 1945* (Chatham, N.J., 1959), 161; and Klehr and Haynes, *American Communist Movement,* 120.

31. Wallace's letter to Stalin, May 11, 1948, and Stalin's response, May 17, 1948, were printed as part of a campaign flyer by the Wallace campaign committee. Copy in Wallace

Papers. Both letters were reprinted in *NYT*, May 18, 1948. For Truman's response to the Wallace-Stalin exchange, see Ferrell, ed., *Truman in the White House*, 257-58.

32. Wallace made this statement in his acceptance speech in Philadelphia on July 24, 1948, manuscript copy in Wallace Papers, reprinted in *NYT*, July 25, 1948.

33. The Survey Research Center at the University of Michigan reported in October 1948 that among the American public there was an "almost unanimous belief that Russia is an aggressive, expansionist-minded nation." It further noted an "overwhelming demand for firmness and increased 'toughness' in relations with Russia" (quoted in Ralph B. Levering, *The Cold War, 1945-1987* [Arlington Heights, 1988], 35).

34. This is the main point in Walton, *Henry Wallace, Harry Truman and the Cold War*, 111-12, 116. See also Kendrick A. Clements, Introduction to *James F. Byrnes and the Origins of the Cold War*, ed. Clements (Durham, 1982), 1-17; and Robert L. Messer, "'Et Tu Brute!': James F. Byrnes, Harry Truman and the Origins of the Cold War," ibid., 19-48. For a slightly different view, see Kofsky, *Harry S. Truman and the War Scare of 1948*.

35. James Rowe to James Webb, "The Politics of 1948," Sept. 18, 1947, copy in interview with Rowe, 129-61. See also "The Wallace Voter and the 1948 Election," n.d. [April 1948], manuscript copy in Subject Files, Clifford Papers. Alonzo Hamby argues that Wallace wanted a Republican victory (*Man of the People*, 454).

36. *NYT*, Aug. 27-Sept. 3, 1948; *Washington Post*, Aug. 30-Sept. 1, 1948. For Wallace's own account of his southern campaign trip, see Wallace interview.

37. *PP: Truman, 1948*, 1.

38. For example, see "File on the Facts," undated manuscript compiled by the Democratic National Committee, copy in Nash Papers. See also *New Republic*, Aug. 4, Jan. 27, 1947; and *Vital Speeches of the Day*, Oct. 18, 1948, 15:51-53.

39. *Wall Street Journal*, Nov. 8, 1948.

40. Report of C.B. Baldwin on the outcome of the 1948 election to the National Committee to Elect Henry Wallace, Nov. 13, 1948, Progressive Party Papers. Wallace made a similar statement before the National Committee of the Progressive party in Chicago on November 13, 1948, copy in Wallace Papers.

41. *Vital Speeches of the Day*, 14:173. See also *New Republic*, Jan. 19, 1948; and C.B. Baldwin's speech at the Progressive party convention, Progressive Party Papers.

42. A large collection of CIO-PAC campaign material designed to fight Taft-Hartley and defeat congressmen who had supported the bill is in UAW President's Office Files: Walter Reuther, Walter Reuther Papers. See also Jack Kroll and Philip Murray to "State, County and City IUC Political Action Committees," July 17, 1947; and Kroll to Reuther, July 23, 1947, ibid.

43. For Murray's anticommunism, see Win Booth to Don Bermingham, May 16, 1947, Frank McNaughton Papers, HSTL. See also Murray's insistence that all CIO officers refrain from joining either the ADA or the PCA in press release, March 14, 1947, CIO Secretary-Treasurer's Files, CIO Papers.

44. See Murray's statement in CIO-PAC press release, Jan. 23, 1948, UAW Political Action Department, Roy Reuther Papers, WPRL. A UAW-CIO press release, March 3, 1948, calls Wallace's third party a "Communist party maneuver designed to advance the foreign policy interests of the Soviet Union" (UAW President's Office Files: Walter Reuther, Walter Reuther Papers.

45. *CIO News*, Jan. 23, 26, 1948. The CIO-PAC engaged in aggressive Wallace bashing. See CIO-PAC publication, "How Sincere Is Wallace?," CIO Secretary-Treasurer's Of-

fice Files, WPRL; UAW-CIO press release, "Political Action Resolution," March 3, 1948, which calls Wallace a communist; and CIO-PAC publication "Who Wants Wallace?" both in UAW Political Action Department Files, Roy Reuther Papers. The CIO-PAC's answer to "Who Wants Wallace?" was "Russia." See also Macdougall, *Gideon's Army*, 1:315.

46. The editor was Len DeCaux. He went from the *CIO News* to *New Republic*. Good sources on the CIO-communist conflict in this period include David Oshinsky, "Labor's Cold War: The CIO and the Communists," in *The Specter: Original Essays on the Cold War and the Origins of McCarthyism*, eds. Robert Griffith and Athan Theoharis, (New York, 1974), 118-51; and Harvey A. Levenstein, *Communism, Anti-Communism, and the CIO* (Westport, Conn., 1981).

47. *Washington Post*, July 23, 1948. The CIO-PAC officially endorsed Truman at the end of August 1948. See press release, Sept. 1, 1948, UAW Political Action Department, Roy Reuther Papers. In September, Murray publicly endorsed the ADA. See Loeb to Murray, Sept. 3, 1948, ADA Administrative Files, ADA Papers.

48. See, for example, George Meany, transcript of radio speech, Sept. 22, 1948, Secretary's Files, Meany Papers. Meany asked: "Is there a Communist fifth column operating in this country today? Do you know whether or not that fifth column has entered a Presidential candidate in this election?"

49. Abels, *Out of the Jaws of Victory*, 224; *NYT*, Oct. 9, 1948.

50. Rowe, "Politics of 1948."

51. *North American Labor*, July-Aug. 1948.

52. Letters, pamphlets, and flyers as examples of the UAW and CIO-PAC get-out-the-vote campaign can be found in UAW Political Action Department, Roy Reuther Papers. See also scrapbook entitled "UAW-CIO Political Action Literature, 1948 Campaign" in UAW Public Relations Department Files: Frank Winn, United Auto Workers Papers, WPRL. Similar material from the AFL get-out-the-vote campaign can be found in Office of the Secretary-Treasurer, 1940-52, George Meany Files, Meany Papers. See particularly mass mailing: Meany to "The Officers of the National and International Unions of the AFL," Sept. 1948.

53. *NYT*, Nov. 4, 1948.

54. Truman interview with R. Alton Lee, Aug. 3, 1961, in Lee, *Truman and Taft-Hartley*, 153.

55. Foster, *Union Politic*, 128. Foster points out that although Truman won in the areas surveyed, the Democrats did worse in all these areas in 1948 than in the 1940 and 1944 presidential elections. See also pages 214-17.

56. Lee, *Truman and Taft-Hartley*, 148. Labor took credit for the Democratic victory. See *New Republic*, Dec. 15, 1948. See also Walter Reuther's claims that labor made the difference, in Reuther to "All International Representatives," Nov. 12, 1948, UAW Political Action Department, Roy Reuther Papers. See also *Memo from PAC*, Nov. 22, 1948, CIO Secretary-Treasurer's Office Files, CIO Papers.

57. Dubovsky and Van Tine, *John L. Lewis*, 475. Labor was not successful in the South, however; see Garson, *The Democratic Party and the Politics of Sectionalism*, 142, 187.

58. *NYT*, Nov. 4, 1948. Historians have heavily sustained the opinion that labor was the deciding factor in the election. See particularly Ross, *Loneliest Campaign*, 254-55; and Richard Kirkendall, "Election of 1948," in *History of American Presidential Elections, 1789-1968*, ed., Arthur M. Schlesinger Jr., and Fred Israel, (New York, 1971), 3099-3145. Alton Lee has pointed out that labor's successes in congressional elections brought Truman large

numbers of votes in a sort of "reverse coattails" that put him over the top in the industrial states (*Truman and Taft-Hartley*), 152. Alonzo Hamby sees labor's support for Truman as part of a larger coalition (*Beyond the New Deal*), 267-327.

59. *NYT*, Nov. 4, 1948.

60. Bernard R. Berelson, Paul F. Lazersfield, and William N. McPhee, *Voting: A Study of Opinion Formation in a Presidential Campaign* (Chicago, 1955), 53.

61. Angus Campbell and Robert L. Kahn, *The People Elect a President* (Ann Arbor, 1952), 28.

62. Lee, *Truman and Taft-Hartley*, 151.

16. Postelection Analysis

1. The 1948 election was the first time since 1916 that a president failed to get a plurality of the votes cast. It was also the closest election since 1916 and the second largest voter turnout in history. The number of eligible voters in the United States had increased by ten million between 1944 and 1948, however, making the ratio of votes cast smaller compared to the 1940 and 1944 elections. See *CQ Presidential Elections: 1789-1991* (Washington, D.C., 1995), 63, 117. *NYT*, Dec. 11, 1948.

2. Those states were Texas, Arkansas, Oklahoma, New Mexico, Arizona, Nevada, Utah, Colorado, Montana, Tennessee, Georgia, Virginia, West Virginia, Connecticut, Vermont, Ohio, Illinois, Missouri, and Florida. See Malcolm Moos, *Politics, Presidents and Coattails* (Baltimore, 1952), 14. In five states both candidates ran behind local candidates. Sixteen states showed fewer votes cast than in 1944. The best postelection analysis is in *NYT*, Dec. 11, 1948. Almost seven hundred thousand votes were cast without a mark for president (ibid.).

3. Moos, *Politics, Presidents and Coattails*, 13-14; Lee, *Truman and Taft-Hartley*, 151-52.

4. From Morris L. Ernst and David Loth, *The People Know Best: The Ballots vs. the Polls* (Washington, D.C., 1949), 131.

5. Ibid., 135. Crossley saw an upsurge in Truman's numbers as the election got close, but he underestimated the significance and did not report it to the press. After the election Crossley argued that the polls had been correct; the people just changed their minds. See *Time*, Nov. 15, 1948.

6. Ernst and Loth, *The People Know Best*, 132; Elmo Roper, *You and Your Leaders* (New York, 1957), 117-19. See also Roper poll in *New York Herald Tribune*, Aug. 12, 1948. Roper's September 9 poll was published in several places. See *Life*, Nov. 1, 1948. Roper, Gallup, and Crossley all cut the 15 percent "undecided vote" from their figures, assuming that number would be split between Dewey and Truman, when at the polls most of that number went to Truman. See *Time*, Nov. 15, 1948.

7. *Public Opinion Quarterly* (Winter 1948-49): 767.

8. Roper, *You and Your Leaders*, 136. Before the election, 22 percent said they expected Truman to win.

9. *Newsweek*, Oct. 11, 1948. See also Clifford, *Counsel*, 235.

10. *Time*, Oct. 18, 1948.

11. Admitted by *Time* in its next issue, Nov. 15, 1948. The day before the election, *Life* (Nov. 1, 1948) put Dewey's picture on its cover with the caption, "The Next President." The *Manchester Guardian* published an article the day before the election by Alistair Cooke entitled "Harry Truman: A Study in Failure," and the *Kiplinger Washington Newsletter* pub-

lished an article on October 30 entitled "What Dewey Will Do." See *Time*, Nov. 15, 1948.

12. Clifford, *Counsel*, 236, 189, 239. A postelection party was planned at the Biltmore Hotel (Democratic National Committee headquarters) after the election, but most campaign workers came expecting to watch Truman be defeated. See Edwards, *Pulling No Punches*, 110.

13. Manuscript of radio address, Nov. 2, 1948, Wallace Papers.

14. McCullough, *Truman*, 697.

15. Pruessen, *Dulles*, 385. A postelection headline in *Christian Century* (Nov. 3, 1948) said, "Mr. Dulles Should Be Named at Once."

16. Clifford, *Counsel*, 239.

17. Smith, *Dewey*, 510; *NYT*, Aug. 1, 1948.

18. *Chicago Tribune*, Nov. 4, 1948.

19. *Public Papers of Thomas E. Dewey*, 6:526, 530.

20. Dewey to Luce, Dec. 15, 1948, Dewey Papers.

21. Quoted in Smith, *Dewey*, 545.

22. *Saturday Evening Post*, Jan. 29, 1949.

23. *NYT*, Feb. 9, 1948.

24. *Time*, Nov. 29, 1948; *U.S. News and World Report*, Feb. 4, 1949.

25. *Time*, Nov. 29, 1948; *American Mercury*, Feb. 1949.

26. *NYT*, Jan. 2, 1945; White, *Taft Story*, 84; Reinhard, *Republican Right*, 57-58.

27. Reinhard, *Republican Right*, 59-60. Liberals in the party compiled their own statement of principles in opposition.

28. Samuel Lubell, *The Future of American Politics* (Garden City, N.Y., 1951), 135.

29. Truman, *Memoirs*, 2:157.

30. Svend Petersen, *A Statistical History of the American Presidential Elections* (New York, 1968), 149. See also Richard O. Davies, "Whistle-Stopping Through Ohio," *Ohio History*, 71, no. 2 (July 1962), 113-23. Davis argues in favor of the Ohio thesis.

31. Abels, *Out of the Jaws of Victory*, 293.

32. Lubell, *Future of American Politics*, 198-200.

33. Wallace was not allowed on the ballot in Illinois. Had he been, he would almost certainly have taken enough votes from Truman to throw Illinois's twenty-eight electors to Dewey. Alonzo Hamby has called Rowe's insistence that the South would not bolt the party "one enormous blooper." See Hamby, *Man of the People*, 431. For a moderation of that statement, see page 465.

34. Lubell, *Future of American Politics*, 49. According to Lubell, Truman won a plurality in the nation's twelve largest cities in 1948 (New York, Chicago, Philadelphia, Pittsburgh, Detroit, Cleveland, Baltimore, St. Louis, Boston, Milwaukee, San Francisco, and Los Angeles).

35. Lubell, *The Future of American Politics*, rev. 3d ed. (1955), 49.

36. Matusow, *Farm Policies*, 180. For a contemporary survey of the farm vote, see *NYT*, Nov. 29, 1948; and *U.S. News and World Report*, Nov. 19, 1948.

37. Matusow, *Farm Policies*, 188; Lubell, *Future of American Politics*, 156-73.

38. Ross, *Loneliest Campaign*, 257-59.

39. Allen Yarnell, *Democrats and Progressives: The 1948 Presidential Election as a Test of Postwar Liberalism* (Berkeley, 1974), 114. For some disagreement, see Hamby, *Beyond the New Deal*, 401.

40. *Life*, Dec. 30, 1946; *Fortune* (Roper), June 1948. Only 27 percent said the United States should not intervene to save Western Europe.

Bibliography

Manuscripts

American Federation of Labor Papers, George Meany Memorial Archives, Silver Spring, Maryland.

Americans for Democratic Action Papers, Wisconsin State Historical Society, Madison, Wisconsin.

CIO Papers, Walter P. Reuther Library, Wayne State University, Detroit, Michigan.

Oscar L. Chapman Papers, Harry S. Truman Library, Independence, Missouri.

Clark Clifford Papers, Harry S. Truman Library, Independence, Missouri.

Thomas E. Dewey Papers, Rush Rhees Library, University of Rochester, Rochester, New York.

George Elsey Papers, Harry S. Truman Library, Independence, Missouri.

Oscar Ewing Papers, Harry S. Truman Library, Independence, Missouri.

Charter Heslep Papers, Harry S. Truman Library, Independence, Missouri.

Joseph Jones Papers, Harry S. Truman Library, Independence, Missouri.

J. Howard McGrath Papers, Harry S. Truman Library, Independence, Missouri.

Frank McNaughton Papers, Harry S. Truman Library, Independence, Missouri.

George Meany Papers, George Meany Memorial Archives, Silver Spring, Maryland.

NAACP Papers, Library of Congress, Washington, D.C.

Philleo Nash Papers, Harry S. Truman Library, Independence, Missouri.

David K. Niles Papers, Harry S. Truman Library, Independence, Missouri.

Papers of the President's Committee on Civil Rights, Harry S. Truman Library, Independence, Missouri.

Progressive Party Papers, Library of Congress, Washington, D.C.

Progressive Party Papers, Manuscript Division, University of Iowa Library, University of Iowa, Iowa City, Iowa.

Records of the Democratic National Committee, Harry S. Truman Library, Independence, Missouri.

John Redding Papers, Harry S. Truman Library, Independence, Missouri.

Roy Reuther Papers, Walter P. Reuther Library, Wayne State University, Detroit, Michigan.

Walter P. Reuther Papers (UAW President's Files), Walter P. Reuther Library, Wayne State University, Detroit, Michigan.

Samuel T. Rosenman Papers, Harry S. Truman Library, Independence, Missouri.

"States' Rights Scrapbook." Mississippi Department of Archives and History, Jackson, Mississippi.

Robert A. Taft Papers, Library of Congress, Washington, D.C.

Harry S. Truman Papers, Harry S. Truman Library, Independence, Missouri.

United Auto Workers Papers (Frank Winn Papers), Walter P. Reuther Library, Wayne State
    University, Detroit, Michigan.
Henry Wallace Papers, Manuscript Division, University of Iowa Library, University of Iowa,
    Iowa City, Iowa.
James E. Webb Papers, Harry S. Truman Library, Independence, Missouri.

Oral Histories

Interviews in Truman Library
Alben Barkley
William Batt Jr.
Andrew J. Biemiller
Clark Clifford
Girard C. Davidson
Oscar R. Ewing
Leon H. Keyserling
Charles Murphy
Richard Neustadt
James Rowe
John Snyder
David Stowe
James Webb
Columbia Oral History Interview with Henry Wallace

Government Publications

Congressional Quarterly
Congressional Record
Federal Register
President's Committee on Civil Rights. *To Secure These Rights: The Report of the President's
    Committee on Civil Rights.* Washington, D.C.: U.S. Government Printing Office, 1947.
    Also New York: Simon and Schuster, 1947.
Public Papers of the Presidents: Harry S. Truman, 1946. Washington, D.C.: U.S. Government
    Printing Office, 1962.
Public Papers of the Presidents: Harry S. Truman, 1947. Washington, D.C.: U.S. Government
    Printing Office, 1962.
Public Papers of the Presidents: Harry S. Truman, 1948. Washington, D.C.: U.S. Government
    Printing Office, 1964.
Public Papers of Thomas E. Dewey. 12 vols. Albany: State of New York, n.d.
U.S. Housing and Home Finance Agency, *Housing of the Nonwhite Population, 1940-1947.*
    Washington, D.C.: U.S. Government Printing Office, 1948.

Dissertations

Mattern, Carolyn J. "Man on the Dark Horse: The Presidential Campaigns of Douglas
    MacArthur, 1944 and 1948." Ph.D. dissertation, University of Wisconsin, 1976.
Poder, Michael P. "The Senatorial Career of William E. Jenner." Ph.D. dissertation, Uni-
    versity of Notre Dame, 1976.

Poole, Walter Sloan. "The Quest for a Republican Foreign Policy, 1941-1951." Ph.D. dissertation, University of Pennsylvania, 1968.

Newspapers and Periodicals

ADA World
American Mercury
Arkansas Gazette
Atlantic Monthly
Baltimore Sun
Chicago Defender
Chicago Tribune
CIO News
Jackson (Miss.) *Clarion-Ledger*
Colliers
Crisis
Ebony
Fortune
Jackson (Miss.) *Daily News*
Life
Louisville Courier-Journal
Memphis Commercial Appeal
Nation
Negro Digest
New Republic
Newsweek
New York Daily News
New York Herald-Tribune
New York Post
New York Times
New York Times Magazine
New Yorker
North American Labor
PM
Pittsburgh Courier
Political Affairs
Public Opinion Quarterly
Reader's Digest
St. Louis Post-Dispatch
Saturday Evening Post
Shreveport Times
Time
UDA Bulletin
U.S. News
U.S. News and World Report
Vital Speeches of the Day
Wall Street Journal
Washington Post

Books and Articles

Abels, Jules. *Out of the Jaws of Victory*. New York: Henry Holt, 1959.

Acheson, Dean. *Present at the Creation: My Years in the State Department*. New York: Norton, 1969.

Alinsky, Saul. *John L. Lewis: An Unauthorized Biography*. New York: Putnam, 1949.

Ambrose, Stephen E. *Eisenhower: Soldier and President*. New York: Simon and Schuster, 1990.

———. *Nixon: The Education of a Politician*. New York: Simon and Schuster, 1987.

Anderson, Patrick. *The President's Men: The White House Assistants of Franklin D. Roosevelt, Harry S. Truman, Dwight D. Eisenhower, John F. Kennedy, and Lyndon B. Johnson*. Garden City, N.Y.: Doubleday, 1968.

Baldwin, David. *Economic Development and American Foreign Policy, 1943-1962*. Chicago: University of Chicago Press, 1966.

Bartley, Ernest R. "The Tidelands Oil Controversy." *Western Political Quarterly* (March 1949): 135-53.

Berelson, Bernard R., Paul F. Lazersfield, and William N. McPhee. *Voting: A Study of Opinion Formation in a Presidential Campaign*. Chicago: University of Chicago Press, 1955.

Berman, William C. *The Politics of Civil Rights in the Truman Administration*. Columbus: University of Ohio Press, 1970.

Bernard, William. *Dixiecrats and Democrats: Alabama Politics, 1942-1959*. Tuscaloosa: University of Alabama Press, 1974.

Bernstein, Barton J. "The Ambiguous Legacy: The Truman Administration and Civil Rights." In *Politics and Policies of the Truman Administration*, edited by Bernstein. Chicago: Quadrangle, 1970.

———. "America in War and Peace: The Test of Liberalism." In *Twentieth Century: Recent Interpretations*, edited by Bernstein and Allen Matusow. New York: Harcourt Brace Jovanovich, 1969.

Bernstein, Carl. *Loyalties: A Son's Memoir*. New York: Simon and Schuster, 1989.

Blum, John Morton, ed. *The Price of Vision: The Diary of Henry A. Wallace, 1942-1946*. Boston: Houghton Mifflin, 1973.

Bohlen, Charles, *Witness to History, 1929-1969*. New York: Norton, 1973.

Bontecou, Eleanor. *The Federal Loyalty-Security Program*. Ithaca, N.Y.: Cornell University Press, 1953.

Brinkley, Alan. *The End of Reform: New Deal Liberalism in Recession and War*. New York: Vintage, 1995.

Brock, Clifton. *The Americans for Democratic Action: Its Role in National Politics*. Washington, D.C.: Public Affairs Press, 1962.

Brown, D. Clayton. *Electricity for Rural America: The Fight for the REA*. Westport, Conn.: Greenwood Press, 1980.

Bunche, Ralph. "A Critical Analysis of the Tactics and Programs of Minority Groups." *Journal of Negro Education* 4 (July 1935): 308-20.

———. "The Programs of Organizations Devoted to the Improvement of the Status of the American Negro." *Journal of Negro Education* 88 (July 1939): 539-47.

Butcher, Harry C. *My Years with Eisenhower: The Personal Diary of Captain Harry C. Butcher, USNR*. New York: Simon and Schuster, 1946.

Byrnes, James F. *All in One Lifetime*. New York: Harper, 1958.

———. *Speaking Frankly*. New York: Harper, 1947.

Campbell, Angus, and Robert L. Kahn. *The People Elect a President*. Ann Arbor: University of Michigan Press, 1952.

Cantril, Hadley. *Public Opinion, 1935-1946*. Princeton: Princeton University Press, 1951.

Chesteen, Richard D. "'Mississippi Is Gone Home!': A Study of the 1948 States' Rights Bolt." *Journal of Mississippi History* 32, no. 1 (Feb. 1970), 43-59.

Clements, Kendrick A. "Introduction" to *James F. Byrnes and the Origins of the Cold War*, edited by Kendrick Clements. Durham, N.C.: Duke University Press, 1982.

Clifford, Clark. *Counsel to the President: A Memoir*. New York: Random House, 1991.

Cohodas, Nadine. *Strom Thurmond and the Politics of Southern Change*. New York: Simon and Schuster, 1993.

CQ Presidential Elections, 1789-1991. Washington, D.C.: Congressional Quarterly Press, 1995.

Curry, George. "James F. Byrnes," in Robert H. Ferrell and Samuel Flagg Bemis, eds., *The American Secretaries of State and Their Diplomacy*. New York: Cooper Square, 1965.

Dalfiume, Richard M. *Desegregation of the U.S. Armed Forces: Fighting on Two Fronts, 1939-1953*. Columbia: University of Missouri Press, 1969.

————. "The 'Forgotten Years' of the Negro Revolution." *Journal of American History* 55, no. 1 (June 1968): 90-106.

Davies, Richard O. "Whistle-Stopping Through Ohio." *Ohio History* 71, no. 2 (July 1962): 113-23.

Democratic National Committee. *Official Proceedings of the Democratic National Convention*. 1948.

Dennis, Eugene. *The Third Party and the 1948 Elections*. New York: New Century, 1948.

Donaldson, Gary A. "The Wardman Park Group and Campaign Strategy in the Truman Administration, 1946-1948." *Missouri Historical Review* 86, no. 3 (April 1992): 282-94.

————. "Who Wrote the Clifford Memo? The Origins of Campaign Strategy in the Truman Administration." *Presidential Studies Quarterly* 23, no. 4 (Fall 1993): 747-54.

Donovan, Robert J. *Conflict and Crisis: The Presidency of Harry S. Truman, 1945-1948*. New York: Norton, 1977.

Dubofsky, Melvyn. *The State and Labor in Modern America*. Chapel Hill: University of North Carolina Press, 1994.

Dubofsky, Melvyn, and Warren Van Tine. *John L. Lewis: A Biography*. New York: Quadrangle, 1977.

Edwards, India. *Pulling No Punches: Memoirs of a Woman in Politics*. New York: Putnam, 1977.

Eisenhower, Dwight D. *Crusade in Europe*. Garden City, N.Y.: Doubleday, 1948.

————. *Mandate for Change*. Garden City, N.Y.: Doubleday, 1963.

Ernst, Morris L., and David Loth. *The People Know Best: The Ballots vs. the Polls*. Washington, D.C.: Public Affairs Press, 1949.

Ferrell, Robert H. *Harry S. Truman: A Life*. Columbia: University of Missouri Press, 1994.

————, ed. *Dear Bess: The Letters from Harry to Bess Truman, 1910-1959*. New York: Norton, 1983.

————, ed. *Off the Record: The Private Papers of Harry S. Truman*. New York: Penguin, 1980.

————, ed. *Truman in the White House: The Diary of Eben A. Ayres*. Columbia: University of Missouri Press, 1991.

Foner, Philip S. *Organized Labor and the Black Worker, 1619-1973*. New York: International Publishers, 1974.

Forrestal, James. *The Forrestal Diaries*. Edited by Walter Millis, New York: Viking, 1951.

Foster, James C. *The Union Politic: The CIO Political Action Committee*. Columbia: University of Missouri Press, 1975.

Gaddis, John Lewis. *Strategies of Containment: A Critical Appraisal of Postwar American National Security Policy*. New York: Oxford University Press, 1982.

Galambos, Louis, and Alfred D. Chandler Jr., eds. *The Papers of Dwight D. Eisenhower*. 13 volumes to date. Baltimore: Johns Hopkins University Press, 1970-.

Garson, Robert A. *The Democratic Party and the Politics of Sectionalism, 1941-1948*. Baton Rouge: Louisiana State University Press, 1974.

Gillon, Steven M. *Politics and Vision: The ADA and American Liberalism, 1947-1985*. New York: Oxford University Press, 1987.

Goldman, Eric F. *The Crucial Decade—And After*. New York: Vintage, 1960.

Gosnell, Harold F. *Truman's Crises: A Political Biography of Harry S. Truman*. Westport, Conn.: Greenwood Press, 1980.

Goulden, Joseph C. *The Best Years, 1945-1950*. New York: Atheneum, 1976.

Green, James R. *The World of the Worker: Labor in the Twentieth Century*. New York: Hill and Wang, 1980.

Griffith, Robert. *The Politics of Fear: Joseph R. McCarthy and the Senate*. Amherst: University of Massachusetts Press, 1970.

Guhin, Michael A. *John Foster Dulles: A Statesman and His Times*. New York: Columbia University Press, 1972.

Gunther, John. *Eisenhower: The Man and the Symbol*. New York: Harper and Brothers, 1952.

Hamby, Alonzo. *Beyond the New Deal: Harry S. Truman and American Liberalism*. New York: Columbia University Press, 1973.

———. *Man of the People: A Life of Harry S. Truman*. New York: Oxford University Press, 1995.

Hartmann, Susan. *Truman and the 80th Congress*. Columbia: University of Missouri Press, 1971.

Heard, Alexander. *A Two-Party South?* Chapel Hill: University of North Carolina Press, 1952

Howe, Irving, and Lewis Coser, *The American Communist Party, 1919-1957*. New York: Praeger, 1962.

Ickes, Harold L. *The Secret Diary of Harold L. Ickes*. 3 vols. New York: Simon and Schuster, 1954.

Kennan, George F. *Memoirs: 1925-1950*. Boston: Little, Brown, 1967.

Key, V.O. *Southern Politics in State and Nation*. New York: Knopf, 1949.

Keyserling, Leon H. "Leon H. Keyserling." In *The Truman White House: The Administration of the Presidency, 1945-1953*, edited by Francis H. Heller. Lawrence: University of Kansas Press, 1980.

Kirkendall, Richard. "Election of 1948." In *History of American Presidential Elections, 1789-1968*, edited by Arthur M. Schlesinger Jr. and Fred Israel. New York: Chelsea House, 1971.

Klehr, Harvey, and John Earl Haynes. *The American Communist Movement: Storming Heaven Itself.* New York: Twayne, 1992.

Kofsky, Frank. *Harry S. Truman and the War Scare of 1948: A Successful Campaign to Deceive the Nation*. New York: St. Martin's Press, 1993.

Krock, Arthur. *Memoirs: Sixty Years on the Firing Line*. New York: Funk and Wagnall's, 1968.

Lawson, Steven F. *Black Ballots: Voting Rights in the South, 1944-1969*. New York: Columbia University Press, 1976.

————. *Running for Freedom: Civil Rights and Black Politics in America Since 1941.* New York: McGraw-Hill, 1991.

Lee, R. Alton. *Truman and Taft-Hartley: A Question of Mandate.* Lexington: University of Kentucky Press, 1966.

————. "The Turnip Session of the Do-Nothing Congress; A Presidential Campaign Strategy." *Southwestern Social Science Quarterly* 44 (Dec. 1963): 256-67.

Leffler, Melvyn P. *A Preponderance of Power: National Security, the Truman Administration, and the Cold War.* Stanford: Stanford University Press, 1992.

Leuchtenburg, William E. *Franklin Roosevelt and the New Deal.* New York: Harper, 1963.

————. *In the Shadow of FDR: From Harry Truman to Ronald Reagan.* Ithaca, N.Y.: Cornell University Press, 1989.

Levenstein, Harvey A. *Communism, Anti-Communism, and the CIO.* Westport, Conn.: Greenwood Press, 1981.

Levering, Ralph B. *The Cold War, 1945-1987.* Arlington Heights, Ill.: Harlan Davidson, 1988.

Lilienthal, David E. *The Journals of David E. Lilienthal.* Vol. 2, *The Atomic Energy Years, 1945-1950.* New York: Harper & Row, 1964.

Lubell, Samuel. *The Future of American Politics.* Garden City, N.Y.: Doubleday, 1951. Rev. 3d ed. 1955.

Lyon, Peter. *Eisenhower: Portrait of a Hero.* Boston: Little, Brown, 1974.

Manchester, William. *American Caesar: Douglas MacArthur, 1880-1964.* Boston: Little, Brown, 1978.

Marable, Manning. *Race, Reform, and Rebellion: The Second Reconstruction in Black America, 1945-1990.* Jackson: University Press of Mississippi, 1991.

Martin, Joseph. *My First Fifty Years in Politics.* New York: McGraw-Hill, 1960.

Matusow, Allen J. *Farm Policies and Politics in the Truman Administration.* Cambridge, Mass.: Harvard University Press, 1967.

————. *The Unraveling of America: A History of Liberalism in the 1960s.* New York: Harper & Row, 1984.

McCoy, Donald R., and Richard T. Reutten. *Quest and Response: Minority Rights and the Truman Administration.* Lawrence: University of Kansas Press, 1973.

McCullough, David. *Truman.* New York: Simon and Schuster, 1992.

Macdougall, Curtis. *Gideon's Army.* 3 vols. New York: Marzani and Munsell, 1965.

Messer, Robert L. "'Et Tu Brute!': James F. Byrnes, Harry Truman and the Origins of the Cold War." In *James F. Byrnes and the Origins of the Cold War,* edited by Kendrick Clements. Durham, N.C.: Duke University Press, 1982.

Miller, Merle. *Plain Speaking: An Oral Biography of Harry S. Truman.* New York: Berkley, 1974.

Millis, Harry A., and Emily Clark Brown. *From the Wagner Act to Taft-Hartley: A Study of National Labor Policy and Labor Relations.* Chicago: University of Chicago Press, 1950.

Moon, Henry Lee. *Balance of Power: The Negro Vote.* Garden City, N.Y.: Doubleday, 1948.

Moos, Malcolm. *Politics, Presidents and Coattails.* Baltimore: Johns Hopkins Press, 1952.

Myrdal, Gunnar. *An American Dilemma.* New York: Harper, 1944.

O'Brien, Michael. *McCarthy and McCarthyism in Wisconsin.* Columbia: University of Missouri Press, 1980.

Oshinsky, David. "Labor's Cold War: The CIO and the Communists." In *The Specter: Original Essays on the Cold War and the Origins of McCarthyism,* edited by Robert Griffith and Athan G. Theoharis. New York: Franklin Watts, 1974.

Parmet, Herbert S. *The Democrats: The Years After FDR.* New York: Macmillan, 1976.

Patterson, James T. *Mr. Republican: A Biography of Robert A. Taft.* Boston: Houghton Mifflin, 1972.

Patterson, Thomas G. *Meeting the Communist Threat: Truman to Reagan.* New York: Oxford University Press, 1988.

Pemberton, William E. *Harry S. Truman: Fair Dealer and Cold Warrior.* Boston: Twayne, 1989.

Petersen, Svend. *A Statistical History of the American Presidential Elections.* New York: Ungar, 1968.

Pfeffer, Paula F. *A. Philip Randolph: Pioneer of the Civil Rights Movement.* Baton Rouge: Louisiana State University Press, 1990.

Phillips, Cabell. *The Truman Presidency: The History of a Triumphant Succession.* New York: Macmillan, 1966.

Porter, Kirk, and Donald B. Johnson. *National Party Platforms, 1840-1964.* Urbana: University of Illinois Press, 1966.

Pruessen, Ronald W. *John Foster Dulles: The Road to Power.* New York: Free Press, 1982.

Redding, John M. *Inside the Democratic Party.* Indianapolis: Bobbs-Merrill, 1958.

Reichard, Gary. *Politics as Usual: The Age of Truman and Eisenhower.* Arlington Heights, Ill.: Harlan Davidson, 1988.

Reinhard, David W. *The Republican Right Since 1945.* Lexington: University Press of Kentucky, 1983.

Roland, Charles P. *The Improbable Era: The South Since World War II.* Lexington: University Press of Kentucky, 1976.

Roosevelt, James. *My Parents: A Differing View.* Chicago: Playboy Press, 1978.

Ross, Irwin. *The Loneliest Campaign: The Truman Victory of 1948.* New York: New American Library, 1968.

Salmond, John A. "The Civilian Conservation Corps and the Negro." *Journal of American History* 52, no. 1 (June 1965): 75-88.

Schapsmeir, Edward L., and Frederick H. Schapsmeir. *Profits in Politics: Henry A. Wallace and the War Years, 1940-1965.* Ames: Iowa State University Press, 1970.

Scheele, Henry Z. *Charlie Halleck: A Political Biography.* New York: Exposition, 1966.

Schmidt, Karl M. *Henry A. Wallace: Quixotic Crusade, 1948.* Syracuse, N.Y.: Syracuse University Press, 1960.

Seidman, Joel. *American Labor from Defense to Reconversion.* Chicago: University of Chicago Press, 1953.

Shannon, David A. *The Decline of Communism: A History of the Communist Party in the United States Since 1945.* Chatham, N.J.: Chatham Bookseller, 1959.

Sitkoff, Harvard. *A New Deal for Blacks: The Emergence of Civil Rights as a National Issue, the Depression Decade.* New York: Oxford University Press, 1978.

Smith, Richard Norton. *Thomas E. Dewey and His Times.* New York: Simon and Schuster, 1982.

Starobin, Joseph. *American Communism in Crisis, 1943-1947.* Cambridge, Mass.: Harvard University Press, 1972.

Stromer, Marvin. *The Making of a Political Leader: Kenneth S. Wherry and the United States Senate.* Lincoln: University of Nebraska Press, 1969.

Theoharis, Athan G. *Seeds of Repression: Harry S. Truman and the Origins of McCarthyism.* Chicago: Quadrangle, 1971.

Truman, Harry S. *Memoirs.* 2 vols. Garden City, N.Y.: Doubleday, 1956.

Truman, Margaret, *Harry S. Truman*. New York: William Morrow, 1972.

Tygiel, Jules. *Baseball's Great Experiment: Jackie Robinson and His Legacy*. New York: Vintage, 1983.

Van Auken, Cecelia. "The Negro Press in the 1948 Presidential Election." *Journalism Quarterly* 26, no. 4 (Dec. 1949): 431-35.

Vandenberg, Arthur Jr., ed. *The Private Papers of Senator Vandenberg*. Boston: Houghton Mifflin, 1952.

Voorhis, Jerry. *Confessions of a Congressman*. Garden City, N.Y.: Doubleday, 1947.

Walton, Richard J. *Henry Wallace, Harry Truman, and the Cold War*. New York: Viking, 1976.

Weiss, Nancy J. *Farewell to the Party of Lincoln: Black Politics in the Age of FDR*. Princeton: Princeton University Press, 1983.

White, Walter. *A Man Called White*. New York: Viking, 1948.

White, William S. *The Taft Story*. New York: Harper & Row, 1954.

Wolters, Raymond. *Negroes and the Great Depression: The Problem of Economic Recovery*. Westport, Conn.: Greenwood Press, 1970.

Yarnell, Allen. *Democrats and Progressives: The 1948 Presidential Election as a Test of Postwar Liberalism*. Berkeley: University of California Press, 1974.

Zieger, Robert H. *The CIO, 1935-1955*. Chapel Hill: University of North Carolina Press, 1995.

Index

Italic numbers refer to photographs.